FICTIONAL FLIGHTS

An Anthology of Short Stories for Nonnative Speakers of English

Howard Sage

New York University

HEINLE & HEINLE PUBLISHERS
A Division of Wadsworth, Inc.
Boston, Massachusetts 02116

The publication of *Fictional Flights* was directed by the members of the Heinle & Heinle ESL Publishing Team:

Erik Gundersen, Editorial Director
Susan Mraz, Marketing Manager
Kristin Thalheimer, Production Editor

Also participating in the publication of this program were:

Publisher: Stanley J. Galek
Editorial Production Manager: Elizabeth Holthaus
Associate Editor: Lynne Telson Barsky
Project Manager: Cindy Funkhouser
Manufacturing Coordinator: Mary Beth Lynch
Photo Coordinator: Martha Leibs-Heckly
Interior Designer and Compositor: Greta D. Sibley
Illustrator: Stephanie Peterson
Cover Designer: Ken Condon

Fictional Flights: An Anthology of Short Stories for Nonnative Speakers of English

Heinle & Heinle is a division of Wadsworth, Inc.

Manufactured in the United States of America.

Library of Congress Cataloging-in-Publication Data

Sage, Howard.
    Fictional flights / Howard Sage.
      p. cm.
    Inlcudes bibliographical references.
    ISBN 0-8384-2646-8
      1. English language—Textbooks for foreign speakers. 2. Fiction-Appreciation.
    3. American fiction. 4. English fiction. 5. Readers. I. Title
    PE1128.S2155   1993
    428.6'4—dc20   92-41840
                                                CIP

ISBN: 0-8384-2646-8
10 9 8 7 6 5 4 3 2 1

Dedication

To my wife Lillian, friend and critical reader, whose support encouraged me during the writing of this book

To Dr. James R. Frakes, whose unfailing energy and unyielding commitment to excellence inspired me

To Dr. Donald A. Sears, whose joy, wit, and acuity while instructing me in Shakespeare, Chaucer, and Milton still buoy me

CONTENTS

Foreword xi

To the Teacher xix

Outer Marker: Entering the World of the Imagination 1

Chapter 1: Departures I 3

    A. Introductions 4
    Jack and the Beanstalk 4
    B. Fact and Fantasy in Fiction 9
    C. The Real versus the True 12
    The Princess and the Pea...13
       Hans Christian Andersen

Chapter Two: Departures II 17

    A. Five Foundations of Fiction Land..18
    B. Building on the Foundations 18
    The Man, the Boy, and the Donkey 19
       Aesop

Chapter Three: Practice Flights I 31

    A. The World of the Job Hunter 32
    Job Hunt...32
       John Zebrowski
    B. Key Moments in the Plot..39
    C. As Time Goes By..40
    D. A Sense of Place...41
    E. The Right Person in the Right Place at the Right Time.................44
    F. Looking Ahead 47

Chapter Four: Practice Flights II 49

    A. Behind the Scenes..50

Feast 50
    Eric Larsen
  B. Exploring the Background of "Feast" 53
  C. Characters: What They Say and Do 54
  D. Flat and Round Characters 56
  E. Setting 59
  F. Plot and Story 60
  G. Subplot (A Second Plot) 61
  H. What's It All About? 62

Chapter Five: Practice Flights III 65
  A. Background: Mexico and the United States 66
  B. The Story from Start to Finish 66
  I See You Never 66
    Ray Bradbury
  C. Plot 70
  D. A Matter of Character 73
  E. Friends and Family 74
  F. The Language of Feelings 74
  G. From Story to Theme 75

Chapter Six: Takeoff 77
  A. Background 78
  The Strawberry Season 79
    Erskine Caldwell
  B. Understanding Character 83
  C. Point of View 83
  D. Structure 84
  E. What's the Problem? 84
  F. Associations of Details 87

Middle Marker: The Entrance Method 91

Chapter Seven: First Flights I 93
  A. Background 94
  The Storm 94
    Kate Chopin
  B. Reviewing the Facts 98
  C. Entrance One: The Parts and the Whole 99
  D. Entrance Two: Character 101
  E. Entrance Three: The Language of "The Storm" 103
  F. Entrance Four: Images and Image Clusters 104
  G. Entrance Five: Symbols 106
  H. Theme 107

Chapter Eight: First Flights II 109

  A. The Action of the Story 110

  A Bag of Oranges 110
     Spiro Athanas

  B. The Problem Itself 117

  C. Entrance One: Structure..118

  D. Entrance Two: Character 120

  E. Entrance Three: Family Dynamics 121

  F. Entrance Four: Ritual, Myth, and Symbol.................................123

  G. Summing Up 127

Chapter Nine: Mid-Journey...129

  A. Crisis...130

  B. The Problem 131

  The Stone Boy 131
     Gina Berriault

  C. Structure...142

  D. Character 144

  E. Theme 144

  F. Symbolism 147

  G. Style 148

Chapter Ten: Solo Flight I...151

  Gerald's Song..152
     Phillip O'Connor

Chapter Eleven: Solo Flight II...157

  Sunday in the Park 158
     Bel Kaufman

Chapter Twelve: Maneuvers I...163

  A. The Action...164

  The Use of Force 164
     William Carlos Williams

  B. The Proper Subject Matter of Fiction...168

  C. Point of View..168

  D. Character Motivation 169

  E. Language and Style 169

  F. Themes and Issues 170

Chapter Thirteen: In Flight...173

  A. The Camera's Angle..174

  Guests of the Nation 174
     Frank O'Connor

B. Encounter: Hobson's Choices 184

C. Background and Allusions 184

D. Structure and Foreshadowing 185

E. Style: The Way It's Said 186

F. Pace 187

G. Imagery 188

H. Theme 189

Chapter Fourteen: Maneuvers II 191

A. Warm-Up: Dealing with Difficult People and/or Situations 192

The Other Laundrette 192
   Helen Harris

B. The Title and Its Meanings 196

C. Setting: The Power of Place 197

D. The Laundrette as Symbol 198

E. Getting to Know You through Words 200

F. Style 200

G. Point of View 200

H. Character Change 201

I. Conflicts in Fiction 201

Chapter Fifteen: Solo Flight III 203

Rope 204
   Katherine Anne Porter

Chapter Sixteen: Maneuvers III 211

A. The World of the Boarding House 212

The Boarding House 212
   James Joyce

B. Narration and Description 218

C. Character and the Story 220

D. Other Routes to Character 221

E. Allusions 222

F. Congruent Patterns 223

G. Structure 224

H. Epiphanies 225

Chapter Seventeen: Advanced Solo 227

Like a Winding Sheet 229
   Ann Petry

Inner Marker: Universal Timeless Challenges.....................................239

Chapter Eighteen: The Territory Ahead 241

    A. The World of Longer Fiction 242
    B. The Author's Background 242
    The Open Boat..243
      Stephen Crane
    C. Images and Image Clusters......................................264
    D. Symbols 266
    E. Structure..267
    F. Voice...268
    G. Character and Point of View....................................270
    H. Theme 270
    I. Closing Thoughts and Future Openings 271

Appendix I: Appearance of Terms by Chapter 273

Appendix II: Selected Articles on the Use of Literature in ESL/EFL......................275

Copyrights and Acknowledgments...278

FOREWORD

by Candace Harper
University of Florida

Dr. Harper's well-known research explores the challenges that second language students face when reading unabridged literature in English. For this Foreword, we have asked Dr. Harper to apply the knowledge and insights she has gained through her research to the work that the author has done in developing Fictional Flights.

Fictional Flights is a guided entry to the world of fiction, designed especially for nonnative readers of English. The author carefully prepares readers for passage into the stories by eliciting personal experiences and affective involvement and provides readers with the critical tools necessary for viewing the stories from multiple perspectives (or "locations"). A major focus of the book is to help readers at intermediate to advanced levels of English proficiency develop their ability and confidence in reading fiction. The writing and discussion activities which accompany the stories are designed to develop oral and written skills through the sharing of readers' critical and aesthetic responses to the stories.

DEVELOPMENTS IN SECOND LANGUAGE READING THEORY AND INSTRUCTION

THE ROLE OF LITERATURE

Developments in reading theory and instruction have opened the door for a broader consideration of what materials are appropriate for second language learners, and the use of fiction in English as a Second Language (ESL) programs has gained widespread popularity in recent years. Short stories are particularly well suited to current instructional trends in ESL classrooms, such as the use of authentic native language materials, and whole language and cooperative learning techniques.

They are an ideal vehicle for developing automaticity in processing written language through independent, sustained silent reading and for developing critical reading skills through individual and teacher-directed group interactions with texts.

THE ROLE OF THE READER

One key development in reading theory should be noted here for its relevance to ESL reading programs. The reading process is currently seen as an interaction between a reader and a text, with efficient readers sampling from the text to confirm expectations. New information is processed in association with existing schematic patterns, or organizations of background knowledge. Ability to understand a text will depend on a reader's language proficiency, motivation and interest, the cohesive and structural qualities of the text, and to a large extent on how much the reader already knows about the topic, or how familiar one is with similar or related topics or texts (such as stories). The realization that a reader's experience plays a critical role in reading comprehension has important implications for reading pedagogy, and for issues of text readability, which has traditionally been defined primarily through surface features of sentence length and word length or frequency.

▪▪▪▪▪▪▪▪▪▪▪▪▪▪▪▪▪▪▪▪▪▪▪▪▪▪▪▪▪▪▪▪▪▪▪▪▪

PROBLEMS WITH USING READABILITY CRITERIA TO SIMPLIFY MATERIALS

RESULTS OF RESEARCH ON READING COMPREHENSION

Anderson and Davison (1988) argue that the variables measured by readability formulas are less important to comprehension than topic knowledge or interest, and studies in both first and second language contexts with adult and young readers have concluded that stories and texts which have been "simplified" (or rewritten in shorter sentences with more common words) are not always more readable than the original versions. They may in fact be more difficult to understand. Johnson (1981) in a study of first and second language adult readers concluded that syntactic and semantic complexity had less effect than did cultural factors on ESL students' comprehension of simplified versus original versions of stories. Blau (1982) reported similar results with adult ESL readers in Puerto Rico. Not only did lower readability levels (as predicted by readability formulas) *not* facilitate the reading comprehension of these ESL students, but the subjective ranking for difficulty of the passages by the students was opposite that suggested by the readability formulas.

In addition to standard simplification procedures, simplified materials are sometimes edited or abridged to remove content which might complicate the reading or extend the length of the text. Such content in fiction may include subplots, culturally specific aspects of a story, character descriptions, or information about the characters' feelings or attitudes. Studies have shown that deletion of such information can result in misunderstanding of characters' motivations (Bruce, 1985; Liebling, 1986).

RESULTS OF RESEARCH ON READER APPRECIATION, READER RESPONSE, AND READER ACHIEVEMENT IN DIFFERENT SKILLS AREAS

One first language study with children reports that, for selected simplified stories, not only was comprehension not affected, but the readers preferred the original versions. This effect was strongest among the average to less able readers (Green & Olsen, 1986). Schlager (1978) also reported that young readers preferred the original to the adapted versions of stories, and that comprehension, reader involvement, and identification with characters in stories were reduced in reading the simplified versions. Harper (1990) noted that the original version of a short story evoked more elaborate responses from adult ESL readers in written response tasks, and Vigil's (1987) study with beginning learners of Spanish found that students in a program using unsimplified texts as the primary instructional materials outperformed those in the regular language program in productive tasks involving reading comprehension, oral proficiency, and writing skills.

▪▴▪▴▪▴▪▴▪▴▪▴▪▴▪▴▪▴▪▴▪▴▪▴▪▴▪▴▪▴▪▴▪▴▪▴▪▴

ADVANTAGES OF UNSIMPLIFIED STORIES IN ESL READING PROGRAMS

The use of unsimplified materials with ESL students has been advocated on the basis that it provides authentic samples of language use, where the focus is on meaning and not on language form. Many researchers and educators feel that reading unsimplified stories in the second language helps to develop vocabulary and cultural knowledge, as well as greater proficiency in critical reading and creative writing skills (Brumfit & Carter, 1986; Collie & Slater, 1987; Di Pietro, 1982; Krashen, 1989; McConochie, 1981; Oster, 1989; Povey, 1979, 1986; Sage, 1987; Stern, 1987).

Several researchers have argued that the answer to the problem of text readability lies in preparing a particular group of readers to meet a text, rather than simplifying a text for readers according to a formula based on syntactic and semantic measures of difficulty (Harper, 1988; Israelite, 1988; Kramsch, 1985). Floyd and Carrell (1987) demonstrated that differences in syntactic complexity had no significant effect on ESL reading comprehension, but that intervention in the form of teacher directed classroom activities did aid in the development of schemata which helped readers overcome difficult linguistic structures in texts. Swaffar (1988) recommends the reading of authentic texts in lieu of simplified materials starting even at elementary levels of language proficiency in order to replace dependence on word for word decoding strategies with training in use of story scripts and schemata to facilitate reading. Schulz (1981) advises that a text should never be dismissed simply because it is linguistically complex.

▲·▲·▲·▲·▲·▲·▲·▲·▲·▲·▲·▲·▲·▲·▲·▲·▲·▲

THE ROLE OF THE TEACHER

The decision to use unsimplified texts with second language learners carries certain responsibilities for a teacher. First is the careful selection of appropriate materials. The appropriateness of materials for any group of readers will be a function of their background experiences, their interest in a particular topic, and their motivation to read, as well as of their level of reading proficiency in the second language. Next, a teacher should provide prereading experiences which stimulate interest and activate or develop needed schematic information. The teacher should also provide "handles" for readers of fiction, where much of the meaning in a story may lie beyond the surface level of plot development. Discussion and writing activities which encourage association and interpretation are important bases for interaction with other readers and for extension of the reading of the story from an efferent (factual) level to a personal and aesthetic level. *Fictional Flights* provides these valuable opportunities for objective and subjective, individual and collective readings.

▲·▲

FICTIONAL FLIGHTS AS A VALUABLE RESOURCE IN A LITERATURE-BASED APPROACH TO ESL INSTRUCTION

THE STORIES

In *Fictional Flights* Dr. Sage has assembled a group of stories which are engaging and understandable in terms of universal human hopes and experiences. The collection includes fables and folk tales as well as modern short fiction and is ordered on the basis of structural and thematic complexity, with the more accessible genres of fable and folk tale leading to the more demanding short stories. Potentially difficult vocabulary are not glossed as Dr. Sage believes (as many teachers do) that most unfamiliar terms may be understood through the story contexts.

THE TEACHER'S GUIDE AND SUGGESTED ACTIVITIES

The Teacher's Guide for *Fictional Flights* provides suggestions on useful approaches for each story, with descriptions of terms and group activities to enhance class readings. The accompanying discussion and writing activities were developed and classroom tested over a period of several years and were included on the basis of their success in facilitating ESL students' readings of the stories. They serve as important links between real world experiences and the fictional "flights," and they provide a context for examining the linguistic, structural, and thematic elements of all of the stories.

READER–TEXT INTERACTION

The greatest strength of *Fictional Flights* as an ESL reading text lies in its emphasis on developing readers' ability to interact with a story—to associate with past experiences and anticipate developments, to identify with characters, and to recognize and respond to the emotional tone of the story. The consistent focus in the readings is on the potential meaning each story holds and on the variety of ways in which readers can learn to approach and access these meanings.

In both the main text and the Teacher's Guide, Dr. Sage provides the tools and procedures through which readers can understand and appreciate the stories. He defines and provides examples of literary terms, using them as means of entry into different stories. The "ingredients" of fiction (such as "plot," "point of view," "symbolism," and "theme," among others) are explained and used to analyze the what, who, and why (action, characters, and message). These elements are not important in themselves; what is important is that they serve as vehicles for passage into the stories.

We believe that the stories and activities in *Fictional Flights* will assist readers in developing the skills and confidence necessary for successful and enjoyable travels through the world of fiction. Bon voyage!

▲▼▲▼▲▼▲▼▲▼▲▼▲
REFERENCES

Anderson, R. C., & Davison, A. (1988). Conceptual and empirical bases of readability formulas. In G. Green & A. Davison (Eds.), *Linguistic complexity and text comprehension: Readability issues reconsidered* (pp. 23–54). Hillsdale, NJ: Erlbaum.

Blau, E. K. (1982). The effect of syntax on readability for ESL students in Puerto Rico. *TESOL Quarterly, 16,* 517–528.

Bruce, B. C. (1985). Stories in readers and tradebooks. In J. Osborn, P. T. Wilson, & R. C. Anderson (Eds.), *Reading education: Foundations for a literate America* (pp. 29–45). Lexington, MA: D. C. Heath.

Brumfit, C. J., & Carter, R. A. (1986). *Literature and language teaching.* Oxford: Oxford University Press.

Collie, J., & Slater, S. (1987). *Literature in the language classroom: A resource book of ideas and activities.* Cambridge: Cambridge University Press.

Di Pietro, R. J. (1982). The multi-ethnicity of American literature: A neglected resource for the EFL teacher. In M. Hines & W. Rutherford (Eds.), *On TESOL '81* (pp. 215–229). Washington, DC: Teachers of English to Speakers of Other Languages.

Floyd, P., & Carrell, P. (1987). Effects on ESL reading of teaching cultural content schemata. *Language Learning, 37,* 89–108.

Green, G. M., & Olsen, M. S. (1986). *Preferences for and comprehension of original and readability-adapted materials.* Urbana, IL: Illinois University, Center for the Study of Reading. (ERIC Document Reproduction Service No. ED 208 656)

Harper, C. A. (1990). A comparative study of the readability and comprehensibility of a simplified and the original version of an American short story with students of English as a foreign language. (Doctoral dissertation, Florida State University, 1990). *Dissertation Abstracts International, 90,* 24095.

Harper, S. N. (1988). Strategies for teaching literature at the undergraduate level. *Modern Language Journal, 72,* 402–408.

Israelite, N. K. (1988). On readability formulas: A critical analysis for teachers of the deaf. *American Annals of the Deaf,* March, 14–18.

Johnson, P. (1981). Effects on reading comprehension of language complexity and cultural background of a text. *TESOL Quarterly, 15,* 169–181.

Kramsch, C. (1985). Literary texts in the classroom: A discourse model. *Modern Language Journal, 69,* 356–366.

Krashen, S. (1989). We acquire vocabulary and spelling by reading: Additional evidence for the input hypothesis. *Modern Language Journal, 73,* 446–447.

Liebling, C. R. (1986). *Inside view and character plans in original stories and their basal reader adaptations* (Technical Report No. 143). Washington, DC: National Institute of Education.

McConochie, J. (1981). All this fiddle: Enhancing language awareness through poetry. In M. Hines & W. Rutherford (Eds.), *On TESOL '81* (pp. 231–240). Washington, DC: Teachers of English to Speakers of Other Languages.

Oster, J. (1989). Seeing with different eyes: Another view of literature in the ESL class. *TESOL Quarterly, 23,* 85–103.

Povey, J. F. (1979). The teaching of literature in advanced ESL classes. In M. Celce-Murcia & L. McIntosh (Eds.), *Teaching English as a second or foreign language* (pp. 162–186). Rowley, MA: Newbury House.

Povey, J. F. (1986). Using literature with ESL students. *ERIC/CLL News Bulletin, 10,* 3–4.

Sage, H. (1987). Incorporating literature in ESL instruction. In *Language in education: Theory and practice.* Englewood Cliffs, NJ: Prentice-Hall.

Schlager, N. (1978). Predicting children's choices in literature: A developmental approach. *Children's Literature in Education, 10,* 136–142.

Schulz, R. A. (1981). Literature and readability: Bridging the gap in foreign language reading. *Modern Language Journal, 65,* 43–53.

Stern, S. L. (1987). Expanded dimensions to literature in ESL/EFL: An integrated approach. *English Teaching Forum,* October, 47–55.

Swaffar, J. K. (1988). Readers, texts, and second languages: The interactive processes. *The Modern Language Journal, 72,* 123–149.

Vigil, V. D. (1987). Authentic text in the college-level Spanish 1 class as the primary vehicle of instruction. (Doctoral dissertation, University of Texas at Austin, 1987). *Dissertation Abstracts International, 88,* 06431.

TO THE TEACHER

Fictional Flights invites you on a journey.

Focusing on a wide array of stimulating and unabridged pieces of literature, *Fictional Flights* is an anthology of short fiction designed specifically to meet the needs of nonnative readers of English. Through reading, examining, and discussing the human experience as presented in the stories, students using this text will learn to consider, crystallize, state, and evaluate the thoughts and feelings that naturally arise when one reads literature.

STRUCTURE OF THE TEXT

The stories in *Fictional Flights* evolve in two distinct ways. First, the content and themes grow from highly transparent narratives about very mundane experience to extremely profound stories about universal and timeless concerns. The techniques of reading fiction also increase in complexity. Basic components necessary to grasp literature are introduced in the early chapters. More sophisticated modes of enjoying and appreciating literature are added in a measured, graded manner in the middle and later chapters. Explanations of key concepts, both of content and technique, recur throughout the book but do not depend on repetition.

AUDIENCE

Fictional Flights is designed to meet the needs of high-intermediate to advanced students of English as a second or foreign language.

'▲'▲'▲'▲'▲'▲'

COMPONENTS

Fictional Flights is a complete and well-integrated program for students and teachers alike. In addition to the student text, an Instructor's Manual and an audio cassette are also available. The Instructor's Manual offers the teacher a wealth of specific suggestions and general guidelines designed to successfully facilitate the classroom use of the student text. The audio cassette, which includes recordings of selected readings, involves students in the aural dimension of literature and emphasizes the significance of literary devices such as intonation, rhythm, and style.

'▲'▲'▲'▲'▲'

APPROACH

As often as possible, students should read the stories in *Fictional Flights* on their own after the teacher has introduced the story in the way she or he prefers. In each chapter, students should be encouraged to draw on their own knowledge and experience in order to facilitate and enhance their interaction with the story.

The willingness of students to reflect on the content of the stories rather than to accumulate knowledge of concepts or terms will make the reading easier and more pleasant. For that reason, the majority of necessary terms are explained as part of the ongoing discussion of stories, not separated from the text, in language as plain as possible. Students should not strive to memorize or study the terms for themselves. The terms are useful only as guides to greater understanding and more enjoyment of the stories.

Instructors should not expect to complete all of the activities in each chapter. Instead, the teacher is encouraged to select the most important and appropriate activities for his or her own particular class.

Enjoy your journey.

ACKNOWLEDGMENTS

I would like to express my appreciation to Erik Gundersen and Lynne Telson Barsky for their unfailing support throughout the writing of this book.

My thanks also go to Kathleen Ossip and Susan Maguire, who had faith in the book in the earliest stages.

For their encouragement throughout the project, I would like to thank John Dumicich and Aurora Wolfgang.

I am grateful to Candace Harper, whose foreword so enhances this book.

For their intelligent and lively participation, I acknowledge the students who read and discussed the stories with me in the Day Intensive Program at New York University's American Language Institute.

OUTER MARKER[1]

Entering the World of the Imagination

Does your classroom have a window? If it does, look outside for a minute or two. What do you see: a building, a piece of sky, a person walking on the street outside? Now imagine that your classroom is moving slowly away from that building, piece of sky, or street. The building is becoming smaller and smaller. The distance between your world in this room and the people and objects outside is becoming greater and greater. The building, the piece of sky, and the street all still exist, are still part of the world, but their location and your location in your classroom are so far apart now that, temporarily, you are in one world and the building, the piece of sky, and the street are in another, separate world. In *your* world, by allowing yourself to imagine, you can do whatever you want, be wherever you wish. For now, the "laws" and rules of that other, faraway world— the laws of gravity, parking, crime and punishment, even health and sickness, do not matter or apply to you.

---

[1]Outer, middle, and inner markers are terms used to indicate certain positions on an airplane's approach to the airport.

CHAPTER ONE

DEPARTURES I

The goals for this chapter are:

To learn the basic elements of short story analysis
To discover how fantasy and truth co-exist in fiction

In this chapter, you will read:

"Jack and the Beanstalk," a fable
"The Princess and the Pea" by Hans Christian Andersen

So they lived on the bag of gold for some time, but at last they came to the end of it, and Jack made up his mind to try his luck once more up at the top of the beanstalk.

"Jack and the Beanstalk"

◆◆◆◆◆◆◆◆◆◆◆◆◆◆◆◆◆◆◆◆◆◆
A. INTRODUCTIONS

1: INTRODUCTIONS TO EACH OTHER AND TO THE WORLD OF THE IMAGINATION

Perhaps you do not know each other's names yet. Instead of telling everybody your name, take a few minutes to remember something you have always wanted to do or something you have always wished would happen to you. After five minutes, tell all your classmates what this fantasy is and briefly explain it. For example, when did you first have this fantasy? Why do you want this fantasy? Enjoy your own and your classmates' journeys into these private (and now shared) imaginary, fantastic worlds.

2: PREPARING TO READ

To prepare to discuss the first story you will read this semester, read aloud "Jack and the Beanstalk" with your classmates. Each of you will read a part, perhaps one or two sentences or a paragraph.

 Now recall the fantasy you and your fellow students told each other today. Did you notice that those fantasies contained some real details taken from and observed in daily life? What were those details? Remember that pure fact and pure fantasy are at opposite ends of the spectrum of reality: most stories combine both. With this idea in mind, reread "Jack and the Beanstalk."

JACK AND THE BEANSTALK

1   There was once upon a time a poor widow who had an only son named Jack and a cow named Milky-White. And all they had to live on was the milk the cow gave every morning, which they carried to the market and sold. But one morning Milky-White gave no milk, and they didn't know what to do.

2   "What shall we do, what shall we do?" said the widow, wringing her hands.

3   "Cheer up, mother, I'll go and get work somewhere," said Jack.

4   "We've tried that before, and nobody would take you," said his mother; "we must sell Milky-White and with the money start shop or something."

5   "All right, mother," says Jack; "it's market-day today, and I'll soon sell Milky-White, and then we'll see what we can do."

6   So he took the cow's halter in his hand, and off he started. He hadn't gone far when he met a funny-looking old man, who said to him: "Good morning, Jack."

7   "Good morning to you," said Jack, and wondered how he knew his name.

8   "Well, Jack, and where are you off to?" said the man.

9   "I'm going to market to sell our cow here."

10   "Oh, you look the proper sort of chap to sell cows," said the man; "I wonder if you know how many beans make five."

11   "Two in each hand and one in your mouth," says Jack, as sharp as a needle.

12   "Right you are," says the man, "and here they are, the very beans themselves," he went on, pulling out of his pocket a number of strange-looking beans. "As you are so sharp," says he, "I don't mind doing a swop with you — your cow for these beans."

13   "Go along," says Jack; "wouldn't you like it?"

14   "Ah! you don't know what these beans are," said the man; "if you plant them overnight, by morning they grow right up to the sky."

15   "Really?" said Jack; "you don't say so."

16   "Yes, that is so, and if it doesn't turn out to be true you can have your cow back."

17   "Right," says Jack, and hands him over Milky-White's halter and pockets the beans.

18   Back goes Jack home, and as he hadn't gone very far, it wasn't dusk by the time he got to his door.

19   "Back already, Jack?" said his mother; "I see you haven't got Milky-White, so you've sold her. How much did you get for her?"

20   "You'll never guess, mother," says Jack.

21   "No, you don't say so. Good boy! Five pounds, ten, fifteen, no, it can't be twenty."

22   "I told you you couldn't guess. What do you say to these beans; they're magical, plant them overnight and — "

23   "What!" says Jack's mother, "have you been such a fool, such a dolt, such an idiot, as to give away my Milky-White, the best milker in the parish, and prime beef to boot, for a set of paltry beans? Take that! Take that! Take that! And as for your precious beans here they go out of the window. And now off with you to bed. Not a sup shall you drink, and not a bit shall you swallow this very night."

24   So Jack went upstairs to his little room in the attic, and sad and sorry he was, to be sure, as much for his mother's sake, as for the loss of his supper.

25   At last he dropped off to sleep.

26   When he woke up, the room looked so funny. The sun was shining into part of it, and yet all the rest was quite dark and shady. So Jack jumped up

and dressed himself and went to the window. And what do you think he saw? Why, the beans his mother had thrown out of the window into the garden had sprung up into a big beanstalk, which went up and up and up till it reached the sky. So the man spoke truth after all.

27   The beanstalk grew up quite close past Jack's window; so all he had to do was to open it and give a jump on to the beanstalk which ran up just like a big ladder. So Jack climbed, and he climbed, and he climbed, and he climbed, and he climbed, and he climbed, and he climbed till at last he reached the sky. And when he got there he found a long broad road going as straight as a dart. So he walked along, and he walked along, and he walked along till he came to a great big tall house, and on the doorstep there was a great big tall woman.

28   "Good morning, mum," says Jack, quite polite-like. "Could you be so kind as to give me some breakfast?" For he hadn't had anything to eat, you know, the night before, and was as hungry as a hunter.

29   "It's breakfast you want, is it?" says the great big tall woman, "It's breakfast you'll be if you don't move off from here. My man is an ogre and there's nothing he likes better than boys broiled on toast. You'd better be moving on or he'll soon be coming."

30   "Oh! please mum, do give me something to eat, mum. I've had nothing to eat since yesterday morning, really and truly, mum," says Jack. "I may as well be broiled as die of hunger."

31   Well, the ogre's wife was not half so bad after all. So she took Jack into the kitchen and gave him a chunk of bread and cheese and a jug of milk. But Jack hadn't half finished these when thump! thump! thump! the whole house began to tremble with the noise of someone coming.

32   "Goodness gracious me! It's my old man," said the ogre's wife, "what on earth shall I do? Come along quick and jump in here." And she bundled Jack into the oven just as the ogre came in.

33   He was a big one, to be sure. At his belt he had three calves strung up by the heels, and he unhooked them and threw them down on the table and said: "Here, wife, broil me a couple of these for breakfast. Ah! what's this I smell?

34   Fee-fi-fo-fum,
       I smell the blood of an Englishman,
       Be he alive, or be he dead
       I'll have his bones to grind my bread."

35   "Nonsense, dear," said his wife, "you're dreaming. Or perhaps you smell the scraps of that little boy you liked so much for yesterday's dinner. Here, you go and have a wash and tidy up, and by the time you come back your breakfast'll be ready for you."

36   So off the ogre went, and Jack was just going to jump out of the oven and run away when the woman told him not. "Wait till he's asleep," says she; "he always has a doze after breakfast."

37   Well, the ogre had his breakfast, and after that he goes to a big chest and takes out of it a couple of bags of gold, and down he sits and counts till at last his head began to nod, and he began to snore till the whole house shook again.

38   Then Jack crept out on tiptoe from his oven, and as he was passing the ogre he took one of the bags of gold under his arm, and off he pelters till he came to the beanstalk, and then he threw down the bag of gold, which of course fell into his mother's garden, and then he climbed down, and climbed down till at last he got home and told his mother and showed her the gold and said, "Well, mother, wasn't I right about the beans? They are really magical, you see."

39   So they lived on the bag of gold for some time, but at last they came to the end of it, and Jack made up his mind to try his luck once more up at the top of the beanstalk. So one fine morning he rose up early, and got on to the beanstalk, and he climbed, and he climbed, and he climbed, and he climbed, and he climbed, and he climbed till at last he came out on to the road again and up to the great big tall house he had been to before. There, sure enough, was the great big tall woman a-standing on the doorstep.

40   "Good morning, mum," says Jack, as bold as brass, "could you be so good as to give me something to eat?"

41   "Go away, my boy," said the big tall woman, "or else my man will eat you up for breakfast. But aren't you the youngster who came here once before? Do you know, that very day, my man missed one of his bags of gold."

42   "That's strange, mum," said Jack, "I dare say I could tell you something about that; but I'm so hungry I can't speak till I've had something to eat."

43   Well, the big tall woman was so curious that she took him in and gave him something to eat. But he had scarcely begun munching it as slowly as he could when thump! thump! thump! they heard the giant's footstep, and his wife hid Jack away in the oven.

44   All happened as it did before. In came the ogre as he did before, said: "Fee-fi-fo-fum," and had his breakfast of three broiled oxen. Then he said: "Wife, bring me the hen that lays the golden eggs." So she brought it, and the ogre said: "Lay," and it laid an egg all of gold. And then the ogre began to nod his head and to snore till the house shook.

45   Then Jack crept out of the oven on tiptoe and caught hold of the golden hen and was off before you could say "Jack Robinson." But this time the hen gave a cackle which woke the ogre, and just as Jack got out of the house he heard him calling: "Wife, wife, what have you done with my golden hen?"

46   And the wife said: "Why, my dear?"

47   But that was all Jack heard, for he rushed off to the beanstalk and climbed down like a house on fire. And when he got home he showed his mother the wonderful hen, and said "Lay" to it; and it laid a gold egg every time he said, "Lay."

48   Well, Jack was not content, and it wasn't very long before he determined to have another try at his luck up there at the top of the beanstalk. So one fine morning, he rose up early and got on to the beanstalk, and he climbed, and he climbed, and he climbed, and he climbed till he got to the top. But this time he knew better than to go straight to the ogre's house. And when he got near it, he waited behind a bush till he saw the ogre's wife come out with a pail to get some water, and then he crept into the house and got into the copper. He hadn't been there long when he heard thump! thump! thump! as before, and in came the ogre and his wife.

49   "Fee-fi-fo-fum, I smell the blood of an Englishman," cried out the ogre. "I smell him, wife, I smell him."

50   "Do you, my dearie?" says the ogre's wife. "Then, if it's that little rogue that stole your gold and the hen that laid the golden eggs he's sure to have got into the oven. And they both rushed to the oven. But Jack wasn't there, luckily, and the ogre's wife said: "There you are again with your fee-fi-fo-fum. Why of course it's the boy you caught last night that I've just broiled for your breakfast. How forgetful I am, and how careless you are not to know the difference between live and dead after all these years."

51   So the ogre sat down to the breakfast and ate it, but every now and then he would mutter: "Well, I could have sworn—" and he'd get up and search the larder and the cupboards and everything, only, luckily he didn't think of the copper.

52   After breakfast was over, the ogre called out, "Wife, wife, bring me my golden harp." So she brought it and put it on the table before him. Then he said: "Sing!" and the golden harp sang most beautifully. And it went on singing till the ogre fell asleep and commenced to snore like thunder.

53   Then Jack lifted up the copper-lid very quietly and got down like a mouse and crept on hands and knees till he came to the table, when up he crawled, caught hold of the golden harp and dashed with it towards the door. But the harp called out quite loud: "Master! Master!" and the ogre woke up just in time to see Jack running off with his harp.

54   Jack ran as fast as he could, and the ogre came rushing after and would soon have caught him only Jack had a start and dodged him a bit and knew where he was going. When he got to the beanstalk the ogre was not more than twenty yards away when suddenly he saw Jack disappear like, and when he came to the end of the road he saw Jack underneath climbing down for dear life. Well, the ogre didn't like trusting himself to such a ladder, and he stood and waited; so Jack got another start. But just then the harp cried out: "Master! Master!" and the ogre swung himself down on to

the beanstalk, which shook with his weight. Down climbs Jack, and after him climbed the ogre. By this time Jack had climbed down, and climbed down, and climbed down till he was very nearly home. So he called out: "Mother! Mother! bring me an axe; bring me an axe." And his mother came rushing out with the axe in her hand, but when she came to the beanstalk she stood stock still with fright, for there she saw the ogre with his legs just through the clouds.

55   But Jack jumped down and got hold of the axe and gave a chop at the beanstalk which cut it half in two. The ogre felt the beanstalk shake and quiver, so he stopped to see what was the matter. Then Jack gave another chop with the axe, and the beanstalk was cut in two and began to topple over. Then the ogre fell down and broke his crown, and the beanstalk came toppling after.

56   Then Jack showed his mother his golden harp, and what with showing that and selling the golden eggs Jack and his mother became very rich, and he married a great princess, and they lived happy ever after.

◆◆◆

B. FACT AND FANTASY IN FICTION

3: A GROUP SUMMARY

Explain to your classmates one event that occurred in the story. If there is some action in the story you don't understand, ask one of your classmates to explain that action.

4: POSSIBLE AND IMPOSSIBLE DETAILS

Some of the people and objects in "Jack and the Beanstalk" are facts of every day life: a mother, a son, bread, and cheese. Other actions and objects mix the factual and the fantastic, for example, snores so loud that they shake a whole house, a hen that lays golden eggs, and a beanstalk tall enough to reach the sky. Make a short list of the actions, objects, and people in the story that you feel are impossible to find in everyday life. For example, can a harp ever call out to its master?

1. _____

2. _____

3. _____

4. _____

5. _____

5: IMPOSSIBLE WORDS

Some idioms state apparent impossibilities, yet these idioms often have a meaning in daily life and are frequently used . For example, "Has the cat got your tongue? " or "Have you swallowed your tongue? " suggests that a person cannot speak. Other examples include "She ran like the wind," "It's raining cats and dogs," and "He is drowning himself in drink." In a dictionary or in a book of idioms in English, find an idiom that suggests impossibilities and explain to the class what it means.

6: FACT AND FANTASY CLOZE

Read the lines below from "Jack and the Beanstalk." First, without looking back at the story, fill in the blanks with FACTUAL words you think best fit. In the second copy of the passage, fill in the blanks with FANTASY words you think best fit. Compare your choices with the story itself and with your classmates' choices. Discuss why one word choice fits better than another word choice.

A. Factual Cloze:

Well, Jack was not content, and it wasn't very long before he _____
(1)

to have another try at his luck up there at the top of the _____ .
(2)

So one fine _____ , he rose up early and _____ to the
(3)   (4)

beanstalk, and he_____ , and he_____ and
(5)   (6)

he _____ , and he _____ till he got to the top.
(7)   (8)

But this time he knew better than to _____ straight to the ogre's
(9)

house. And when he got near it, he_____ behind a bush till he
(10)

_____ the ogre's wife come out with a pail to get some
(11)

_____ , and then he crept into the house and got into the copper.
(12)

He hadn't been there long when he heard _____ _____
(13)   (14)

_____ as before, and in _____ the ogre and
(15)   (16)

his wife.

B. Fantasy Cloze:

Well, Jack was not content, and it wasn't very long before he _____
(1)

to have another try at his luck up there at the top of the _____ .
(2)

So one fine_____ , he rose up early and _____ to the
(3)   (4)

beanstalk, and he_____ , and he _____ and
(5)   (6)

he_____ , and he _____ till he got to the top.
(7)   (8)

But this time he knew better than to _____ straight to the ogre's
(9)

house. And when he got near it, he_____ behind a bush till he
(10)

_____ the ogre's wife come out with a pail to get some
(11)

_____ , and then he crept into the house and got into the copper.
(12)

He hadn't been there long when he heard _____ _____
(13)   (14)

_____ as before, and in _____ the ogre and
(15)   (16)

his wife.

◆◆◆◆◆◆◆◆◆◆◆◆◆◆◆◆◆◆◆◆◆◆◆◆◆◆◆◆◆◆◆◆◆◆◆

C. THE REAL VERSUS THE TRUE

You have discussed how the real in "Jack and the Beanstalk" differs from the story's fantasy elements. The "real" also differs from the "true." While hens which lay golden eggs are not real, that is, do not exist, they may still be true. Stating that some event, person, character, or detail "rings true" doesn't mean that the event actually happened or that the person or character actually lived. Rather, "true" means that events, details, and persons that don't have a physical, observable reality still suggest insight that reveals something essential about life.

7: GIFTS FROM OUT OF THE BLUE OR MY GOLDEN HEN

Now think about the "truth" of the beanstalk and the hen that lays the golden eggs. Try to recall moments in your life, perhaps as a child, when you had great hopes or great ideas for doing something very important but needed more money than you had to carry out your plan. You started to invent ways to get this money. What were some of the plans you made or visions you had about how the money would come into your hands? Write some of them below.

I hoped to receive money by

1. _____

2. _____

3. _____

4. _____

5. _____

8: SENT FROM ABOVE

Human beings have always dreamed of ways money would come to them, even imagining it falling from the sky into their hands. For example, a popular song of the 1930s by the American singer Bing Crosby is called "Pennies from Heaven." Can you think of other things people have expected might come from the heavens? Add your own examples below.

1. _____

2. _____

3. _____

As you read the story below, you will have a chance to see a delicate combination of the "real" and the "true" in fiction and to observe how the two aspects, while different, work together smoothly.

THE PRINCESS AND THE PEA
Hans Christian Andersen

1   There was once a prince who wanted to marry a princess; but she was to be a *real* princess. Though he travelled about, all through the world, to find a real one, there was always something wrong. There were princesses enough, but whether they were *real* princesses he could not quite make out: there was always something that did not seem quite right. So he came home again, and was quite sad, for he wished so much to have a real princess.

2   One evening a terrible storm came up; it lightened and thundered, and the rain streamed down; it was quite fearful! Then there was a knocking at the town gate, and the old king went out to open it.

3   It was a princess who stood outside. But, mercy! how she looked from the rain and the bad weather! The water ran down from her hair and clothes; it ran in at the tops of her shoes and out at her heels; and yet she declared that she was a real princess.

4   "Well, we shall soon find that out," thought the old queen. But she said nothing, only she went out into the bed-chamber, took off all the bedding, and put a pea on the bedstead; then she took twenty mattresses and laid them on the pea, and then twenty eider-down featherbeds upon the mattresses. This was where the princess was to lie all night.

5   In the morning she was asked how she had slept.

6   "Oh, miserably!" answered the princess. "I scarcely closed my eyes all the night long. Goodness only knows what was in my bed. I lay upon something hard, so that I am black and blue all over. It is quite dreadful!"

7   They saw at once that she was indeed a real princess, for through the twenty mattresses and the twenty eider-down feather-beds she had felt the pea. No one but a real princess could be so sensitive.

8   So the prince took her to be his wife, for now he knew he had found a real princess; and the pea was put into the museum, where it may still be seen, unless someone has stolen it.

9   Look you, this is a true story.

9: "IMAGINARY TOADS IN REAL GARDENS"

With your partner, think about the following questions about "The Princess and the Pea." Then, discuss the answers with your classmates.

1. What are the "real" elements in the story?

   Model: **a storm**

   _____ _____ _____

   Explain to your partner(s) why you feel they are "real."

2. What actions, characters, and details of the story seem unlikely or impossible? Why do you feel they are so?

3. Remember the beanstalk and the hen that laid the golden eggs. Can you connect the "impossibilities" in "The Princess and the Pea" to something "true" to life?

4. Describe the characters, backgrounds, likes and dislikes, and experiences of the prince and the princess.

5. Based on your information, do you believe they are well-suited to one another? Do you think they will have a satisfying marriage and life together? Why do you think so?

A Note to Take with You on Your Journey

In the fiction you will be reading, the "real" actions, people, and details will be fewer or greater depending on the story. When fewer "real" actions occur, the story may seem to pull you away from the "real" world, and you may want to resist this pulling. At these times, try to remember Jack's beanstalk and the hen that lays the golden eggs. Recall that though Jack, his beanstalk, and his hen may never have existed, you know, through your own experiences and those of others, their "truth." Such "truth" in fiction combines with the "real" to make fiction what it is, the story teller's fullest possible picture of life at that time.

10: WRITING ACTIVITY

A Beanstalk I Had in My Mind: A Three-Paragraph Essay

Paragraph One: Explain your "beanstalk," something you considered impossible at one time in your life. Identify it and explain what it is. For example, it may be swimming a distance you thought you could never swim, getting a job you thought out of your reach, or conquering a fear that once ruled you.

Paragraph Two: Explain why you thought your "beanstalk" could not become a reality.

Paragraph Three: Explain how you feel now. Do you still think your "beanstalk" is impossible, or have you changed your mind? Why or why not?

Model Topic: **I once didn't believe a man could climb up the side of a 107-floor building.**

CHAPTER TWO
DEPARTURES II

The goals for this chapter are:

To understand the characters, plot, and setting of a story

To begin reading fiction effectively

In this chapter, you will read:

"The Man, the Boy, and the Donkey" by Aesop

*The man said: "Aren't you ashamed of yourself
for overloading that poor Donkey of yours
— you and your hulking son?"*

"The Man, the Boy, and the Donkey"

◆◆◆
A. FIVE FOUNDATIONS OF FICTION LAND

When you walk through an airport almost anywhere in the world, you recognize familiar areas: the ticket counter, the baggage claim area, a restaurant or snack bar, and a gift shop. The world of fiction also has some recognizable areas: (1) setting, (2) events or action, (3) details, (4) plot, and (5) character, as well as additional areas. These five areas can be found in "The Princess and the Pea."

Settings: a town gate during a very bad storm, a bedroom, a museum.

Actions: a prince travels the world looking for a real princess to marry; a princess arrives in town during a storm and sleeps the night at the castle; traveling; sleeping; arranging a marriage.

Details: thunder, lightning, wet hair, twenty mattresses, black and blue marks on the princess's delicate skin, a pea.

Plot (the dramatic arrangement of the action): a prince has been traveling the world looking for a princess to marry. By chance, a woman who says she is a princess arrives at the town gate wet and cold from the rain. The plot continues with the princess's sleepless night, the queen's "test" (putting a pea under the princess's twenty mattresses) to find out if she is a real princess, her awakening the next morning, body aching from the pea which disturbed her all night, and, finally, the prince's decision that she is a real princess whom he can and will marry.

Characters: The prince, princess, king, and queen begin and carry out all the action of the plot. They have desires (to find a princess), problems (it is difficult to find one), opportunities (a princess arrives who may be the right one), and plans to solve their problems (test the princess). Finally, they get results (they find a princess and the prince marries her.)

◆◆◆
B. BUILDING ON THE FOUNDATIONS

Of the main distinct areas of fiction, the setting, events, details, plot, and character are the most important. From this chapter to Chapter Five most of your attention will focus on these elements of fiction as well as on time, subplots, and structure. The special focus of this chapter is The Who, Character; the What, Plot; and the Where, Setting; three aspects of Aesop's "The Man, the Boy, and the Donkey," a Sixth Century B.C. fable.

THE MAN, THE BOY, AND THE DONKEY
Aesop

1   A man and his son were once going with their Donkey to market. As they were walking along by its side a countryman passed them and said: "You fools, what is a Donkey for but to ride upon?"

2   So the Man put the Boy on the Donkey and they went on their way. But soon they passed a group of men, one of whom said: "See that lazy youngster, he lets his father walk while he rides."

3   So the Man ordered his Boy to get off, and got on himself. But they hadn't gone far when they passed two women, one of whom said to the other: "Shame on that lazy lout to let his poor little son trudge along."

4   Well, the Man didn't know what to do, but at last he took his Boy up before him on the Donkey. By this time they had come to the town, and the passers-by began to jeer and point at them. The Man stopped and asked what they were scoffing at. The men said: "Aren't you ashamed of yourself for overloading that poor Donkey of yours—you and your hulking son?"

5   The Man and Boy got off and tried to think what to do. They thought and they thought, till at last they cut down a pole, tied the Donkey's feet to it, and raised the pole and the Donkey to their shoulders. They went along amid the laughter of all who met them till they came to Market Bridge, when the Donkey, getting one of his feet loose, kicked out and caused the Boy to drop his end of the pole. In the struggle the Donkey fell over the bridge, and his fore-feet being tied together he was drowned.

6   "That will teach you," said an old man who had followed them:

7   "Please all, and you will please none."

THE WHO

1. Full-Dimensional (Round) Characters: **Full** or **round** characters, usually opposed to one-dimensional or **flat** characters, are complete human beings whose thoughts, feelings, and actions are changing all the time. For this reason, we do not always know what they are going to do and we are sometimes surprised or even shocked by their thoughts, words, or actions. Because they are not persons with only one characteristic who rarely or never change, they reveal themselves more fully and allow us to know them better than flat characters.

1: BECOMING THE CHARACTERS

The title of the story, "The Man, the Boy, and the Donkey," pulls readers toward its three main characters.

   a. With the others in your group, become one of the main characters in this story: the man, the boy, the donkey (the donkey is also a character), one of the two women, or a man passing by. Think about what you, the character, feel, speak, and do. Why do you feel, speak, and act that way? For example, if you are the man, why do you put your boy on the donkey? How do you feel about the other characters? Consider what kind of human beings they are. What kinds of desires, needs, concerns, and goals do they have?

   b. Then, tell the students in the other groups how your character (use the pronoun "I") thinks and feels. Finally, discuss why this character speaks and acts as she or he does. After listening to the other characters speak, discuss with your classmates what kinds of desires, needs, concerns, and goals their characters have. Evaluate the other characters, expressing your admiration, respect, pity, dislike, or apathy for them.

---

2. *One-Dimensional (Flat) Characters:* When a writer shows the reader *only* one part of a character (for example, that the character is a follower, and for the entire story, the character does nothing other than act as a follower), the reader has not met a character but only *the idea* of a character. Such characters, called "flat" characters, are difficult or impossible to understand and to believe in, making it difficult to "speak" in their voices.

THE WHAT

1. *Definition:* The "what" or **plot** is the fictional element closest to the "who." Plot and character exist side by side; a change in one usually affects the other. A series of events, called a **narrative,** is not always the same thing as a plot. What makes the events in any short story, like "The Man, the Boy, and the Donkey," a plot? The people, the scene, and the actions share a common time period. Nevertheless, this in itself doesn't make this series of events a plot. Activity 2 will help you answer the question: What constitutes a plot?

2: WHAT KIND OF STORY IS IT, ANYWAY?

Below you will find two accounts of the same events. Although they seem basically the same, they have small but important differences. Read both accounts. Make a list of the events of each account. Then compare the two lists. How are they different? What effect do these differences have on the two accounts and on you as the reader?

Account A: It rained last night. I was at the diner on Highway 1 at 6 P.M. When I came out, my car wouldn't start. My girlfriend wasn't home. I asked Elaine for a ride to the gas station to get some help. Elaine took me to the station and then left to go to the movies. The service station repairman came to the diner and fixed my car. At the movies, Elaine met my girlfriend. She told my girlfriend what had happened to me and how she helped me. Later I found out that my girlfriend was very angry at me.

Account B: At 6 P.M. I was at the diner eating during a cold, heavy rain. When I went out to start my car, I found it wouldn't start. I tried to call my girlfriend to help me, but she wasn't home. Then, suddenly I saw Elaine drive up to the diner. She was stopping after work for a snack before going to the movies. When I told her what had happened to my car, she offered to take me to the service station. She drove me there and left for the movies. The repairman came with me to the diner and, after a half hour, started my car. While he was fixing my car, a bad thing was developing. Elaine had run into my girlfriend at the movies and told her about my car and about driving me to the diner. My girlfriend has known Elaine since she was a child. They have always been in the same classes and tried to get better grades on every test. My girlfriend became very angry at me and asked me why I didn't try to find her instead of asking Elaine for help.

Which account is a plot? Which is simply a series of events sharing the same time period? What are the differences between the two?

---

2. *Plot and Story:* Any recorded series of events, even one which is not a plot, is often loosely called a **story**. The word "story," used in this sense, does not mean a short story like those you will be reading in this book. It refers only to a series of events. A plot, then, has several important elements not found in a story:

1. A "why," a reason or explanation why the characters act as they do, sometimes called the character's **motivation**;

2. A strong connection, usually a cause-effect relationship, between one action and those that follow it, sometimes called **causality**;

3. A carefully arranged sequence of events in which the relationship between the chronological order of the action and the relative importance of the events is clear.

3A: PLOTS OR STORIES

Read the accounts below. Decide if each is a plot or a story. What elements make the account a plot, or what missing elements make the account only a story? Explain your decision.

1. A man opens a door, enters a room, and sees a bleeding person lying on the floor with a gun next to him. The door on the other side of the room closes, and a man is seen running out. The gun on the floor is still warm from being shot, and the smell of gunpowder is in the air.

2. It is ten P.M. on a dark, almost deserted suburban street. A woman is walking very rapidly down the street. A man is following one hundred yards behind her, trying to catch up. He has his hand in the air, as if to signal her. She keeps looking back but won't stop.

3. A man rings the outside bell of apartment 3-A in a city building. There is no answer. Later, as he waits, the outside door is opened and he walks upstairs to the apartment. He rings the bell, but no one answers. Two pairs of shoes are in the hall outside the apartment door. The man goes downstairs again, exits the building, and waits. A woman wearing one pair of the shoes he has seen comes out. When he asks if his friend is there, she doesn't answer and leaves.

4. A businessman is late to a local airport for his flight on a small, private plane. Suitcase in hand, he hurries out to the runway, but the plane is already in the air. Disappointed and angry at himself, he begins to walk away, cursing the plane and the situation. Suddenly, the plane explodes and is completely destroyed, broken into pieces of wreckage. He gets on his knees on the runway and thanks God for saving his life. On his knees and with his head down, he is struck on the head by one of the pieces of the exploding plane.

3B: FOLLOW-UP

Choose one of the accounts above which you decided was a story, not a plot. Do what is necessary to change it into a plot. Consider, for example, what else you need to know about this event and the people in the story.

I need to know the following about

The Characters	The Time
1. _____	1. _____
2. _____	2. _____
3. _____	3. _____
4. _____	4. _____
5. _____	5. _____

The Reasons for the Actions	The Cause-Effect Relationship between Actions
1. _____	1. _____
2. _____	2. _____
3. _____	3. _____
4. _____	4. _____
5. _____	5. _____

What other information about the events and the people in this story do you need in order to make it into a plot?

Write your new version, your plot, below.

_____
TITLE OF MY PLOT

_____

_____

_____

_____

_____

_____

_____

_____

_____

_____

4: PLOT, REVIEW AND APPLICATION FOR CLASS DISCUSSION

Earlier in this chapter you read Aesop's "The Man, the Boy, and the Donkey." Do the events in Aesop's fable form a plot, or are they only a story?

THE WHERE

The **scene** of the story, where the story takes place, is a third element basic to fiction. The "where," like the "who" and the "what" discussed above, is an essential aspect of fiction.

A strong "where," a good scene, appeals to your visual sense. As you read it, you visualize a clear picture complete with all the details. The author may sometimes put many details in that picture and sometimes only a few, but even when only a few details are given, the scene always suggests many more.

"The Man, the Boy, and the Donkey" contains not one but several different scenes: a road leading to the market, the town, and the Market Bridge.

5: DEVELOPING A PICTURE

Imagine the Market Bridge as the man, the boy, and the donkey approach it. With your classmates, develop a picture of the scene. What do you see there? What buildings are there? What are the people wearing and doing? What is being sold? Add a detail or part to the scene your classmates are creating. Continue adding until the scene seems complete to you. Imagine, for example, these parts of the scene at the Bridge:

- Stone steps leading to and from the Bridge
- A long, narrow boat crossing under the Bridge

Now continue to add details to the scene.

As you read the stories in this book, you will come across many "wheres" or scenes. One of the first things you should do when you begin a story is to find out what the scene or scenes of the story are. Knowing where the action (the "what") of the story takes place, where the characters work and live will help you better enjoy and understand the story.

MORE ABOUT PLOT: ITS FLEXIBILITY IS NOT SET IN STONE

Most people accept the idea of the beginning, middle, and end of a story, a play, a piece of music, a ballet, or a film. Yet it is perfectly possible to imagine a different order of events; for example, giving the ending of a story at the beginning or returning to the beginning in the middle of a story. Many readers disagree about the way a particular story ends or don't agree with the direction the action of a story takes. In short, one plot rarely pleases everybody. In addition, the arrangement of events in a short story is to some extent culturally based. Differences of opinion may be the beginning of an opportunity for readers to see plot as something flexible, that is, grasping the notion of an "elastic" plot enables one to look at a particular story and see that it can begin and end in many different ways.

6: REVISING A PLOT

The story of Atalanta, a heroine of classical Greece, has been told and retold by such authors as Ovid, Apolladorus, and Hesiod. The essence of the story's action is as follows:

Several men wanted to marry Atalanta because of her great hunting and wrestling ability. She devised a method to put them off, saying that she would marry anyone who could defeat her in a foot race. She knew no man could do it. Many tried and lost. Finally, one, Melanion, planned a way to defeat her. He brought three golden apples with him to the race. As they raced, he threw one golden apple in front of her. She stooped to pick it up and he caught up to her. Soon after, he threw the second a little to the side. She moved to pick it up and he went ahead of her. However, she caught up with him. The third golden apple he threw far to the side of the race path. She ran to get it, and Melanion crossed the finish line ahead of her. She married him, and her freedom and athletic triumphs were over.

Atalanta's story does not have to remain the same as when written. Rearrangement is possible, actions can be added or removed, new characters and new aspects of old characters can appear, the scene can shift to another country, or the ending can change. Changing what you wish, rewrite Atalanta's story. You may wish to make an outline in the space below:

Beginning Actions	Mid-Actions	Concluding Actions
_____	_____	_____
_____	_____	_____
_____	_____	_____
_____	_____	_____
_____	_____	_____
_____	_____	_____
_____	_____	_____
_____	_____	_____
_____	_____	_____
_____	_____	_____
_____	_____	_____
_____	_____	_____
_____	_____	_____
_____	_____	_____
_____	_____	_____
_____	_____	_____
_____	_____	_____
_____	_____	_____

Write your "new" story here. When you have finished, compare your version of Atalanta with some of your classmates' versions. How are they different? Does different mean better or worse? Why or why not?

_____

_____

_____

_____

_____

_____

_____

_____

_____

_____

_____

_____

_____

_____

_____

_____

_____

_____

_____

_____

_____

_____

_____

_____

Guidelines for Reading Fiction

1. Read the entire story through once. Try to get a general sense of all the characters, the story line (plot), and the structure of the story. Do not stop for difficult words which may interfere with your understanding the action and overall movement.

2. Write a brief synopsis (summary) of what occurred in the story and the principle characters involved.

3. Make a list of questions you have about the story, questions of fact (what happened) and questions of interpretation (what does it mean?). Read through the story again with these questions in mind and try to answer them. To help you later locate difficult words, note all such words by underlining or another easy-to-find mark.

4. Go back to parts of the story that were difficult for you. Analyze those parts with reference to difficult sentences or difficult words. Use your technique of guessing from context to discover the meaning of those words. If you still can't find their meanings, use the dictionary.

5. Make a chart of the major events in the story. Look at it carefully to see what changes in people or situations it reveals. Then ask yourself what these changes mean or suggest. Does the story have a beginning, middle, and end? Which part is most important?

6. Concentrate on the language of the story. Has the author used a kind of language associated with a particular subject matter or aspect of life (religion, politics, myth, science, etc.)? What relation does this language have to the story?

7. Are there any kinds of language or references to your sensory experience that the author keeps repeating? These **image clusters** may help you understand the direction of the story.

8. Who is telling the story, a character or the author? How do you know? How does this **point of view** influence the way the story is told?

9. Is one character more important than the others? Why?

10. How much time passes during the story?

11. What is the overall tone or mood of the story?

CHAPTER THREE
PRACTICE FLIGHTS I

The goals for this chapter are:

To identify key moments in the plot of a story

To understand time, setting, and characters of a story

In this chapter you will read:

"Job Hunt" by John Zebrowski

"I say, Mr. Armstrong, I come by you house, you Big Boss, I say to you, I wannit job by powerhouse, you give me slip paper, I go inside gate, I get job."

"Job Hunt"

◆◆◆◀

A. THE WORLD OF THE JOB HUNTER

When jobs are hard to find, when many people are looking for work, or when the jobs available are not well-known or well-advertised, then the expression "job hunt" may apply to the search for work. What do the words "Job Hunt," the title of the story, suggest to you?   The expressions below are associated with job hunting:

job lead: some information or hint that lets a job seeker know there is a job free, such as someone telling his friend about a free job at his work.

strategy: a method or way a worker uses to try to get a job, for example, buying the newspaper the evening before she or he will search for a job.

knowing the right people: being familiar with or close to persons in important positions who are able to help someone job hunting.

shape up: a line of potential workers forming at a factory where jobs are thought to be available, usually in the early morning. Workers are picked from those who appear.

Most job seekers develop a strategy when hunting for a job, ranging from the ordinary, such as reading the job ads in the newspaper, to the very creative; a musician, for example, may send a copy of a composition she or he wrote to the director of a major orchestra. Most job-hunting strategies, however, are conventional rather than unique.

JOB HUNT
John Zebrowski

1   Uncle Bruno's job in the Punxsutawney mines ended and after waiting for a few weeks he realized that he would not be called back soon and that he had to do something. He asked the local priest to write his brother Joe in Wyandotte asking, How were things there?

2   Joe's priest wrote back for him and said that though things were not exactly booming it was possible to get some kind of a job, and anyway he could always stay with them until he found a place. That's what families were for—to stick together in a crisis, praise God, and may Providence bless you all, and so forth.

3   "I go," Uncle Bruno said to Stryjna. "After while you will come."

4   In spite of Uncle Bruno's original intentions over Stryjna's money when they married he had not squandered it, and they still had it all, plus a little

more they had saved since then. So they had train fare and much more to spare, and they both knew they could make the move and arrive at Joe's with capital besides.

5   "Ve go by bank tomorrow," Stryjna said. "Gettit money."

6   So they did and Uncle Bruno left Punxsutawney and that was the winter he came to Wyandotte to my father's house. And with a little money ahead it explains why he was not so desperate as some men about a job. But it does not explain his particular unique approach to job hunting.

7   He asked my father about the various factories and other employing institutions in the area and I could see him making quiet calculation as to their possibilities. But it was not until my father mentioned the Edison power station out on the channel near Trenton that Uncle Bruno's eyes glittered with a new animation and his manner became enthusiastic.

8   "How da git dis place?" he asked.

9   My father told him about the jitney service that way, how you catch a yellow jitney on Biddle Avenue practically any time day or night, pointing out that you could even bargain out the fare sometimes with the driver, and to this Uncle Bruno nodded with relish and winked at my father, as if anticipating a friendly fracas over a nickle or dime of fare.

10   The next morning Uncle Bruno arrived at the Edison Company power station. Dawn was just breaking and in the cold gray light the huge red-brick building with its three tall chimneys was impressive against the streaked and cloudy sky. It had a solid massive and substantial look, and Uncle Bruno approvingly associated it with other institutions like banks and churches. He started down the side street toward the building.

11   At the hiring gate he was startled to see that there were several hundred men huddling in the cold like a great mass of sheep.

12   "Crise sakes," he said to himself. "Is no for Bruno dis wait like bunch sheeps." He thereupon decided to ask a few questions. This must be indeed a desirable employer who could attract so many men at so early an hour, and it might be worth finding out a few facts.

13   The guard finally came out, menacing in manner out of the contumely of his own security.

14   "What the hell's eatin' you buddy?" he glowered.

15   "Who's Big Boss dis place?" Uncle Bruno asked.

16   "You mean the Shift Foreman?" the guard asked. "He ain't hirin' today. I told all you guys to go home. Ain't no use hangin' around."

17   "Screw Foreman," Uncle Bruno said. "Me wannit know name Big Fella Boss by da whole goddamn place."

18   "O.K., Big Shot," the guard leered at him. "You want Mr. Armstrong. He's Chairman of the Board of Directors."

19   "Otts my man," Uncle Bruno said. "Me wannit see."

20   "Lots of luck, pal," the guard derided him. "He ain't here. You'll find him at the Wyandotte Merchants' Bank. He owns that too." And he turned around amid the huge laughter of the assembled men and clattered back up the stairs into his warm guard's hut.

21   "Some nut," he said to the other guard. "Wants to know the name of the Big Boss so I told him to go see Old Man Armstrong at the Bank."

22   "Them nutty Polacks," the other guard said.

23   Uncle Bruno had meantime already left the laughter at the gate and was pushing his way back through the insults.

24   "Get a fifty out of him for me, pal," one said.

25   "Ask him to send up a bucket of hot coffee out here," another spoke up. And worse from some of the others.

26   On the main street Uncle Bruno caught a jitney back to town.

27   "I go Wyandotte Merchants' Bank," he told the driver.

28   "I'll let you off right in front of the place," the driver said. "But it don't open till ten o'clock."

29   "Otts all right," Uncle Bruno said. "Is be open, I be there." By now his determination was high, he was not to be denied.

30   At ten o'clock promptly when the guard threw open the bank doors Uncle Bruno was at the head of the little cluster of clients shivering in the bleak winter sun. Uncle Bruno's face was red from the cold and his nose was cold and his breath was frosty, but he was not cold. Not he. He was going to get in and see this Armstrong no matter what.

31   He entered the bank and paused. Which way? There were the private offices, there on the left, and there was another guard holding up his belly.

32   "Me wannit see Mr. Armstrong," Uncle Bruno said.

33   "Is that so?" the guard said. "You got an appointment?"

34   "Me wannit see."

35   "Mr. Armstrong is a busy man."

36   "Me busy too," Uncle Bruno said. "Is my life. Is my time. Is my business for me big business. Me wannit see Mr. Armstrong."

37   "What do you want to see him about?" the guard persisted.

38   "Is my business," Uncle Bruno stubbornly refused to tell. He would not deal with a servant regardless of gun and uniform. After all, Uncle Bruno was not educated but he came of an old family used to command.

39   "Unless you can state the nature of your business with Mr. Armstrong," the guard said, suddenly formalizing the situation by reciting his memorized speech, "I cannot permit you to enter the waiting room to request an appointment."

40   The language did not all come through to Uncle Bruno, but he realized from the change in tone and vocabulary that he had run into the final opposition from this pot bellied flunky, and there was no point in resorting to violence or any further altercation. He'd have to outwit him.

41   "O.K.," Uncle Bruno said, "Me wannit see Mr. Armstrong get job by house shovel up snow."

42   The guard smirked in triumph. "You don't have to see Mr. Armstrong about *that*," he said in scorn. "You can ask his butler. But I'll bet you you don't get hired, buddy."

43   "What place Mr. Armstrong live?" Uncle Bruno asked, ignoring the guard's discouragement and condescension.

44   "Three twenty-five Superior Boulevard," the guard answered. You never know about them nutty Polacks, he thought.

45   Uncle Bruno left the bank more determined than ever to see this Armstrong now. Whether he dented the man or not or even got to talk to him, Uncle Bruno felt he owed it to himself to try. He would. That evening at dinner he'd go over and breast the Big Man in his own home at his own table and put the question to him. At worst, if he lost his temper, he'd throw him off the premises.

46   By now the situation had reached the point in Uncle Bruno's mind where he would not brook opposition up to the final defeat or victory. He had to see the thing through. First, he would see where this Armstrong lived, and then he'd lay his plans for how to grab him off. Uncle Bruno was no respecter of status or position or even brains. He had some of his own, and his major respect was for power and authority—the which he wanted to invade or violate and subdue to his desires.

47   He caught another jitney out toward Superior Boulevard. He'd see where this Armstrong lived and look around. He might get an idea as to what to do or how to proceed—and by becoming familiar with the scene he'd ease some of the pressure on himself when he got into motion later.

48   Superior Boulevard turned out to be a fine residential neighborhood, the finest in Wyandotte, with spacious lawns, old and spreading elms and oaks and chestnuts, now barren, and large, gabled brick and stone houses with leaded windows and giant doors of mellow oak and beveled glass. This was the neighborhood built a generation or more ago by the people who founded and now owned the city. And there was 325—another large and spacious home with that solid substantial look that impressed Uncle Bruno as favorably as Mr. Armstrong's power plant and bank. He would see this man and he would speak to him. *Alea iacta est.* He crossed the Rubicon of his desire at that instant and ceased being a citizen engaged in quest of a job. He now was a Man of Dedication. He now was a man on the make and no banker-chairman-citizen Mr. Armstrong could say him nay.

49   He walked past the place looking it over, walked down the block briskly, turned a corner and walked on, then crossed the street and walked back. Uncle Bruno knew he could not stand around, giving the appearance of loitering. But to be moving briskly and purposively was the right thing to do.

These well-to-do neighborhoods could get the cops down on you faster than anything. He decided not to approach the house or the butler. The walk was already shoveled neatly and anyway Uncle Bruno had no intention of asking for a job shoveling snow. Nor was he about to diminish the surprise of his appearance by revealing himself now to be recognized later. He was after a permanent position at the power station, maybe the last job he'd ever seek, not some casual piece of odd labor.

50   There was the living room, on the right through those handsome bay windows, and evidently the gable at the left was the dining room. He'd be able to see Armstrong tonight when he came. He had an inspiration! Surely to approach the butler now would be to tip his hand. He would carry on with his plan tonight. Meantime, he'd go back to Joe's house and rest.

51   "How da go?" Joe asked.

52   "Otts all right," Bruno replied. "Me fix it up by Armstrong inna dinnertime." As if it were all settled and just awaited some final detail for consummation.

53   They spent the rest of the afternoon in pleasant, idle reminiscence and conversation, and I remember Uncle Bruno was lively and animated, exuding an air of vigor and drive and impending attack sure to be a triumph. Occasionally he would take a short swig of whiskey from the pint bottle in his coat pocket. But never enough for it to show except in a heightened liveliness. And along about dark he asked my mother for a sandwich to eat, and a little later he took off.

54   Uncle Bruno walked up to the Armstrong door and rapped sharply on the oval glass, using his special cocked knuckle technique.

55   "Yes?" the butler acknowledged Uncle Bruno's presence, unctuously but with a grain of caution. After all, who might this stranger in strange uniform be? Uncle Bruno had put on his sky-blue Polonais Volontaires uniform, complete with black leather leggings, visored cap, and overcoat with leather belt.

56   "Mr. Armstrong, please," said Uncle Bruno, trying with all the knowledge of English in his possession to keep words to a minimum, aware that his usual speech was only a garbled approximation of English.

57   "May I say who is calling?"

58   "Bruno Zebrowski," and he snapped a two-finger salute sharply to his visor.

59   The butler withdrew behind his composure, confused by this uniformed stranger, but obliged to do his duty.

60   He walked up to Armstrong's chair and stooped over. The candlelight glowed mellow in the walnut-paneled dining room. "Mr. Armstrong," he said, "beggin' your pardon, but a Bruno Zebrowski wishes to see you."

61   "What's his business?"

62   "I don't know, sir, but he is wearing some kind of foreign soldier's uniform."

63   "I see," said Mr. Armstrong. "Well, ask him to tell you what it's about. I'm at dinner now."

64   The butler returned to the living room where he had seated Uncle Bruno.

65   "Mr. Armstrong would like to know the nature of your business."

66   "Is business by Mr. Armstrong. Is my business. Is special business."

67   The butler grimaced with a querulous questioning look, but, used to being commanded by his superiors, he accepted the reply and strode back majestically in all his servant's pride over to Mr. Armstrong's chair, where he told his master what had transpired. "Well, then, ask him to wait till I finish with my dinner and see if he won't have something."

68   Ah, now Uncle Bruno's pride towered high. Of course he accepted refreshment—what else but a cognac and a cigar? Not since a wild leave in Paris had he had so fine a liquor or so noble a cigar. *Psiakrew, cholera!* This was life. And he basked in the radiance of his initiative and arrogance. What other common laborer but an illiterate aristocrat like Bruno Zebrowski could be invited to partake of vintage cognac and choice cigars right in the home of the city's leading and wealthiest citizen? On the strength of nothing more than sheer bravado—and imagination?

69   Finally dinner was over and Mr. Armstrong came into the room, a man obviously used to authority, but a man of great calmness and kindness. A man of steely benevolence.

70   "Sir," he said to Uncle Bruno, extending his hand, "I am James Armstrong." Uncle Bruno stood up and casually touched his Polonais Volontaires cap visor with two fingers in the regulation salute. Then he shook Armstrong by the proffered hand.

71   "Hoddy do," he said.

72   "Now, sir, what can I do for you."

73   "Dis morning," Uncle Bruno said, "over by power house man by gate say: Mr. Armstrong is Big Fella dis place. Is true?"

74   Armstrong look puzzled. But he understood.

75   "Yes, of course, I'm Chairman of the Board there. But I don't participate actively in the day-to-day management."

76   "Otts all right," Uncle Bruno said. "No make difference by me. By gate is couple hundred guys lookit for by job catchem. Stand by gate in cold, wait somebody lift it up finger say, Come here. Is big bunch sheeps."

77   "What is it you are trying to tell me, sir?" Could this be a complaint of mistreatment?

78   "I say, Mr. Armstrong, I come by you house, you Big Boss, I say to you, I wannit job by powerhouse, you give me slip paper, I go inside gate, I get job."

79   Armstrong's face underwent a transformation. From a puzzled attentive somehow confused expression all at once it dawned on him that this man had with colossal effrontery invaded his home at the dinner hour to ask for

some ordinary, unskilled job at the powerhouse. Good Lord! What a fantastic situation! And all at once he leaned back and laughed uproariously, holding his sides and roaring loudly in a manner his family had not heard for twenty years. And Uncle Bruno, sensing the man had realized the trap he'd found himself in, joined in, stomping his feet and grabbing Armstrong by the arm, they looked at each other like two conspirators and laughed till tears ran down their cheeks and they were out of breath, both of them stomping their feet, like little children, clasping and unclasping each other on the arm, patting each other on the back, slapping their thighs, and laughing, laughing, while the family stood in the doorway to the dining room and the butler and servants stood watching. And they too joined in, at first smiling and then laughing at the infectious and joyous and hilarious laughter until the whole house shook and reverberated with howls and roars of joyous mirth.

80   Finally, finally, after a half dozen attempts to stop, Armstrong managed to stop.

81   "Well, sir," he said, breathlessly, holding his sides helplessly. "I haven't had this good a laugh in I don't know how long. And just for that I'll see what I can do. What can *you* do?"

82   "Nothing," Uncle Bruno said. "No go school. No speak English good. Smart by da head but no can do."

83   "Yes, of course," Armstrong said, comprehending the quality of this man, with guts and brains, but unequipped. "All right," he said, "let's get you in to talk to the right people there, and they'll see how they can use you best." He walked over to his desk and sat down and wrote a note on his personal stationery. He then put it in an envelope and addressed it to Employment Manager.

84   "Show *this* at the gate tomorrow," he said, chuckling, "and they'll certainly let you in. And good luck. I really admire you."

85   "Thanks," Uncle Bruno said, meeting Armstrong's eyes in a gaze of camaraderie and equality. "Thanks, you good man."

86   "Well, sir," Armstrong said. "Lets have one more cognac for good luck. And have another cigar, please. You're a rare one, you are."

87   And in the morning, Uncle Bruno triumphantly walked through the mob of sheep at the gate, sneered at the guards, and got in to see the right people, who placed him in the right job, the only one available at the time— Dynamo Oiler, a simple job of some minor complexity and judgment, but allowing scope for occasional inattention. For Uncle Bruno it was right up his alley.

◆◆◆◆◆◆◆◆◆◆◆◆◆◆◆◆◆◆◆◆◆◆◆◆◆◆◆◆◆◆◆◆◆◆◆◆
B. KEY MOMENTS IN THE PLOT

The story "Job Hunt" is a narrative. Does it also have a plot? When you look carefully at some important moments in the story, what do you find? When Uncle Bruno, his wife, the workers, the guard at the factory, or Mr. Armstrong speak or act, why do they do so? Study the passages below taken from the story. Do you find a reason for the actions in the story? Is "Job Hunt" more than a narrative? Does it contain at least one essential element of a plot?

1: KEYS TO THE PLOT

Find the place in the story where each passage below appears. Explain the meaning of each passage. Finally, discuss the passages and decide if there is a reason or motivation for the actions related. If so, explain what it is.

1. Joe's priest wrote back for him and said that though things were not exactly booming it was possible to get some kind of a job, and anyway he could always stay with them until he found a place.

2. "Ve go by bank tomorrow," Stryjna said. "Gettit money."

3. At the hiring gate he was startled to see that there were several hundred men huddling in the cold like a great mass of sheep.
   "Crise sakes," he said to himself. "Is no for Bruno dis wait like bunch sheeps."

4. "Get a fifty out of him for me pal," one said.
   "Ask him to send up a bucket of hot coffee out here," another spoke up.
   And worse from some of the others.

5. "Unless you can state the nature of your business with Mr. Armstrong," the guard said, …"I cannot permit you to enter the waiting room to request an appointment."
   "Well, sir," he said, breathlessly, holding his sides helplessly. "I haven't had this good a laugh in I don't know how long. And just for that I'll see what I can do. What can *you* do? "

▶◆◆◆◆◆◆◆◆◆◆◆◆◆◆◆◆◆◆◆◆◀
C. AS TIME GOES BY

> In the famous American film, *Casablanca*, starring Humphrey Bogart and Ingrid Bergman, a song, "As Time Goes By," is played many times, either in part or in its entirety. Whenever the tune is played, it suggests that time within the story has moved forward. For example, it may indicate a change from one evening to the next evening or signal that something important in the characters has changed or will change. It may also indicate that one character has changed her or his mind about something or has discovered something she or he didn't know the day before. In a short story, as in the film *Casablanca,* the passage of time is very important. In "Job Hunt," it is clearly marked and, therefore, emphasized. These markers signal some movement of the characters or change in the action. Recognizing these time signals and connecting them to changes in characters or advances in the action of the story is one way to decipher the story's meaning.

2: MORE THAN MARKING TIME

On the left are listed some time markers used in the story. On the right are some important thoughts and actions from the story. Looking through the story carefully, connect a time marker to the correct thought or action and write the number of the time marker in the blank on the right. The time markers are not listed in the order they occurred in the story.

Time Marker	Thought or Action
Model	
1. after waiting for a few weeks	Uncle Bruno realizes he will not be rehired in the mines and decides to look for new work in a different place. **1**
2. along about dark	"Uncle Bruno triumphantly walked through the mob of sheep at the gate."____
3. at the gate tomorrow	Uncle Bruno waits for the bank to open. ____
4. and in the morning (2nd morning)	Uncle Bruno first arrives at the Edison Company Power Station. ____

5. at ten o'clock promptly

Uncle Bruno is told to come to the factory at this time and bring the letter Mr. Armstrong gave him. ____

6. that evening at dinner

Uncle Bruno eats a sandwich and leaves for Mr. Armstrong's house. ____

7. the next morning

The time Uncle Bruno fixes, after his visit to the bank, for his visit to Armstrong's house. ____

After you have completed the matching activity, ask yourself the questions below:

1. How much time does Uncle Bruno need for each decision he makes? Do you consider this (a) too long a time, (b) too short a time, or (c) just the right amount of time? Why?

2. Does Mr. Armstrong's response to Uncle Bruno appear too fast? Do you think in a non-fictional situation he would have taken more time?

3. What does the word "decisive" mean? Based on their decision-making process, do you think Uncle Bruno and Mr. Armstrong are decisive people?

♦♦♦♦♦♦♦♦♦♦♦♦♦♦♦♦♦♦♦♦♦♦
D. A SENSE OF PLACE

In addition to time, a change of place may also stimulate and be stimulated by the action of a story. In the first sentence of "Job Hunt," the reader learns that in his home area Uncle Bruno cannot find work again and has decided to move. What kind of place does Uncle Bruno come from? What kind of world is he going to? These are questions about the story's setting, another important part of the short story.

In "The Man, the Boy, and the Donkey," you visualized the setting. Another way to approach setting, however, involves words. The words the author uses to describe the people, the buildings, the weather, the transportation, and the natural sur-roundings of the area, for example, reveal much about the setting. If the reader carefully chooses and studies the meaning and sound of the essential words relating to those people and buildings, the weather, and so on, the nature of the story's set-ting will emerge.

3: PLACING THE STORY[1]

Read each sentence below and look at the underlined words. By noticing the information **implied** in the words—for example, weather conditions, cultural characteristics, and division of power— learn as much as you can about the setting. Then write what you have learned about the setting from them. Look at the model paragraph below.

Model: Uncle Bruno was at the head of the little cluster of clients shivering in the <u>bleak winter sun.</u>

The action of the story occurs in a place where there is a definite winter season. In such a place, work is sometimes seasonal. That is, people cannot plant crops and harvest all year, so there must be other work available. In addition, such a place must have the facilities and bear the expense of a heating system, of fuel oil. Probably some of the workers in the area have jobs related to producing fuel for the area. Finally, although the sun may shine, it remains cold and "bleak," in other words, sad. It is sometimes very difficult for people to survive physically and psychologically in such a setting.

1. "<u>Me wannit see</u> Mr. Armstrong get job by house shovel up snow."

   _____

   _____

   _____

   _____

   _____

   _____

2. Superior Boulevard turned out to be a fine residential neighborhood, the finest in Wyandotte, with spacious lawns, old and <u>spreading elms and oaks and chestnuts, now barren</u>, and <u>large, gabled brick and stone houses</u> with leaded windows and giant doors of mellow oak and beveled glass. This was the neighborhood built a generation or more ago by the people who <u>founded</u> and now <u>owned the city.</u>

   _____

   _____

   _____

[1]The word "story" here and throughout the remainder of this book differs from the word "story" (as opposed to plot) explained in the previous chapter. Story is now used to mean the narratives you will be reading in each chapter of this text.

_____

_____

_____

_____

3. He asked the <u>local priest to write his brother</u> Joe in Wyandotte asking, How were things there?

_____

_____

_____

_____

_____

4. But it was not until my father mentioned the <u>Edison power station</u> <u>out on the channel near Trenton</u> that Uncle Bruno's eyes glittered with a new animation and his manner became enthusiastic.

_____

_____

_____

_____

_____

_____

5. "Lots of luck, pal," the guard derided him. "He <u>ain't</u> here. You'll find him at the <u>Wyandotte Merchants' Bank. He owns that too.</u>"

_____

_____

_____

_____

_____

_____

_____

6. "What place Mr. Armstrong live?" Uncle Bruno asked, ignoring the guard's discouragement and condescension.

"Three twenty-five Superior Boulevard," the guard answered. You never know about them <u>nutty Polacks, he thought</u>.

_____

_____

_____

_____

_____

_____

7. Dawn was just breaking and in the <u>cold gray light</u> the <u>huge red-brick building</u> with its <u>three tall chimneys</u> was impressive against the <u>streaked</u> and <u>cloudy sky</u>. It had a solid <u>massive</u> and <u>substantial look</u>, and Uncle Bruno approvingly associated it with other <u>institutions like banks and churches</u>.

_____

_____

_____

_____

_____

_____

◆◆◆

E. THE RIGHT PERSON IN THE RIGHT PLACE AT THE RIGHT TIME

How important is setting to a story? In some stories, setting may become so vivid and so important that it seems to become a character in the story. Characters, however, are usually the most important elements in a work of fiction.

A person or a character who gets the most benefit from the time and place she or he occupies is said to be "in the right place at the right time." Uncle Bruno is such a character. Is he lucky to meet up with Mr. Armstrong and get a job at Edison Company power station? Or, on the other hand, do his attributes make him a successful job hunter? Evaluate Uncle Bruno the way an employer might conventionally evaluate a job applicant, through a job application such as the one below.

4: UNCLE BRUNO'S JOB APPLICATION

Review the story before completing the application. Examine Uncle Bruno's words and actions as he moves his home, consults family about job opportunities, and approaches prospective employers. Think about his personal attributes. What are his strong and weak points? Imagining you are Uncle Bruno, fill out the application for a job at the Edison Company power station.

Application for Employment
PLEASE PRINT CLEARLY

Personal

Date _____

Name ___<u>Zebrowski Bruno</u>___ Social Security Number _ _ _ - _ _ - _ _ _ _

Present Address _____
                 NO.   STREET

               _____
                  CITY   STATE   ZIP

Telephone _____

Are you legally eligible for employment in the U.S.A.? _____

Date of Birth _____

Position Applied For _____ Salary Sought _____

Were you previously employed by us? _____ If yes, when? _____

(TURN OVER)

Record of Education

School	Name and Address of School	Degree or Diploma
Elementary		
Junior High		
High		
College		
Graduate School		

Job History

List latest position first and work backward.

Employer	Date	Position	Reason for Leaving

Why do you feel you are qualified to work for the Edison Company power station?

_____

_____

_____

_____

_____

_____

How did you hear about the Edison Company power station?

Advertisement __ Personal Reference __ Other _____

After you have completed your application carefully, exchange it with a classmate. Evaluate the application from the employer's point of view. Which of Uncle Bruno's qualities would make him an asset to the company? Which might not fit or even be detrimental to the Edison Company power station? Do you agree with Mr. Armstrong's judgment of Uncle Bruno? Would you have helped him, as Mr. Armstrong did, to get the job? Remember that, when recruiting and hiring workers, many employers look for a good "fit" or good "match," that is, a strong relationship between what the company needs and what the job applicant can offer.

F. LOOKING AHEAD

This chapter addressed how plot, time, setting, and characters affect the development of a story. In the next chapter, you will meet more methods to help you more easily approach these elements as well as some new ones, such as subplot and theme. Try them all out, adding some of your own questions and methods to understand the next story, "Feast." With confidence and imagination, you will see the story open and reveal its riches to you.

CHAPTER FOUR

PRACTICE FLIGHTS II

The goals for this chapter are:

    To further explore characters and setting of a story

    To discover the relationship between the plot and subplot

In this chapter, you will read:

    "Feast" by Eric Larsen

Before Christmas she announced a special treat. A group of live Eskimos was to visit the class. We would be able to see them in the flesh.

"Feast"

◗◆◆◆◆◆◆◆◆◆◆◆◆◆◆◆◆◆◆◆◆◆◆◆◆
A. BEHIND THE SCENES

In "Feast" Eric Larsen has written what seems to be a simple story of one school day in the sixth grade, perhaps one school day he himself experienced. You probably can remember some of your own grade school days, although none may have been as unusual as this one. No matter how similar this school, teacher, and day may be to your own, they contain certain items special only to them. To appreciate them and to understand the story better, you need to find out something about the background of the story.

FEAST
Eric Larsen

1   In the sixth grade I had a teacher whose name was Christine Cutter. Even then I felt she was an earnest and idealistic young woman; a miniature silver cross hung each day from a fine chain around her neck; and she was fond of wearing a blue blazer that had the gold-embroidered emblem of the college she had graduated from sewn over her left breast. The college was named after one of the female saints, and its emblem depicted an open book radiating beams of light outward and also upward toward heaven, which was represented by three hovering gold clouds.

2   Miss Cutter felt that learning should be a meaningful experience. She endeavored to reveal the excitement of life to us, and to expand our vision to the point where we were aware of the great feast of knowledge the world has to offer. She attempted to bring things into the classroom, and she took us in turn outside to see things in the world. We went on outings to factories and fire departments and courthouses. Once we went to a local dairy, and Miss Cutter was fascinated by seeing the white bubbling milk flowing through transparent pipes under the ceiling.

3   Before Christmas she announced a special treat. A group of live Eskimos was to visit the class. We would be able to see them in the flesh.

4   The day they were to arrive started out warm and gray. A light mist was falling, and if you turned your face upward you could feel it touching your skin, but still it was hard to tell if it felt more like cool air or water. By the middle of the morning, from inside the steam-heated classroom, you could see that it was getting thicker; it was starting to form drops and beads as it drifted against the windowpanes. Then it turned to snow, shapeless heavy flakes falling straight down.

5   We ate lunch as usual in a room in the basement that was used the rest of the day as a gymnasium for the lowest three grades. Suspended under the ceiling there was a jungle of steampipes that made hissing sounds and dripped water down onto the pressboard tables that held our meals.

6   In the afternoon the disappointment grew general when it became clear that the visitors were going to be late. We read over the chapter on Eskimos again in our book, and Miss Cutter pointed out once more how the women chew on the hides of animals in order to make them soft. Then as we studied further with bowed heads she paced around the room, glancing at the clock and gazing out the steamed windows at the thickly falling snow outdoors. She stood with her arms folded together so that her breasts were like two cats sleeping in a cradle.

7   She gave us a recess in spite of the snow, and let us stay out longer than usual. It seemed dark outdoors and there was a particular hush in the air that seemed to absorb the sound of our voices and make our shouts sound as though they came from a great distance. The snow was already several inches deep over the ground, and heavy and damp.

8   Some of the girls began building snowmen, and others began games of Fox and Goose. The boys had a game of what we called Victim. Each of us chose a victim and attempted to bring him down in the snow. Everyone was a victim and a chaser at once, although the swiftest runners were seldom brought down.

9   Tim Greves was hurt. Someone hit him in the face and he had a cut lip and bloody nose. He was very small, even for his age, and he wailed in surprise and fear. The blood went down his chin and onto his coat until Tracey Cook put her arm around his shoulder and bent down and told him to lean forward. Then the blood dripped onto the snow, and she walked with him into the school with her arm around his shoulder.

10   We milled around not knowing what to do. It seemed strange outdoors, growing darker and the snow falling heavily down through the hushed air. Tracy Cook came back and stood with us. She had light hair and blue eyes, and flakes of snow caught in the lashes of her eyes and clung there a moment before they melted.

11   A drop of Tim Greve's blood had fallen on the white fur cuff of her coat and she scrubbed at it with snow a moment but then gave up. We were standing by the flag pole and Wendell Cleaver dared people to put their tongues on it. It was made of steel and no one would do it. He grabbed someone and started forcing his face up against it until Tracy Cook told him to quit it and after a minute or two he did. Of course he was doing it for her. We made a game of trying to see the top of the pole, but the snow fell into your eyes so it was hard to keep them open when you turned your face upward to look.

12   At last Miss Cutter called and we went back inside. It was already the end of the afternoon, and she made us sit down without taking off our coats. It was hot in the room. People's faces were red and burning, and everyone was wiping his hands under his nose. There was the smell of wet wool in the air.

13   There was only one Eskimo. She was a tiny figure, almost like a doll, padded and bulky in leggings and parka made of brown animal hide trimmed with fur at the wrists and the ankles and waist. There was fur around her hood, too, so that her small round face looked out at us from behind a perfect circle of gray fur. Her skin was weathered and almost black, soft and creased like the leather on the seats of antique cars. Her tiny black eyes jumped around the room as though she were afraid.

14   We stared at her.

15   The bell had already rung, but Miss Cutter placed the tiny Eskimo on a chair in the front of the room. Her feet failed to touch the floor, and her small brown hands, like paws with their short stubby fingers, rested together in her lap. Miss Cutter squatted down beside her and showed her how to open her mouth and bare her teeth. She did it herself several times before the Eskimo understood and opened her mouth up and stretched her lips back with her fingers the way Miss Cutter had done.

16   Then we filed past one by one and looked into her face. With her little black eyes fixed on us as though in terror, we looked into the opened privacy of her mouth to see the way her small brown teeth were worn down to almost nothing, just rows of stubs flattened and worn away down to the gums.

17   After we had seen, we went out of the classroom and into the hallway and out the door of the school again. When I stepped out, it seemed colder than before; after the steaming classroom the air was like ice water against my heated face, and I met it with relief and breathed it in as if I were thirsty for its coolness.

18   Others came out the door. The snow was still falling, perhaps more heavily, and the air was hushed and growing dark; it would be an early dusk. We began running across the snow-covered yard toward where the buses were waiting for us with their engines running and their small yellow lights shining through the snow. There was the jingle of the loose clasps on our boots as we ran, and one of the drivers called out with a curse that we ought to hurry at that because the roads were already hardly passable and school should have been canceled hours before.

◆◆

B. EXPLORING THE BACKGROUND OF "FEAST"

Read the brief background descriptions concerning "Feast."

1. Small Christian colleges in the midwestern United States.

   Throughout the United States and especially in the midwestern United States, there are many small Christian colleges. These colleges, which are often church-affiliated, may serve 500, 1000, 2000 students, or more. The students attending these colleges not only receive a basic liberal arts education but often study religion courses connected to the sponsoring church. These colleges often serve the communities around them and help provide an education for students who don't have the financial resources or the desire to travel far from home.

2. Eskimo background and cultural characteristics.

   Eskimos are a group of people living in northern Canada, Greenland, Alaska, and eastern Siberia. They are generally believed to be the original inhabitants of North America, the ancestors of the Indians. They are believed to have migrated from Siberia to Alaska thousands of years before the Vikings. Aboriginal Canadians, the Indians, and the Eskimos combined make up less than two percent of the Canadian population.

3. Busing to schools in rural areas of the United States.

   In many rural areas, that is, areas where few people live, each town or community may not have its own school. Rather, one central school serves many communities, and students are bussed from their homes to the central school. The students may travel many hours and miles each day to reach the school, and in bad weather—which is usual—the travel conditions are even worse.

4. Academic training of elementary school teachers in the United States.

   As part of their education for teaching, elementary school teachers in the United States have for a long time had to follow a carefully prescribed curriculum. As part of their training, elementary-school teachers are required to go to college, where they may study a major subject such as English or mathematics. In addition, they are required to complete a minimum of usually four education courses and to practice teach at a school. Thus, the emphasis in their teaching education is on teacher training as much as or more than on mastery of their major subject.

1: LETTER TO YOUR GRANDPARENTS

It is your first year in junior high school. Last week, your grandparents, who live about four hours' driving distance from your home, wrote a postcard to you. Your grandmother asked you how you like your new sixth-grade class. After reading "Feast," imagine you were at school the day of the actions in the story.

Write a letter to your grandparents telling them in your own words what happened that day. Tell not only what happened but how you feel about what you saw and heard. You do not need to report everything that happened. Write them only what you think is important and what they would like to know about your school day. The outline below gives you some advice about how to organize your letter.

Dear Grandma and Grandpa,

Paragraph One	**Greetings to your grandparents, general news.** I hope you are fine.
Paragraph Two	**What happened one day at school.** I want to tell you something that happened in my class last week. Miss Cutter, our teacher, had told us we were going to have a visitor.
Paragraph Three	**How did you feel about the day at school?**
Paragraph Four	**Closing to the letter, for example, their opinion about the Eskimo incident and when they are coming to visit you.**

◆◆
C. CHARACTERS: WHAT THEY SAY AND DO

To understand any short story, becoming familiar with the characters is extremely important. You can learn about a character in many ways, for example, (1) where the character was born and lives; (2) the character's appearance, such as height, weight, color of eyes and hair, etc.; (3) what kinds of clothes the character wears; (4) the character's friends, family, coworkers, etc.; (5) the character's education, if you know it; (6) his or her religion, if it is known; (7) what the character says and how she or he says it; and, of course, (8) what the character does—his or her actions. Those actions, which often reveal much about the character's entire life, including many of the areas just mentioned—education, religion, place of birth, and residence—can help you better understand the character.

2A: ACTIONS SPEAK LOUDER THAN WORDS

The story, "Feast," contains no dialogue; the characters never speak. We hear only the words of the unnamed narrator, one of the students himself, telling us what he and the other characters did that day.

In each question below, you will find an action or actions of a character in "Feast" summarized. For each action, four opinions about the character appear. The basis of each opinion is only the character's action. Although all the opinions may contain some truth, circle the letter of the sentence expressing the opinion which in your view *best* fits the action and the character. Discuss your answers with your classmates.

Model:

Although it was hot in the classroom, Miss Cutter made the students sit down without taking off their coats.

   A. The school day was almost over and Miss Cutter didn't want to waste time having students take off and put on their coats again.

   B. Since it was late in the day, Miss Cutter was tired and simply didn't remember to have the students remove their coats.

   C. Miss Cutter was nervous because the Eskimo had not arrived.

   D. Many of the students had colds, so Miss Cutter thought it was better for their health if they didn't take off and put on their coats frequently in a short time.

Answer: **C**

1. Miss Cutter often wore a blue blazer with the emblem of the college she had graduated from sewn on and a chain with a silver cross around her neck.

   A. Miss Cutter remembered her college days with happiness.

   B. Because Miss Cutter was a new teacher on a low salary, she had to wear a few simple outfits again and again.

   C. Miss Cutter's mother had sewn the emblem of the college on her sweater and she liked to remember her mother.

   D. Miss Cutter was a sincere and proud Christian.

2. When Tim Greaves had a cut lip and bloody nose, Tracy Cook put her arm around his shoulder and tried to comfort him.

   A. Tracy Cook is older than Tim and likes to be his protector.

   B. Tracy Cook is the leader whom the whole class admires and looks up to as a model.

   C. Tracy Cook wants to be Tim Greaves' girlfriend.

   D. Tracy Cook is a very well-behaved child who wants to be the teacher's favorite.

3. Miss Cutter asks the Eskimo woman to open her mouth and show her teeth, and when the woman doesn't understand, shows her how to do it.

   A. Miss Cutter wants the students to see things with their own eyes, so they will learn better.

   B. Miss Cutter thinks Eskimos are inferior and should be studied so their superiors can learn about them.

   C. Miss Cutter is worried because it is snowing, and she wants to finish the lesson as soon as possible so the students can go home.

   D. Miss Cutter herself has never seen an Eskimo's teeth face to face and is very curious to look at them.

4. The Eskimo's tiny, black eyes moved continuously around the room.

   A. The Eskimo is afraid of the students, the teacher, and the unfamiliar situation.

   B. The Eskimo doesn't know why she has been asked to come to the school and is waiting anxiously to see what will happen.

   C. The Eskimo, curious about the students and the teacher, wanting to know them better, is looking around to observe as much as possible about them.

   D. The Eskimo, worried about the bad weather and getting home, would like to leave as soon as possible.

5. The students walked past the Eskimo one by one and looked into her face and mouth.

   A. The students want to learn firsthand about the Eskimo's teeth, which they had been studying.

   B. The students are bored and want to get the lesson finished as soon as possible.

   C. The students have been told by the teacher to get in a line and look in the Eskimo's open mouth. They are afraid not to obey.

   D. The students think an Eskimo is like an animal and examine her mouth as they would examine a snake's, a cat's, or any animal's body.

◆◆
D. FLAT AND ROUND CHARACTERS

In Chapter Two, you observed two kinds of characters: complete characters and ideas of characters. They are, respectively, **round** and **flat** characters. A round character is one whose next actions are not easy to predict, who is likely to grow and change throughout a story. A flat character is one in whom the reader finds only one personality trait or one unchanging desire, for example, selfishness, or jealousy.

2B: CHARACTER SHAPE

Decide if each of the characters in "Feast" is primarily round or flat. Under the appropriate column, explain why you believe the character is either round or flat. Remember that an important change in a character usually indicates she or he is a round character.

Model:

Christine Cutter, Teacher

Round	Flat
She has many different characteristics including shyness, curiosity, activity.	During the story she has only one purpose, to bring the Eskimo to the class so the students can look in her mouth.

Now continue giving examples of the roundness and flatness of **the teacher, Christine Cutter.**

Round	Flat
The Eskimo	
The Students Tim Graves	
Tracy Cook	

◆◆◆◆◆◆◆◆◆◆◆
E. SETTING

Stories typically have a the geographical location and a specific environment or region in which they occur (tropical, arctic, city, country, suburb). In addition, a story typically has a specific location such as a factory, a house, or, in the case of "Feast," a school.

Furthermore, a story may actually have more than one setting or location even within a specific location. That is, the setting may change during the story. For example, while part of the action of "Feast" occurs inside the school, another part occurs outside. If the story were to continue, perhaps the setting would shift to the school bus taking the children home or to the children's homes themselves. Setting, then, has both importance and variety.

3: LOCATING THE SCENE

The checklist below contains many possible qualities of any story setting. Not all of them apply to the setting of "Feast." Put a check next to any which seem to be true of "Feast." You may look back at the story. Try to find a sentence or some words from the story to support your decision. If you are not sure of a word, look it up in an English dictionary.

a.
_____ Urban
_____ Rural
_____ Suburban

b.
_____ Northern
_____ Central
_____ Southern

c.
_____ Very poor
_____ Working class
_____ Middle class
_____ Upper middle class
_____ Upper class

d.
_____ Pioneer town
_____ Traditional
_____ Modern

e.
_____ Primarily white
_____ Mixed races
_____ Primarily black
_____ Primarily Asian
_____ Primarily Eskimo

f.
_____ Very populated
_____ Moderately populated
_____ Sparsely populated

g.
____ Coastal area
____ Prairie
____ Mountain area

h.
____ Primarily farming community
____ Primarily business community
____ Primarily professional community
____ Primarily residential community
____ Other

i.
____ Original settlers
____ First generation immigrants
____ Second or later generation immigrants

◆◆◆◆◆◆◆◆◆◆◆◆◆◆◆◆◆◆◆◆

F. PLOT AND STORY

In fiction, a character usually has a reason or **motivation** for his or her behavior.

Motivation: The reasons, apparent or actual, which cause a character to speak or act as she or he does. Motivation may be psychological; e.g., jealousy; physical, e.g., thirst; social or moral, e.g., patriotism.

4: STIMULUS AND RESPONSE

a. In "Feast," Miss Cutter invites an Eskimo to the classroom, although the students may not be very interested in the experience and although it may be embarrassing and even humiliating to the Eskimo.

Why does she do this? Become Miss Cutter. You are invited to a meeting of teachers to explain one of your lessons and your teaching method in that lesson. Before the meeting, you have been asked to write a 150-word summary of your speech. Everything you say or write should be from Miss Cutter's point of view. Use the first person, for example, "I think," "I consider," when you speak or write in her voice. In the summary, explain why you decided to invite the Eskimo to your classroom. You should include the following issues:

• the educational value of the lesson

• the students' response to the lesson

• the Eskimo's attitude to the lesson

• the overall evaluation of success or failure of the lesson

b. When you have completed (a), ask yourself the following questions:

    1. Would you expect most teachers to create and teach a lesson of this type?

    2. Do Miss Cutter's actions make sense? Would you expect Miss Cutter to create and teach a lesson of this type? Is there a relationship between Miss Cutter's character (background, education, religion) and her actions?

    3. Review the idea of story and plot explained in Chapter Two. Is the relationship between Miss Cutter's character and her actions close enough to call this story a plot?

◆◆◆◆◆◆◆◆◆◆◆◆◆◆◆◆◆◆◆◆◆◆◆◆◆◆◆◆◆◆◆
G. SUBPLOT (A SECOND PLOT)

Many readers of fiction expect only one plot per story. They are familiar with one plot which follows a straight line. The story "Feast" begins as if it will satisfy these readers: the plot moves in a straight line. The teacher and the children are waiting for the Eskimo to arrive. When the Eskimo is late arriving, the story pauses and takes a slight turn: in spite of the bad weather, the children are sent out to recess, for a longer time than usual, and begin playing games. This pause or turn, a **subplot,** is a short section which is different from but relates to the main action of the story. How does the main plot become stronger and clearer to the reader because of the action of the subplot?

Subplot: A short, second story inside the main story supporting the main plot in one or more ways, sometimes by similarities, sometimes by differences.

5: MAKING CONNECTIONS

Read the two lists below. On the left are actions from the main story. On the right are summaries of some actions from the subplot. Draw a line between actions or situations which closely relate to each other. They should not be exactly the same.

Main Story	Subplot
A. Tim Greves was hurt and cried in surprise and fear.	___ The bus driver shouts to the students with a curse to come to the bus quickly and that school should have been canceled before because of the snow.
B. After Tim Greves is hurt, the students don't know what to do and stand around waiting.	___ The Eskimo girl's dark eyes look at the students in terror.

C. Wendell Cleaver dares people to put their tongues on the cold flag pole.

—— The narrator is glad to feel the cold air, like ice water, hit his face after being in the overheated room.

D. Miss Cutter calls the students back inside because it is already late afternoon.

—— The students one by one walk past the Eskimo girl, who holds her mouth open, and look at her teeth.

E. The boys play a game of Victim in which everyone chooses a victim and tries to push him down in the snow.

—— The students stare at the Eskimo girl whose mouth they will soon look into.

◀◆◆◆◆◆◆◆◆◆◆◆◆◆◆◆◆◆◆◆◆◆◆◆◆◆◆◆◆◀

H. WHAT'S IT ALL ABOUT?

Your study of a story does not end when you have understood its separate parts. Understanding each part in and of itself is not the same as understanding how all the parts come together to form a whole story with a clear meaning. "What's it all about?" is a typical and good question to ask even after you have read and studied a story.

You do not have to reach a final conclusion about the meaning of the story; however, one way to test if you have understood the main direction of the story is to write a **theme statement**. A theme statement is a one-sentence statement of the main idea of the story. It should not repeat the actions of the story nor mention the characters' names. It should be general but clear to someone who has not read the story. For example, one possible theme of the story appears in item number 1 below.

6: CREATING THEME STATEMENTS

Each group of words below, from "Feast," relates in an important way to the theme of the story. Write a one-sentence theme statement of your own connected to each group of words. You do not need to use the exact words.

Model:

1. a meaningful experience

   Children do not always know the importance of some events they have experienced until much later in their lives.

2. chew on hides of animals to make them soft

_____

_____

_____

3. chose a victim

_____

_____

_____

4. the swiftest runner

_____

_____

_____

5. blood had fallen on the white fur cuff of her coat

_____

_____

_____

6. the opened privacy of her mouth

_____

_____

_____

7. school should have been canceled hours before

_____

_____

_____

8. the college was named after one of the female saints

_____

_____

_____

CHAPTER FIVE
PRACTICE FLIGHTS III

The goals for this chapter are:

To understand the connection between language and plot

To explore the problems and themes of the story

In this chapter, you will read:

"I See You Never" by Ray Bradbury

"I have been here thirty months," said Mr. Ramirez quietly, looking at Mrs. O'Brian's plump hands.

"That's six months too long," said one policeman.

"I See You Never"

◆◆◆

A. BACKGROUND: MEXICO AND THE UNITED STATES

According to U.S. Immigration and Naturalization Service (INS) statistics, as reported in the 1990 *Statistical Abstract of the United States,* by the time of the report almost 20,000 aliens from Mexico, had been located by the INS. These statistics, reported *The New York Times* on October 12, 1991, led U.S. army reservists to begin building a ten-foot-high steel panel fence near the border in Otay Mesa, California, to try to prevent the use of that route by illegal aliens from Mexico. The same newspaper, on January 19, 1992, stated that many immigrants were crossing the border on their way to join Magnolia, the oldest Hispanic community in Houston, Texas. One of those immigrants, reports the newspaper, says her life in the U.S. is not easy but is better than what she had back home.

◆◆◆

B. THE STORY FROM START TO FINISH

Although citizens from Mexico and the U.S. do not share a common language, they do share a very long common border. In "I See You Never," Mr. Ramirez has crossed that border and has been staying in the United States illegally. "I See You Never" is fiction with a solid basis in fact.

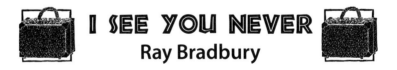

I SEE YOU NEVER
Ray Bradbury

1   The soft knock came at the kitchen door, and when Mrs. O'Brian opened it, there on the back porch were her best tenant, Mr. Ramirez, and two police officers, one on each side of him. Mr. Ramirez just stood there, walled in and small.

2   "Why, Mr. Ramirez!" said Mrs. O'Brian.

3   Mr. Ramirez was overcome. He did not seem to have words to explain.

4   He had arrived at Mrs. O'Brian's rooming house more than two years earlier and had lived there ever since. He had come by bus from Mexico City to San Diego and had then gone up to Los Angeles. There he had found the clean little room, with glossy blue linoleum, and pictures and calendars on the flowered walls, and Mrs. O'Brian as the strict but kindly landlady. During

the war he had worked at the airplane factory and made parts for the planes that flew off somewhere, and even now, after the war, he still held his job. From the first he had made big money. He saved some of it, and he got drunk only once a week—a privilege that, to Mrs. O'Brian's way of thinking, every good workingman deserved, unquestioned and unreprimanded.

5 Inside Mrs. O'Brian's kitchen, pies were baking in the oven. Soon the pies would come out with complexions like Mr. Ramirez'—brown and shiny and crisp, with slits in them for the air almost like the slits of Mr. Ramirez' dark eyes. The kitchen smelled good. The policemen leaned forward, lured by the odor. Mr. Ramirez gazed at his feet, as if they had carried him into all this trouble.

6 "What happened, Mr. Ramirez?" asked Mrs. O'Brian.

7 Behind Mrs. O'Brian, as he lifted his eyes, Mr. Ramirez saw the long table laid with clean white linen and set with a platter, cool, shining glasses, a water pitcher with ice cubes floating inside it, a bowl of fresh potato salad and one of bananas and oranges, cubed and sugared. At this table sat Mrs. O'Brian's children—her three grown sons, eating and conversing, and her two younger daughters, who were staring at the policemen as they ate.

8 "I have been here thirty months," said Mr. Ramirez quietly, looking at Mrs. O'Brian's plump hands.

9 "That's six months too long," said one policeman. "He only had a temporary visa. We've just got around to looking for him."

10 Soon after Mr. Ramirez had arrived he bought a radio for his little room; evenings, he turned it up very loud and enjoyed it. And he bought a wrist watch and enjoyed that too. And on many nights he had walked silent streets and seen the bright clothes in the windows and bought some of them, and he had seen the jewels and bought some of them for his few lady friends. And he had gone to picture shows five nights a week for a while. Then, also, he had ridden the streetcars—all night some nights— smelling the electricity, his dark eyes moving over the advertisements, feeling the wheels rumble under him, watching the little sleeping houses and big hotels slip by. Besides that, he had gone to large restaurants, where he had eaten many-course dinners, and to the opera and the theater. And he had bought a car, which later, when he forgot to pay for it, the dealer had driven off angrily from in front of the rooming house.

11 "So here I am," said Mr. Ramirez now, "to tell you I must give up my room, Mrs. O'Brian. I come to get my baggage and clothes and go with these men."

12 "Back to Mexico?"

13 "Yes. To Lagos. That is a little town north of Mexico City."

14 "I'm sorry, Mr. Ramirez."

15 "I'm packed," said Mr. Ramirez hoarsely, blinking his dark eyes rapidly and moving his hands helplessly before him. The policemen did not touch him. There was no necessity for that.

16   "Here is the key, Mrs. O'Brian." Mr. Ramirez said. "I have my bag already."

17   Mrs. O'Brian, for the first time, noticed a suitcase standing behind him on the porch.

18   Mr. Ramirez looked in again at the huge kitchen, at the bright silver cutlery and the young people eating and the shining waxed floor. He turned and looked for a long moment at the apartment house next door, rising up three stories, high and beautiful. He looked at the balconies and fire escapes and back-porch stairs, at the lines of laundry snapping in the wind.

19   "You've been a good tenant," said Mrs. O'Brian.

20   "Thank you, thank you, Mrs. O'Brian," he said softly. He closed his eyes.

21   Mrs. O'Brian stood holding the door half open. One of her sons, behind her, said that her dinner was getting cold, but she shook her head at him and turned back to Mr. Ramirez. She remembered a visit she had once made to some Mexican border towns—the hot days, the endless crickets leaping and falling or lying dead and brittle like the small cigars in the shopwindows, and the canals taking river water out to the farms, the dirt roads, the scorched landscape. She remembered the silent towns, the warm beer, the hot, thick foods each day. She remembered the slow, dragging horses and the parched jack rabbits on the road. She remembered the iron mountains and the dusty valleys and the ocean beaches that spread hundreds of miles with no sound but the waves—no cars, no buildings, nothing.

22   "I'm sure sorry, Mr. Ramirez," she said.

23   "I don't want to go back, Mrs. O'Brian," he said weakly. "I like it here, I want to stay here. I've worked, I've got money. I look all right, don't I? And I don't want to go back!"

24   "I'm sorry, Mr. Ramirez," she said. "I wish there was something I could do."

25   "Mrs. O'Brian!" he cried suddenly, tears rolling out from under his eyelids. He reached out his hands and took her hand fervently, shaking it, wringing it, holding to it. "Mrs. O'Brian, I see you never, I see you never!"

26   The policemen smiled at this, but Mr. Ramirez did not notice it, and they stopped smiling very soon.

27   "Goodbye, Mrs. O'Brian. You have been good to me. Oh, goodbye Mrs. O'Brian. I see you never!"

28   The policemen waited for Mr. Ramirez to turn, pick up his suitcase, and walk away. Then they followed him, tipping their caps to Mrs. O'Brian. She watched them go down the porch steps. Then she shut the door quietly and went slowly back to her chair at the table. She pulled the chair out and sat down. She picked up the shining knife and fork and started once more upon her steak.

29   "Hurry up, Mom," said one of the sons. "It'll be cold."

30   Mrs. O'Brian took one bite and chewed on it for a long, slow time; then she stared at the closed door. She laid down her knife and fork.

31 "What's wrong, Ma?" asked her son.

32 "I just realized," said Mrs. O'Brian—she put her hand to her face—"I'll never see Mr. Ramirez again."

1: THE MAIN PROBLEM IS...

Most short stories tell of a problem or difficulty. Decide what the problem is in "I See You Never." Write it down in a few words or sentences. Be prepared to read and explain your idea of the problem to your classmates.

Model: **Mr. Ramirez has a visa problem.**

2: REVIEWING THE FACTS

Answer the questions below as specifically as possible. In your answer use the same verb tense used in the question.

1. What job did Mr. Ramirez have during the war?

_____

_____

_____

2. From which area of Mexico does Mr. Ramirez come?

_____

_____

_____

3. How long has Mr. Ramirez been living at Mrs. O'Brian's rooming house?

_____

_____

_____

4. What did Mrs. O'Brian notice when she visited Mexico? Why do you think she remembers these details so well?

_____

_____

_____

5. What did Mrs. O'Brian say to Mr. Ramirez before the police took him away?

_____

_____

_____

6. While Mr. Ramirez is getting ready to go with the police, what are Mrs. O'Brian's children doing?

_____

_____

_____

7. What do you imagine Mr. Ramirez will do when he returns to Mexico?

_____

_____

_____

◆◆◆◆◆◆◆◆◆◆
C. PLOT

```
LANGUAGE
```

3: MOVING THINGS ALONG

In earlier chapters you saw how a character's motivation can advance the plot. The choice of language can also move the plot ahead.

Each of the idioms below from "I See You Never" is connected to an action of the story. (1) In a dictionary or a dictionary of idioms, find out first what the idiom means. (2) State to which part of the plot it relates. (3) Finally, use the idiom in a sentence of your own about the story.

Model: held his job. **To hold one's job means to keep or maintain one's job, to not be fired or removed from one's job. This relates to the job Mr. Ramirez had during the war and which he continued to work at after the war.**

Sample Sentence: **Because he was a good worker, he held his job even after the war ended.**

1. come out

   _____

   _____

   _____

2. got around to

   _____

   _____

   _____

3. slip by

   _____

   _____

   _____

4. driven off

   _____

   _____

   _____

5. rising up

   _____

   _____

   _____

6. go back

   _____

   _____

   _____

7. look in

   _____

   _____

   _____

4. THE QUESTION OF TIME

The above idioms relate to actions which move the plot forward. How much time actually passes in the story?

THE BEGINNING, MIDDLE, AND END

Not all stories have a traditional beginning, middle, and end, but most do. Each reader may have a slightly different idea about when the beginning of a story finishes and the middle begins. Similarly, readers may differ on when the middle of a story gives way to the ending.

5: THE FIRST, LAST, AND IN BETWEEN

Below some actions from "I See You Never" are listed out of order. Next to each action put a B (beginning), an M (middle), or an E (end) to indicate when the action takes place in the story. In this way, you are dividing the story into three parts and can more clearly see its structure. Then list all the actions according to their groups and in the order in which they occur.

Model: Mr. Ramirez returns the key to Mrs. O'Brian. (**M**)

1. After Mr. Ramirez is gone, Mrs. O'Brian's son tells her to eat her dinner because it is getting cold.

2. The knock of the police officers comes at the door.

3. Mr. Ramirez buys a radio for his room.

4. The pies are baking in the oven.

5. Mrs. O'Brian tells Mr. Ramirez, "I wish there was something I could do."

6. Mr. Ramirez looks at the kitchen and thanks Mrs. O'Brian.

7. Mr. Ramirez tells Mrs. O'Brian "I see you never."

Beginning	Middle	End
	Mr. Ramirez returns the key to Mrs. O'Brian.	

_____

_____

_____

_____

_____

_____

_____

Review the sections in which you have placed the actions and the order in which the action occurs. What do you notice about the beginning, middle, and end of the story? How did you decide in which section the actions belong?

◆◆◆◆◆◆◆◆◆◆◆◆◆◆◆◆◆◆◆◆◆◆◆◆◆◆◆◆◆◆◆
D. A MATTER OF CHARACTER

6: MY FAVORITE CHARACTER

Pick your favorite character in the story and explain your choice to a classmate. What in the character appeals to you? Give reasons for your decisions and support those reasons with examples. Write only notes to be used when you explain your opinion to your classmates. The characters are listed below:

Mr. Ramirez

Mrs. O'Brian

The two policemen

Mrs. O'Brian's children

◆◆◆◆◆◆◆◆◆◆◆◆◆◆◆◆◆◆◆◆◆◆◆◆◆◆◀
E. FRIENDS AND FAMILY

In many countries, family is the most important part of a person's life. A family member is someone whom one will be loyal to and defend and support in all situations, right or wrong. A close friend may become, in a loose sense, a "brother" or "sister" and be as important or even more important to someone than a blood relation. With your classmates, discuss which—family or friends—have been more important to you. Do you think your experience is universal?

7: FRIENDS OR FAMILY

Closeness between people means that they feel very connected to each other because of, among other things, shared experiences, opinions and background. Such sharing is possible by both friends and family members. In "I See You Never," Mr. Ramirez and Mrs. O'Brian have become very close. Although Mrs. O'Brian has children whom she loves, she seems very distant from them because she is so upset about Mr. Ramirez's deportation.

Relationships with friends and family members have similarities and differences. In an essay, compare the two kinds of relationships. Which one, in your opinion, is stronger? You may use but are not limited to examples from the story. Be sure you have a clear introduction, middle, and conclusion and full, specific support.

◆◆◆◆◆◆◆◆◆◆◆◆◆◆◆◆◆◆◆◆◆◆◆◆◆◆◆◆◆◀
F. THE LANGUAGE OF FEELINGS

8: WORDS WHICH FEEL

Certain words in "I See You Never" carry the emotional meaning of the story. In the sentences below, fill in the blanks with words that you think best carry the feeling of the sentence. Compare your choices with the actual text and discuss the similarities and differences between the two.

Model: "I don't want to go back, Mrs. O'Brian," he said _____ .

Choices: **warmly, easily, slowly, softly.** *Author's Choice:* weakly.

1. The kitchen smelled good. The policemen leaned forward, _____ by the odor.

2. "I'm packed," said Mr. Ramirez hoarsely, blinking his dark eyes rapidly and moving his hands _____ before him.

3. "Mrs. O'Brian!" he cried suddenly, tears rolling out from under his eyelids. He reached out his hands and took her hand _____ , shaking it, wringing it, holding to it.

4. And he [Mr. Ramirez] had bought a car, which later, when he forgot to pay for it, the dealer had driven off _____ from in front of the rooming house.

5. Soon after Mr. Ramirez had arrived he bought a radio for his little room; evenings, he turned it up very loud and _____ it.

◆◆◆◆◆◆◆◆◆◆◆◆◆◆◆◆◆◆◆◆◆◆◆◆◆◆◆◆
G. FROM STORY TO THEME

9: THEMES BY AND FOR YOU

Below are three themes of "I See You Never." Is one more fitting than the others? Why? If you have other themes in mind, revise some of the theme statements or create your own.

1. The feelings and desires of human beings are never as powerful as government laws.

2. Nothing lasts forever, although people sometimes forget this truth.

3. Inequality between countries affects people every day of their lives.

ADDITIONAL THEMES

4._____

5._____

6._____

CHAPTER SIX
TAKEOFF

The goals for the chapter are:

To discover how point of view influences events of a story

To explore how nonverbal language is expressed in fiction

In this chapter, you will read:

"The Strawberry Season" by Erskine Caldwell

Another thing we had a lot of fun out of was what we called "strawberry-slapping." One of us would slip up behind a girl while she was stooping over filling her baskets and drop a big juicy ripe strawberry down her dress.

"Strawberry Season"

♦♦♦♦♦♦♦♦♦♦♦♦♦♦♦♦♦♦
A. BACKGROUND

Erskine Caldwell (1903–1987) is best known as an American southerner whose subject matter is primarily life in his own part of the country. The characters of his novels and stories are often the poor and poorly educated workers during the Great Depression (1929–1933) and the two decades following it. At the same time, many southerners and others disapproved of Caldwell's picture of the South. They felt he depicted the South as a primitive, violent place whose population was mostly illiterate. Others thought Caldwell's work and the way it was promoted were immoral because of, for example, book covers emphasizing sex and violence. Interestingly, Caldwell's writing was highly regarded by William Faulkner and has been extremely popular with and also highly regarded by Japanese readers and critics.

1: OBSERVING CHANGE

Walk or ride slowly, on a bicycle perhaps, around an area familiar to you, a street, a road, a small section of town, a bridge. Take the time to notice what is changing, both living and non-living things. For example, are all the signs and advertisements the same as they were last week or last month? Are there any new stores? If a new season is beginning, is there anything new growing? Did you see a new face? Notice even the smallest changes, such as a bit of paint peeling off a building. Finally, think about yourself as you walk. How are you different today than you were yesterday? How are you different after your walk than before you started? "Strawberry Season" depicts a young couple's understanding of their own changes.

It is important to do this activity very slowly. Otherwise, you may miss changes that need time to be noticed.

Worksheet for Activity 1

1. I walked or rode to _____

2. Some things and people I noticed were

   _____

   _____

   _____

3. They were changing in the following ways

   _____

   _____

   _____

2: LIFE NEAR THE EARTH

The story, "Strawberry Season," focuses on a special kind of life and work found in all countries: farming and the farmer. Imagine the life of farm workers. Make a list of the good points and the bad points of being a farm worker. Would you like to be a farmer? Why or why not?

The story "Strawberry Season" reflects the importance of agriculture and crops to the South and the lives of those who helped cultivate those crops. If you can, read an article about strawberry picking or go to a farm and spend a morning picking strawberries.

 # THE STRAWBERRY SEASON
Erskine Caldwell

1   Early in the spring when the strawberries began to ripen, everybody went from place to place helping the farmers gather them. If it had been a good season for the berries and if there were many berries to pick, there would sometimes be as many as thirty-five or forty people in one field. Some men brought their families along, going from one farm to the next as fast as the berries could be gathered. They slept in barns or any place they could find. And, because the season was so short, everybody had to work from sunrise to sunset.

2   We used to have the best times picking strawberries. There were always a lot of girls there and it was great fun teasing them. If one of them stooped over a little too far and showed the least bit of herself, whoever saw her first shouted as loudly as he could. The rest of us would take up the yell and pass it all over the field. The other girls would giggle among themselves and pull their skirts down. The girl who had caused the shouting would blush and hurry away to the packing shed with a tray of baskets. By the time she returned some other girl had stooped over too far and everybody was laughing at her.

3   There was a girl named Fanny Forbes who was always showing some of herself by stooping over too far. Everybody liked Fanny.

4   Another thing we had a lot of fun out of was what we called "strawberry-slapping." One of us would slip up behind a girl while she was stooping over filling her baskets and drop a big juicy ripe strawberry down her dress. It usually stopped midway of her back and there we slapped it good and hard. The mashed strawberry made a mess. The red juice oozed through

the cloth and made a big round stain. If the berry was against the skin it was even worse. Very few girls minded that though. Everybody wore his old clothes in the fields and it did not matter about the stain. The worst part was being laughed at. Everybody stopped picking berries to laugh. When that was over, everybody went back to work and forgot it until somebody else got strawberry-slapped. We had a lot of fun picking strawberries.

5   Fanny Forbes got more strawberry-slappings than any other girl. All the boys and men liked her and she never became angry. Fanny was good-looking, too.

6   One day I went to a field where I knew the strawberry crop was good. It was a small field of only two or three acres and few people ever bothered to go there. I decided to go before somebody else did.

7   When I reached the field, Fanny was finishing the first two rows. She had thought of having the whole field to herself, just as I had thought of doing. We did not mind the other being there as long as no one else came.

8   "Hello, Fanny," I said, "What made you think of coming over here to Mr. Gunby's place today?"

9   "The same thing that made you think of it, I guess," she answered, blowing the sand off a handful of berries and putting them into her mouth.

10   We started off side by side. Fanny was a fast picker and it was all I could do to keep up with her.

11   About an hour before noon the sun came out hot and the sky became cloudless. The berries were ripening almost as fast as we could gather them. Fanny filled a dozen boxes from her next row. She could pick all day and never have a single piece of vine among her berries. She used only the thumb and the next two fingers, making a kind of triangle that grasped the berry close to the stem and lifted it off. She never mashed a berry like some people were forever doing.

12   I had never before noticed it in any other field, but today Fanny was bare-legged. In the afternoon it was much cooler without stockings, of course, and it was the best way to keep from wearing them out in the knees. She saw me looking at her bare legs and smiled just a little. I wanted to tell her how nice-looking they were but I did not dare to.

13   The midafternoon was even hotter than it had been at twelve o'clock. The slight breeze we had felt in the morning was gone and the sun hung over us like a burning glass. Fanny's legs were burned brown.

14   Before I knew what I was doing I stole up behind Fanny and dropped a great big juicy berry down the open neck of her dress. It frightened her at first. Believing that I was several rows away she thought it was a bug or insect of some kind that had fallen down the opening of her dress. When she jumped up and saw me standing behind her however she laughed and

reached down into the bosom of her waist for the berry. I was certain I saw it under her dress. Before she could reach it with her hand I slapped it as hard as I could. I thought surely she would laugh as she had always done when somebody strawberry-slapped her, but this time she did not laugh. She sat down quickly, hugging herself tightly. I then realized something was wrong. She looked up at me and there were tears in her eyes. I fell on my knees beside her. I had slapped her breasts.

15   "What's the matter, Fanny?" I begged. "Did I hurt you? I didn't mean to. Honest, I didn't mean to."

16   "I know you didn't mean to," she said, the tears falling on her lap, "but it did hurt. You mustn't hit me there."

17   "I'll never do it again, Fanny. I promise I won't."

18   "It's all right now," she smiled painfully. "It still hurts a little though."

19   Her head fell on my shoulder. I put my arms around her. She wiped the tears from her eyes.

20   "It's all right now," she repeated. "It will stop hurting soon."

21   She lifted her head and smiled at me. Her large round blue eyes were the shade of the sky when the sun has begun to rise.

22   "I'll never strawberry-slap you again as long as I live, Fanny," I pleaded, hoping she would forgive me.

23   Fanny unbuttoned the dress down to her waist. The berry was mashed beneath her underclothes. The scarlet stain looked like a morning-glory against the white cloth.

24   "I'll have to unfasten this too, to get the berry out," she said.

25   "Let me get it," I urged. "You don't want the juice all over your fingers.

26   She unfastened the undergarment. The berry lay crushed between her breasts. They were milk-white and the center of each was stained like a mashed strawberry. Hardly knowing what I was doing I hugged her tightly in my arms and kissed her lips for a long time. The crushed strawberry fell to the ground beside us.

27   When we got up, the sun was setting and the earth was becoming cool. We found our boxes and baskets of berries and walked across the fields to the barn. When we got there, Mr. Gunby counted them and paid us the money we had earned.

28   We went through the barnyard to the front of the house and stood at the gate looking at each other for several minutes. Neither of us said anything. Fanny had once said she had never had a sweetheart. I wish she had been mine.

29   Fanny turned and went down the road in one direction and I went up the road in another. It was the end of the strawberry season.

3: THE LANGUAGE OF THE EARTH

In this story, many idiomatic words and phrases especially connected to land and growing crops appear. Using context as a guide, identify the meaning of the underlined words taken from the story. Then circle the letter of the word or phrase most similar to the underlined word or phrase.

Model: One of us would <u>slip up</u> behind a girl while she was stooping over filling her baskets and drop a big juicy ripe strawberry down her dress.

   A. hide

   (B.) move quietly

   C. crawl on hands and knees

1. She had thought of <u>having the whole field to herself</u>.

   A. buying the field

   B. eating all the strawberries she picked

   C. being alone in the field picking the strawberries

2. Fanny was a fast picker and it was all I could do to <u>keep up with her</u>.

   A. pick strawberries at the same speed as Fanny

   B. pay attention to her

   C. keep her in my sight

3. Before I knew what I was doing I <u>stole up</u> behind Fanny and dropped a great big juicy berry down the open neck of her dress.

   A. took one of her strawberries

   B. moved up quietly behind her

   C. hid myself

4. The berries were <u>ripening</u> almost as fast as we could gather them.

   A. becoming ready to be picked and eaten

   B. falling

   C. breaking

5. The red juice <u>oozed</u> through the cloth and made a big round stain.

   A. tore

   B. broke

   C. leaked

B. UNDERSTANDING CHARACTER

4: A CLOSE LOOK AT THE CHARACTERS

In a single sentence for each observation, (1) write down something specific—a detail or a characteristic—about Fanny and the narrator respectively. (2) Then write down something general about each character. Write your observations about the characters in separate, complete sentences. Use lively, strong verbs whenever possible.

Model:

Specific: Fanny *picked* strawberries rapidly and neatly.

General: Fanny *worked* carefully.

C. POINT OF VIEW

5: WHO NARRATES "THE STRAWBERRY SEASON"?

If a different character told the story, how would the action change? Identify a new narrator from the list of characters below. Then, describe how the story might change based on that character's point of view.

Model: **If Mr. Gunby told the story, he might emphasize the money he was losing while Fanny and the narrator weren't working.**

Mr. Gunby, owner of the field

Fanny

A neighbor

A strawberry in the field with the narrator and Fanny

Another girl watching secretly

Another boy watching secretly

The narrator ten years later

◆◆◆◆◆◆◆◆◆◆◆◆◆◆◆◀

D. STRUCTURE

A short story the length of "The Strawberry Season" is one uninterrupted narrative. Once Caldwell begins the story, he wants the action to move along quickly. Therefore, the story moves from one scene to the next without any formal divisions. Yet, there is a beginning, middle, and end; furthermore, the narrator becomes more and more deeply involved in the action.

6: THE PARTS AND THE WHOLE

Divide the story into sections, that is, areas of the story that are clearly different from each other and move the story forward. State precisely how each section differs from the others. Consider the narrator's deepening involvement as one criterion for making divisions. How many paragraphs are there in each section?

Section

1. Background of strawberry picking and memories of past strawberry seasons, Paragraphs 1 and 2.

2.

3. (optional)

4. (optional)

▶◆◆◆◆◆◆◆◆◆◆◆◆◆◆◆◆◆◆◆◆◆◆◆◆◆◆◆◆◆◆

E. WHAT'S THE PROBLEM?

7: UNDERSTANDING THE PROBLEM

At the left are several quotations from "Strawberry Season." At the right is a list of problems stated rather generally. Choose the letter of the problem on the right most closely connected with each quotation on the left and write it in the blank.

Model:

1. We went through the barnyard to the
   front of the house and stood at the gate
   looking at each other for several minutes.
   Neither of us said anything. __a__   a. embarrassment

2. There were always a lot of girls there and it was great fun teasing them. _____

    b. Separation after being very close to someone.

3. Fanny Forbes got more strawberry–slappings than any other girl. All the boys and men liked her and she never became angry. Fanny was good-looking, too. _____

    c. Guilt and sorrow.

4. Fanny turned and went down the road in one direction and I went up the road in another. It was the end of the strawberry season. _____

    d. Attraction to the opposite sex during adolescence.

5. "I'll never do it again, Fanny. I promise I won't." _____

    e. The desire to be more popular, friendlier, and more beautiful than others.

6. She saw me looking at her bare legs and smiled just a little. I wanted to tell her how nice-looking they were but I did not dare to. _____

    f. Finding a way to have fun while working very hard.

8: THE POWER OF TOUCH

Look up the following uses of the word "touch" in an English-English dictionary: soft touch, touch it up, touching (adjective). To observe its special use, see how many more idioms using variations of "touch" you can find.

9: REACTING TO TOUCH

The central action of "The Strawberry Season" is not what anyone says but a touch. The main characters speak only 103 words to each other through the entire story.

Imagine that the actions below happened to you. Write a short dialogue with a partner in which you react to the situation.

1. In a crowded department store a stranger puts his/her arm on your shoulder to indicate she or he wishes to pass. You don't like strangers touching you.

2. On a first date, your partner takes your hand as you are walking down a busy street. In your country, it is not usual for a person to take your hand on the first date.

3. A fellow student of the opposite sex kisses you in class when you say you have passed a test. You are very embarrassed by the public demonstration of affection.

4. A waitress or waiter in a restaurant sees that you have a crumb of food on your shirt or blouse and removes it with his or her hand. You are surprised she or he didn't ask you before touching you.

5. A friend you haven't seen for a long time hugs you tightly on the street when you meet. In your country people don't hug each other in public.

10: A SLICE OF LIFE

In this short story the narrator gives us what has been called "a slice of life," a piece or part of a larger life experience. Before the story begins, that is, before we meet Fanny and the narrator, both have led full lives. Based on your knowledge of their lives, write a paragraph (150 words) in which you describe a typical day for both Fanny and the narrator. Select a name for the narrator.

Fanny's Day

_____

_____

_____

_____

_____

_____

The Narrator's Day

_____

_____

_____

_____

_____

_____

◆◆◆◆◆◆◆◆◆◆◆◆◆◆◆◆◆◆◆◆◆◆◆◆◆◆◆◆◆◆
F. ASSOCIATIONS OF DETAILS

11: A STRAWBERRY IS NOT ONLY A STRAWBERRY: ASSOCIATION OF DETAILS

Observe the details of the strawberry drawn below.

What associations come to mind as you observe the drawing? Try the same thing with the strawberry of the story. What flavors, colors, tastes, and feelings does it have for you? What associations has it gathered for you throughout the story? Make a vertical list of associations (each of only one or two words) of the strawberry and its season. For example:

tender

proud

juicy

Compare your list with your classmates' lists and notice how the strawberry has accumulated meaning.

12: INTERVIEW WITH THE AUTHOR

a. Choose a partner or meet with the partner assigned by your teacher. Imagine that one of you is the author of "The Strawberry Season," Erskine Caldwell. The other is an interviewer for a magazine. As the interviewer, prepare questions you would like to ask the author about his story. As the author, give the best answers you can to the interviewer's questions.

_____

_____

_____

_____

_____

_____

_____

_____

_____

_____

_____

_____

_____

_____

_____

_____

_____

_____

_____

b. After completing the interview, consider the questions below.

Author: Do you think the interviewer understands your story?

Interviewer: Do you think the author had a clear intention in writing the story? Did he succeed in communicating it?

13: POST-INTERVIEW

Choose your favorite sentence in the story and tell the class why you liked it.

14: MORE WRITING

Seasons may be defined traditionally as periods of a year (Spring, Summer, etc.) or uniquely as periods of one's life. Describe an important season in your life and tell why it was special and important.

MIDDLE MARKER

The Entrance Method

Until this point, for each story you have read, the information and guidance you needed to understand and appreciate the story were explained and given to you. You were told which step to take next in your discussion of the story, and you were given all the information you needed about that step. Then you were able to do the activities which were part of that stage of understanding the story.

In this chapter, a new method, the "entrance" method, is introduced, one which you will use for the remainder of the book. You will be taught how to choose the best entrance to the story you are studying. Instead of being led step by step through the story, you will be asked to decide what are the easiest and most useful ways to approach a particular story. The best entrance or entrances to begin with are those that allow you to understand the most about a story with the least difficulty. Some of the possible approaches are already well known to you, for instance, plot, character, scene, time, structure, and point of view. In many chapters, approaches you do not yet know will be explained and presented.

CHAPTER SEVEN
FIRST FLIGHTS I

The goals for this chapter are:

To discover how different sections of a story are related

To explore affective language: images and symbols

In this chapter, you will read:

"The Storm" by Kate Chopin

"May I come and wait on your gallery till the storm is over, Calixta?" he asked.
"Come `long in, M`sieur Alcée."

"The Storm"

A. BACKGROUND

Kate Chopin's (1851–1904) fiction holds the interest of many readers today for two reasons: First, born in St. Louis and residing in New Orleans most of her life, she is an important American writer from the South. Second, she writes from a woman's perspective. Chopin wrote about the Cajuns and Acadians, the latter Louisianians descended from French-speaking immigrants from Acadia (Nova Scotia). In her most important novel, *The Awakening,* she portrays a woman very unhappy with marriage, motherhood, and the role of women as she experienced it. In "The Storm" Chopin directly presents the issue of a woman's right to choose to do what she wishes and what gives her pleasure, whether or not society approves of her choices.

Note: Why are there so many French words in a story written in English? Does Kate Chopin's background and the setting of her stories have something to do with the French influence?

THE STORM
Kate Chopin

I

1   The leaves were so still that even Bibi thought it was going to rain. Bobinôt, who was accustomed to converse on terms of perfect equality with his little son, called the child's attention to certain sombre clouds that were rolling with sinister intention from the west, accompanied by a sullen, threatening roar. They were at Friedheimer's store and decided to remain there till the storm had passed. They sat within the door on two empty kegs. Bibi was four years old and looked very wise.

2   "Mama'll be 'fraid, yes," he suggested with blinking eyes.

3   "She'll shut the house. Maybe she got Sylvie helpin' her this evenin'," Bobinôt responded reassuringly.

4   "No; she ent got Sylvie. Sylvie was helpin' her yistiday," piped Bibi.

5   Bobinôt arose and going across to the counter purchased a can of shrimps, of which Calixta was very fond. Then he returned to his perch on the keg and sat stolidly holding the can of shrimps while the storm burst. It shook the wooden store and seemed to be ripping great furrows in the distant field. Bibi laid his little hand on his father's knee and was not afraid.

II

6   Calixta, at home, felt no uneasiness for their safety. She sat at a side window sewing furiously on a sewing machine. She was greatly occupied and did not notice the approaching storm. But she felt very warm and often stopped to mop her face on which the perspiration gathered in beads. She unfastened her white sacque at the throat. It began to grow dark, and suddenly realizing the situation she got up hurriedly and went about closing windows and doors.

7   Out on the small front gallery she had hung Bobinôt's Sunday clothes to air and she hastened out to gather them before the rain fell. As she stepped outside, Alcée Laballière rode in at the gate. She had not seen him very often since her marriage, and never alone. She stood there with Bobinôt's coat in her hands, and the big rain drops began to fall. Alcée rode his horse under the shelter of a side projection where the chickens had huddled and there were plows and a harrow piled up in the corner.

8   "May I come and wait on your gallery till the storm is over, Calixta?" he asked.

9   "Come 'long in, M'sieur Alcée."

10   His voice and her own startled her as if from a trance, and she seized Bobinôt's vest. Alcée, mounting to the porch, grabbed the trousers and snatched Bibi's braided jacket that was about to be carried away by a sudden gust of wind. He expressed an intention to remain outside, but it was soon apparent that he might as well have been out in the open: the water beat in upon the boards in driving sheets, and he went inside, closing the door after him. It was even necessary to put something beneath the door to keep the water out.

11   "My! what a rain! It's good two years sence it rain' like that," exclaimed Calixta as she rolled up a piece of bagging and Alcée helped her to thrust it beneath the crack.

12   She was a little fuller of figure than five years before when she married; but she had lost nothing of her vivacity. Her blue eyes still retained their melting quality; and her yellow hair, dishevelled by the wind and rain, kinked more stubbornly than ever about her ears and temples.

13   The rain beat upon the low, shingled roof with a force and clatter that threatened to break an entrance and deluge them there. They were in the dining room—the sitting room—the general utility room. Adjoining was her bed room, with Bibi's couch along side her own. The door stood open, and the room with its white, monumental bed, its closed shutters, looked dim and mysterious.

14   Alcée flung himself into a rocker and Calixta nervously began to gather up from the floor the lengths of a cotton sheet which she had been sewing.

15   "If this keeps up, *Dieu sait*[1] if the levees goin' to stan' it!" she exclaimed.

---

[1] God knows.

16   "What have you got to do with the levees?"

17   "I got enough to do! An' there's Bobinôt with Bibi out in that storm—if he only didn' left Friedheimer's!"

18   "Let us hope, Calixta, that Bobinôt's got sense enough to come in out of a cyclone."

19   She went and stood at the window with a greatly disturbed look on her face. She wiped the frame that was clouded with moisture. It was stiflingly hot. Alcée got up and joined her at the window, looking over her shoulder. The rain was coming down in sheets obscuring the view of far-off cabins and enveloping the distant wood in a gray mist. The playing of the lightning was incessant. A bolt struck a tall chinaberry tree at the edge of the field. It filled all visible space with a blinding glare and the crash seemed to invade the very boards they stood upon.

20   Calixta put her hands to her eyes, and with a cry, staggered backward. Alcée's arm encircled her, and for an instant he drew her close and spasmodically to him.

21   *"Bonte!"*[2] she cried, releasing herself from his encircling arm and retreating from the window, "the house'll go next! If only I knew w'ere Bibi was!" She would not compose herself; she would not be seated. Alcée clasped her shoulders and looked into her face. The contact of her warm, palpitating body when he had unthinkingly drawn her into his arms, had aroused all the old-time infatuation and desire for her flesh.

22   "Calixta," he said, "don't be frightened. Nothing can happen. The house is too low to be struck, with so many tall trees standing about. There! aren't you going to be quiet? say, aren't you?" He pushed her hair back from her face that was warm and steaming. Her lips were as red and moist as pomegranate seed. Her white neck and a glimpse of her full, firm bosom disturbed him powerfully. As she glanced up at him the fear in her liquid blue eyes had given place to a drowsy gleam that unconsciously betrayed a sensuous desire. He looked down into her eyes and there was nothing for him to do but to gather her lips in a kiss. It reminded him of Assumption.[3]

23   "Do you remember—in Assumption, Calixta?" he asked in a low voice broken by passion. Oh! she remembered; for in Assumption he had kissed her and kissed and kissed her; until his senses would well nigh fail, and to save her he would resort to a desperate flight. If she was not an immaculate dove in those days, she was still inviolate; a passionate creature whose very defenselessness had made her defense, against which his honor forbade him to prevail. Now—well, now—her lips seemed in a manner free to be tasted, as well as her round, white throat and her whiter breasts.

---

[2]An exclamation. Goodness!
[3]A holiday commemorating the ascent of the Virgin Mary to heaven. A feast celebrating the event is held on August 15.

24   They did not heed the crashing torrents, and the roar of the elements made her laugh as she lay in his arms. She was a revelation in that dim, mysterious chamber; as white as the couch she lay upon. Her firm, elastic flesh that was knowing for the first time its birthright, was like a creamy lily that the sun invites to contribute its breath and perfume to the undying life of the world.

25   The generous abundance of her passion, without guile or trickery, was like a white flame which penetrated and found response in depths of his own sensuous nature that had never yet been reached.

26   When he touched her breasts they gave themselves up in quivering ecstasy, inviting his lips. Her mouth was a fountain of delight. And when he possessed her, they seemed to swoon together at the very borderland of life's mystery.

27   He stayed cushioned upon her, breathless, dazed, enervated, with his heart beating like a hammer upon her. With one hand she clasped his head, her lips lightly touching his forehead. The other hand stroked with a soothing rhythm his muscular shoulders.

28   The growl of the thunder was distant and passing away. The rain beat softly upon the shingles, inviting them to drowsiness and sleep. But they dared not yield.

29   The rain was over, and the sun was turning the glistening green world into a palace of gems. Calixta, on the gallery, watched Alcée ride away. He turned and smiled at her with a beaming face; and she lifted her pretty chin in the air and laughed aloud.

III

30   Bobinôt and Bibi, trudging home, stopped without at the cistern to make themselves presentable.

31   "My! Bibi, w'at will yo' mama say! You ought to be ashame'. You oughtn' put on those good pants. Look at 'em! An' that mud on yo' collar! How you got that mud on yo' collar, Bibi? I never saw such a boy!" Bibi was the picture of pathetic resignation. Bobinôt was the embodiment of serious solicitude as he strove to remove from his own person and his son's the signs of their tramp over heavy roads and through wet fields. He scraped the mud off Bibi's bare legs and feet with a stick and carefully removed all traces from his heavy brogans. Then, prepared for the worst—the meeting with an over-scrupulous housewife, they entered cautiously at the back door.

32   Calixta was preparing supper. She had set the table and was dripping coffee at the hearth. She sprang up as they came in.

33   "Oh, Bobinôt! You back! My! but I was uneasy. W'ere you been during the rain? An' Bibi? he ain't wet? he ain't hurt?" She had clasped Bibi and was kissing him effusively. Bobinôt's explanations and apologies which he had been

composing all along the way, died on his lips as Calixta felt him to see if he were dry, and seemed to express nothing but satisfaction at their safe return.

34   "I brought you some shrimps, Calixta," offered Bobinôt, hauling the can from his ample side pocket and laying it on the table.

35   "Shrimps! Oh, Bobinôt! you too good fo' anything!" and she gave him a smacking kiss on the cheek that resounded. *"J'vous reponds,*[4] we'll have a feas' to night! umph-umph!"

36   Bobinôt and Bibi began to relax and enjoy themselves, and when the three seated themselves at table they laughed much and so loud that any-one might have heard them as far away as Laballière's.

IV

37   Alcée Laballière wrote to his wife, Clarisse, that night. It was a loving letter, full of tender solicitude. He told her not to hurry back, but if she and the babies liked it at Biloxi, to stay a month longer. He was getting on nicely; and though he missed them, he was willing to bear the separation a while longer, realizing that their health and pleasure were the first things to be considered.

V

38   As for Clarisse, she was charmed upon receiving her husband's letter. She and the babies were doing well. The society was agreeable, many of her old friends and acquaintances were at the bay. And the first free breath since her marriage seemed to restore the pleasant liberty of her maiden days. Devoted as she was to her husband, their intimate conjugal life was something which she was more than willing to forego for a while.

39   So the storm passed and everyone was happy.

B. REVIEWING THE FACTS

1: THE TRUE AND THE FALSE

Are the following statements true or false? In the blanks, write T for true or F for false.

_____ 1. Calixta and Bobinôt have been married for five years.

_____ 2. Bobinôt and Bibi try to come home during the storm.

_____ 3. Calixta invited Alcée to come in to the house.

---

[4]I'm telling you.

_____ 4. Clarisse and Alcée don't have any children.

_____ 5. This was the first time Alcée and Clarisse had been separated during their marriage.

_____ 6. Alcée is very calm and relaxed as he sits down in in a rocking chair.

_____ 7. Bibi and Bobinôt are afraid Calixta will be angry at them because of their dirty clothes.

_____ 8. Bobinôt brings Calixta a gift of some candy because he is late coming home.

_____ 9. Calixta's fear of the storm leads her to make love with Alcée.

_____ 10. Bobinôt knows that Calixta and Alcée have made love but doesn't tell Calixta he knows.

C. ENTRANCE ONE: THE PARTS AND THE WHOLE

2: A PLACE FOR EVERYTHING AND EVERYTHING IN ITS PLACE

"The Storm" is divided into five numbered divisions, each adding to the movement and purpose of the story.

Review all five parts of "The Storm." Make a list of the actions in each section. Be sure you can explain the actions in all the sections and what importance those actions have for the entire story. Can the actions in one section be moved to another section of the story? Why or why not?

3: PAIRING THE PARTS

Consider the similarities and differences between the five sections of the story. Notice the connections between sections which have some aspects in common. Which sections seem most to belong together? (Sections which are of similar length or include similar actions or characters remind the reader of each other.) For example, does the following pairing make sense? Why or why not?

Sections I and III:

Bobinôt and Bibi are the main characters in these two sections.

In Section I Bobinôt buys the can of shrimps at the store and in Section III he gives the shrimps to Calixta.

Some additional pairings are listed below. See if you can find out what they have in common. Write down what you discover.

Sections IV and V:

_____

_____

_____

Sections II and IV:

_____

_____

_____

Sections II and V:

_____

_____

_____

4: ANTICIPATION AND REMEMBRANCE

An action that occurs early in a story may prepare the reader for something that will happen later. In the left column some actions from the earlier part of the story are listed. Connect them to actions that occur later in the story in the right column.

Earlier	Later
Alcée carries in Bobinôt's pants from the porch so they won't get wet.	Alcée encourages Clarisse to extend their separation by a month.
Bobinôt and Calixta are separated because of the sudden storm.	Calixta puts something beneath the door to shut the house completely after Alcée has entered.
Bobinôt tells Bibi that Mama will shut the house if there is a storm.	Bobinôt criticizes Bibi for wearing his good pants and dirtying them in the storm.

Now add your own related earlier and later actions.

D. ENTRANCE TWO: CHARACTER

5: ROLE PLAYING

Choose one of the situations below. With one of your classmates play the role of one of the characters in the story and tell your partner how you feel in the situation. For example, imagine you are Bobinôt at Friedheimer's store during the storm. Tell Mr. Friedheimer what you are thinking and feeling.

1. Calixta at home before Alcée arrives.
2. Bibi on arrival home after the storm.
3. Alcée writing to his wife.
4. Clarisse receiving Alcée's letter.
5. Alcée leaving Calixta after the storm.
6. Your own choice of a situation from the story.

6: A MOMENT LATER

Imagine the moment just after the story ends. Put yourself in the position of the characters. What do you intend to do (a) immediately, (b) tomorrow, (c) next week, and (d) next year? Write your answers in the table below.

Character	Immediately	Tomorrow	Next Week	Next Year
Bibi				

Character	Immediately	Tomorrow	Next Week	Next Year
Bobinôt				
Calixta				
Alcée				
Clarisse				

■.■

E. ENTRANCE THREE: THE LANGUAGE OF "THE STORM"

Using language as another "entrance" to this story, consider these three areas: (1) basic vocabulary, (2) the meaning of lively and powerful verbs, and (3) significant sentences.

7: CRUCIAL WORDS

Using the list of subjects below, choose the subject area which best describes the underlined words.

Engineering, physical action, religion, morality, psychology, language, packaging of food and drink, agriculture and farming, appearance

Word	Subject Area
Model: She unfastened her <u>white sacque</u> at the throat.	Clothing
1. Bobinôt and Bibi, trudging home, stopped without at the <u>cistern</u> to make themselves presentable.	
2. If she was not an immaculate dove in those days, she was still <u>inviolate</u>; a passionate creature whose very defenselessness had made her defense, against which his honor forbade him to prevail.	
3. They sat within the door on <u>two empty kegs</u>.	
4. It [the storm] shook the wooden store and seemed to be ripping <u>great furrows</u> in the distant field.	
5. Her blue eyes still retained their <u>melting quality</u>; and her yellow hair, <u>dishevelled</u> by the wind and rain, <u>kinked</u> more stubbornly than ever about her ears and temples.	
6. Alcée's arm <u>encircled</u> her, and for an instant he drew her close and <u>spasmodically</u> to him.	
7. The generous abundance of her passion, without guile or trickery, was like a <u>white flame</u> which penetrated and found response in depths of his own sensuous nature that had never yet been reached.	
8. The <u>growl of the thunder</u> was distant and passing away.	

8: THE MEANING OF LIVELY AND POWERFUL VERBS

From the list of verbs, fill in the blanks. Check your choices against the verbs actually used in the story.

> *Model:* The rain __**beat upon**__ the low, shingled roof with a force and clatter that threatened to break an entrance and deluge them there.

Verb list: snatched • clasped • sprang up • heed • struck

1. The playing of the lightning was incessant. A bolt _____ a tall chinaberry tree at the edge of the field.

2. Alcée _____ her shoulders and looked into her face.

3. They did not _____ the crashing torrents, and the roar of the elements made her laugh as she lay in his arms.

4. She _____ as they came in.

5. Alcée, mounting to the porch, grabbed the trousers and _____ Bibi's braided jacket that was about to be carried away by a sudden gust of wind.

9: FAVORITE SIGNIFICANT SENTENCES

Look over the story and choose one sentence that seems particularly interesting and important to you. Look at it again for a few minutes. Be ready to explain to the class everything you understand and why you like it.

F. ENTRANCE FOUR: IMAGES AND IMAGE CLUSTERS

Another, special kind of language used fully in the story is called **imagery,** a word or group of sensory words which refer strongly to the senses (sight, hearing, touch, sound, and taste). A picture affecting the reader more emotionally than intellectually is called an **image** or, when joined with other images, an **image cluster**.

10: PLAYING WITH IMAGES AND IMAGE CLUSTERS

a. The following passages have many images in them. See how many you can find and try to guess what they suggest.

1. Her blue eyes still retained their melting quality; and her yellow hair, dishevelled by the wind and rain, kinked more stubbornly than ever about her ears and temples.

2. Bobinôt, who was accustomed to converse on terms of perfect equality with his little son, called the child's attention to certain sombre clouds that were rolling with sinister intention from the west, accompanied by a sullen, threatening roar.

3. The rain was coming down in sheets, obscuring the view of far-off cabins and enveloping the distant wood in a gray mist. The playing of the lightning was incessant. A bolt struck a tall chinaberry tree at the edge of the field. It filled all visible space with a blinding glare and the crash seemed to invade the very boards they stood upon.

4. When he touched her breasts they gave themselves up in quivering ecstacy, inviting his lips. Her mouth was a fountain of delight. And when he possessed her, they seemed to swoon together at the very borderland of life's mystery.

5. She unfastened her white sacque at the throat. It began to grow dark, and suddenly realizing the situation she got up hurriedly and went about closing windows and doors.

b. Share your guesses and discuss them with the entire class.

11: CLOZE

Without looking at the story, fill in the blanks with words you think fit well. Then compare your choices with those in the story.

His voice and her own startled _____ as if from a trance,
                                      (1)

_____ she seized Bobinôt's vest. Alcée, _____ to the
        (2)   (3)

porch, grabbed the trousers and _____ Bibi's braided jacket that was
                                        (4)

about to be carried away _____ a sudden gust _____
                                  (5)   (6)

wind. He expressed an intention to remain _____ , but it was soon
                                                   (7)

apparent that he _____ as well have been out _____ the
(8)   (9)

open: the water _____ in upon the boards in driving sheets, and he
(10)

went _____ , closing the door _____ him.
(11)   (12)

G. ENTRANCE FIVE: SYMBOLS

Another, more complex use of language is a **symbol**. Like image clusters, symbols accumulate meaning in the story by being placed near other symbols and by being repeated in different situations, with different characters, and with different surroundings. In contrast to images and image clusters, symbols usually replace or stand for what they represent.

For example, notice the language below from "The Storm":

> They did not heed the *crashing torrents,* and the roar of the elements made her laugh as she lay in his arms. She was a *revelation* in that dim, *mysterious* chamber; as white as the couch she lay upon. Her firm, elastic flesh that was knowing for the first time its birthright, was like a creamy lily that the sun invites to contribute its breath and perfume to the *undying life of the world* (author's italics).

Alone, each word or phrase is simply an image. Together, in relation to the title and the action of the story, does the language have any symbolic meaning greater than the literal words? For example, what are "crashing torrents"? When are "crashing torrents" found? Is there anything in the action of the story represented by these symbols?

12: LOCATING SYMBOLIC LANGUAGE (ORAL REPORT)

Find a sentence or a paragraph in "The Storm" which makes use of symbolic language. Prepare at home a one-minute oral report in which you explain the use of the symbolic language to your classmates. Ask each other questions about your reports.

13: WRITING ABOUT SYMBOLIC LANGUAGE

Some of the areas of symbolic language in this story are:

Clothes (especially pants)

The opening and closing of windows, doors, and gates

The storm

Religion (especially Assumption)

Water and fountains

a. Add to this list any other symbolic aspect you find.

_____

_____

_____

b. Now, in a paragraph of at least 150 words, complete the sentence below:

_____ is an important symbolic aspect of Kate Chopin's "The Storm" because...

Give reasons and examples to support your main idea.

H. THEME

14: MORE PRACTICE WITH THEME STATEMENTS

A theme is the essence of the story stated in a single sentence. Prepare to state the theme by asking yourself a question about the story, one that you might have asked when you began studying it. Now that you have read the story, your question is now the central problem of the story. A related question is, "Whose problem is it?" With these questions in mind, take five minutes on your own to write down in a single sentence the theme of Kate Chopin's "The Storm."

Model:

Question: **Why does Alcée suggest Clarisse stay away an additional month?**

Problem: **Alcée must deal with his actions and feelings toward Calixta and his feelings toward his own wife, Clarisse.**

Theme: **Couples must find the closeness that makes them comfortable in their relationship.**

Theme: _____

CHAPTER EIGHT
FIRST FLIGHTS II

The goals for this chapter are:

To discover the structural and mythic patterns of a story

To learn how to identify with characters in a story

In this chapter, you will read:

"A Bag of Oranges" by Spiro Athanas

The boy sat in the chair, in the warmth of his father's body, and watched his mother clear the table.

"A Bag of Oranges"

A. THE ACTION OF THE STORY

"A Bag of Oranges" is short, but it includes many events. Some of them seem to happen suddenly and some don't seem closely related to the main action. These actions occur throughout the entire story: beginning, middle, and end.

 # A BAG OF ORANGES
Spiro Athanas

1   The city market was crowded. The boy, Nikos Pappanoulos, bobbed and weaved among the shoppers. He held a blue cloth sack tightly; his father walking briskly ahead carried three others. Skip stepping, the ten-year-old tried to keep up with his father's long stride. Stavro Pappanoulos strode easily, cutting a smooth path through the thick crowd like a plow turning earth. Something about the set of his shoulders said, "Step aside," and people did. The boy was proud of this father's stocky strength, yet at the same time it made him uneasy.

2   Nikos loved the market, loved coming to shop with his father on Saturday mornings. He loved the smells and bright fall colors of apples, pears, pumpkins, of the fresh fruits and vegetables in the October morning air. The market was like a magic farm indomitably growing and prospering in the heart of the rotting slum.

3   The boy's father knew many of the truck farmers who displayed their colorful harvests in pyramids, bunches, or boxes in the open-air market. He was especially friendly with a gray, old Albanian who hawked strawberries.

4   "Lulustrouthia! Lulustrouthia!" the gaunt, hooknosed farmer yelled. And it worked. No one could hear that cry against the other banal sounds without investigating.

5   "Lulustrouthia? That's Albanian for the freshest, juiciest, sweetest strawberries ever grown," was his stock reply, uttered rather condescendingly to the fat matron who stood before him. "Fifteen cents a box." She bought a box and waddled away, biting off the stems of the unwashed strawberries and popping the fruit into her mouth.

6   "Twenty cents for two?" The boy's father plunked down two shiny dimes next to the rows of boxes overflowing with plump strawberries.

7   "No, no, Stavro Pappanoulos, thirty cents for two! Two times fifteen is thirty." He said this distinctly and rocked back on his heels delighted with his arithmetic.

8   "Twenty-two."

9   "Thirty."

10 "Twenty-five!"

11 "Sold!" The old Albanian adroitly slid the dimes into his money pouch.

12 "Sonofabitch," his father mumbled as he flipped a nickel to the Albanian.

13 "Move away from the stand now, Stavro Pappanoulos, I don't want people to see how you rob me—Lulustrouthia! HEY LULUSTRRROUTHIA!"

14 The boy watched and listened to this dialogue, intrigued—and a little frightened. But the smile on his father's lips as they walked away reassured him.

15 When the sacks were at last filled and the boy held the one bag of oranges that could not be coaxed into any of them, he and his father made their weekly visit to the Greek coffeehouse across the street. To get there they had to pass through the enclosed end of the U-shaped market, the only part the boy didn't like. It was poorly lighted. The chicken house, butcher shop, and fish market all reeked of death. The boy ran ahead of his father, out the double door, and again into the light. He waited at the curb for his father. Stavro took his hand and strode into the street, defying traffic. He seemed to delight in making cars stop to let him pass.

16 In the coffeehouse, the boy sat on a corner of his father's chair. Stavro unbuttoned his pinstriped suit coat and removed his gray hat. As he sipped dark, viscous coffee, the boy ate from the bag of peanuts given him by his uncle, Peter Pappas, proprietor of the coffeehouse. Peter was Stavro's brother, but had shortened his name "for business purposes."

17 The boy, dark and quiet and shy, watched the men at the other tables playing backgammon and pinochle. The men at Stavro's table spoke in low confiding tones.

18 "Michales is dying, you know." Peter clenched the stub of his cigar between his teeth.

19 "It's that woman," a slight bald man chirped. The boy didn't know him. "He's not enough man for Aphrodite."

20 "No one is enough man for Aphrodite, eh Stavro?" Peter nudged his brother.

21 "Old ladies, all of you. Gossiping old ladies." Stavro spat between the space in his front teeth into a cuspidor, smiling mischievously. The talk continued. They spoke of politics and business and gambling. Stavro sat like a rock with his legs corralling the four brimming cloth sacks. He lit a Fatima and put one of his hands gently on the boy's head. The boy enjoyed the talk and sometimes felt he was being allowed to hear all the secrets of the world, and was only mildly frustrated by the mysteries he could not understand.

22   "Time to go, Nikos." Stavro ran his fingers through his own thick, black hair and put on his hat. "I need a haircut," he said, to no one in particular.

23   Nikos was glad to be in the fresh air again when they left. It was even sweeter after being in the mustiness of his uncle's tiny coffeehouse. And he ran ahead of his father again, this time to the bus stop at the corner.

24   The bus was crowded. There were many elderly women and young girls with bright packages returning from downtown shopping trips, but only a few men. It was midafternoon in October, and the bus was uncomfortably warm. The boy sat beside his father on the long seat at the rear.

25   The bus jolted over the city streets, jerking to an abrupt halt at nearly every corner, picking up and surrendering passengers. The boy was holding the oranges so lightly that when the bus lurched into motion after one of the stops, the bag was thrust forward and five oranges bounded into the aisle. Like pin balls, they careened off the brackets and poles. The boy regained control of the bag before any more could escape, and his father scampered down the aisle chasing oranges.

26   On his hands and knees, Stavro Pappanoulos ducked beneath a seat on which two old ladies sat, to their mild humor and fussy dismay, and emerged with three of the oranges. The two others had rolled farther down the aisle. He picked up one, and as he started for the other, a neatly dressed young man reached down from where he was sitting and took it up. Stavro quickly grabbed the young man's wrist and began squeezing. The man gasped slightly, opening his mouth in a grimace of pain and disbelief. Stavro tightened his grip and stared menacingly into the pink face. Finally the young man's grasp was loosened by the pressure and he dropped the orange. Stavro picked it up and walked back to his seat at the rear of the bus. The young man stared after him, his mouth still open, rubbing his wrist briskly.

27   "You know," he began, "I mean anyone could see—I wasn't about to steal your precious orange!"

28   A wave of laughter ran through the bus. Stavro Pappanoulos looked at the man mildly and popped the five oranges back into the boy's bag, carefully folding over the top. He settled himself in his seat once again and looked satisfied. The young man shrugged his shoulders and turned around. There were a few whispers and a few more smiles.

29   The boy felt every whisper piercing his skin, every smile was a slap. His ears burned with embarrassment and shame. The remainder of the trip was an agony. Even the backs of the old gray heads, the light ponytails, the clean shaven necks, seemed to mock the boy. For the first time in his life he hated his father.

30   At their stop, the boy and his father had to pass the young man to get to the door. The boy, mortified, walked by stiffly, staring straight ahead, his head ringing, tears in his eyes. He felt the shadow and weight of his father

behind him, placid and unashamed. Oh how he hated him and his smug, foreign stupidity! Why did he have to be *his* father?

31   Once on the sidewalk the boy dared not look back at the bus as it coughed and whined away for fear it too would mock him. He walked behind his father now, crying silent hot tears. His father turned once and must have noticed the tears, but said nothing.

32   At the gate to their front yard the boy's older sister bounded out to greet them and leaped with remarkable agility onto her father's back. Viki, who was twelve, snuggled her head in Stavro's neck and kissed him affectionately. And as they both laughed, Stavro carried her up the stairs to the porch where the boy caught up with them. Viki jumped from her father's back, snatched the bag of oranges from her brother, and disappeared into the house. Stavro put his bags down for a moment and placed a hand on the boy's head. The boy sprang to him, putting arms around his father's neck and wrapping his legs around his hard body.

33   In this way, they arrived at the kitchen—the boy still clinging to his amused father.

34   "Look at my monkey!" Stavro said to his wife. And the boy was delighted to be his father's monkey again. It was so easy and natural he could scarcely believe the emotions he experienced moments ago were real. Had he really thought he hated his father?

35   The boy's mother was looking at the oranges Viki had given her. She took a few out of the bag.

36   "And what happened to these, Stavro? Did you sit on them on the way home?"

37   "Some dropped. It is of no importance." Stavro looked at the boy.

38   "Well, we can't eat these, but I can use them for juice. Viki, why don't you go to the store and buy a dozen for Poppa's lunches?" Viki frowned, but she knew it was not a question. She went to her mother's purse in the hall closet, removed a dollar, and left for the store.

39   "And you Nikos, be a good boy and bring in the cans from the alley. If you leave them they will get dented worse than they are.

40   The late afternoon sun, subdued by the October mist, hung quietly just above the horizon. It was getting dark earlier. The boy sent a flattened bottle cap skimming down the vacant alley. Then he carried in the empty battered trash cans, one at a time. He stopped after his third and last trip to watch a lone gray pigeon gracefully circle his backyard. In a flutter of furious motion the fat bird ascended to the gutter atop the three-story house and settled gently on the edge. It flicked its nervous head from side to side. And the boy remembered the trap his father had made on the roof: kernels of corn leading to a chicken-wire box. He remembered pigeon soup. There had been the need.

41   He felt a sudden chill, an inner void; and he began to run. Up the brick

wall and over the mound, the swelling where the roots of the gnarled oak had had their say; up the porch stairs, two, three steps at a time: the agile, plastic ten-year-old, a piece of tempered wire.

42   Near the top of a second flight of stairs, still trying to outrun his own insides, the boy heard the soft, familiar voices: his mother and father as they communed over coffee. He stopped running. Slowly, carefully he walked the brown crack in the flowered linoleum down the hall to the kitchen. A sheer drop of ten thousand feet on either side.

43   "Did you bring in the cans?" The boy nodded and his mother smiled her approval. She wiped a loose, dark hair from her smooth brow.

44   The boy moved from the doorway to the table. His father sat there easily, his legs spread. And the boy remembered the coffeehouse; remembered the mischief in his father's eyes as the men spoke of "Aunt" Aphrodite; remembered the dying Michales.

45   "Coffee?"

46   "Yes, black coffee," the boy said quietly.

47   "So it's *black* coffee is it; a man's drink." His mother already moving toward the cupboard—petite, slender in a bright print dress. Dark smiling eyes, affectionate, maternal. She filled a hand-painted demitasse from a copper pot at the stove and brought it to the boy.

48   He sipped. It was bitter, the price of being a man.

49   "I'm going now to get a haircut. Borsch will be closed in half an hour." The boy's father finished his coffee in one long swallow and pushed himself up heavily. Thick, dark, quiet, he spoke a familiar word to his wife, a parting —and he was gone. The boy sat in the chair, in the warmth of his father's body, and watched his mother clear the table.

50   "Why don't you play outside, now?"

51   "Nobody's around."

52   "Viki will be back soon."

53   He watched his mother wash the cups at the sink. And he thought of his "Aunt" Aphrodite, again. Aphrodite Skouras was not a relation, but she was a very close friend of the family. She read fortunes in the swirling patterns of coffee grounds made in empty cups. On more than one occasion the boy had sat in a corner of the kitchen and watched the cluster of women and girls clinging to her every word. He had watched amused, amazed, and sometimes, frightened. At last they would discover him, usually it was his mother, for she was the most skeptical and paid the least attention, and he was ushered from the room. For days afterwards he would hear talk of "Aunt" Aphrodite's predictions. Now he remembered that her last visit had caused a pall to settle over the company. The bright sarcasm and laughter of his mother seemed false in the face of the dark future Aphrodite must have forecast.

54   The boy's mother began to hum a particularly gay Greek tune as she worked at the sink. But somewhere, deep in the boy's mind, the song was transformed into a wail. And then it broke upon a distant reality. Suddenly the room was filled with the sound—screaming terrifically, ominously. And then, abruptly, it subsided to a low, soft moan.

55   "Go to the window and see." His mother, urgent, always frightened by sirens. She listened intently.

56   The boy rushed to a living room window, pushed aside the long hand-crocheted curtain and parted the blind. He saw nothing unusual in the street below except the autos backed up, bumper to bumper. But it was Saturday and theirs was a busy street.

57   Back in the kitchen he said nothing. The wailing sound was gone. His mother wiped the worn oilcloth that covered the solid oak table. She stopped midway in the arc of a smooth stroke, "Shhh."

58   The boy had not uttered a sound. He held his breath. His mother lifted her head and seemed to prick her ears listening to something he could not hear. She held the hand with which she sought to quiet him poised above the table—motionless. "What?" The boy said, "I don't hear anything."

59   "Nothing. Nothing at all." His mother finished wiping the table and went back to her work. The boy saw her knitted brow reflected in the mirror above the sink. She did not hum any more.

60   The boy sat in his father's chair sipping the thick coffee; both had lost their warmth. He watched his mother's efficient hands preparing mousaka at the sink for their evening meal, and thought of nothing.

61   The noise of the front door slamming against the wall echoed violently in the hollow stairwell. The boy had often heard it slammed shut, but this was a different, urgent sound which compelled both him and his mother to rush to the stairs. "Momma, oh Momma, Momma," it was a thin hysterical voice that came to them. They watched Viki, alert and afraid. Her mouth formed the words but she did not, could not speak. Her body writhed and her face twisted but no sound came. Finally, "It's Poppa. Oh, Momma, Poppa!"

62   His mother's eyes were glazed black, wild with terror. She clasped her hands together and ran down the stairs. The boy, rooted to the spot, faced his sister. He began to shake. His neck felt stiff. Then he saw the empty bag Viki clutched to her breast as she rocked side to side. The bottom had torn out. She followed his eyes to the tear. "The oranges! I lost them. Oh Poppa!" The tears now began to flow down her flushed face, from terrified eyes.

63   The boy wanted to know, but he did not dare ask. He watched and waited. Viki put the bag on the dining room table and turned back to face the boy. He still could not move. "I saw his hat. The people were in a circle and there was Poppa's hat. I didn't believe it was Poppa's at first. But I knew it was. I knew it was his gray hat. " She paused and sobbed and wiped the tears from her

frightened face. "Then I saw Poppa. He wasn't bleeding. He looked okay. Like he was asleep. Like he was lying in the street asleep. Nikos, Nikos," She went to the motionless, terrified boy and put her hands on his shoulders. "Poppa's been hit by a car, Nikos. He couldn't talk or see, but maybe it's not bad. There wasn't any blood. He looked okay, Nikos. He's okay." She began to choke on her fear, her deep hurt.

64   The boy felt a drop of perspiration slip down his side. He could hear and feel his heart work faster, faster. And he broke away from his sister; running stumbling down the stairs to the front porch.

65   He could make nothing out of what he saw in the street. There was a car double-parked in the next block, but police and people milled about on the corner. He could not see his mother amongst them. Too late, he was confused and bewildered. He had made up his mind to run down to the corner. But he found he couldn't run. And then he knew he didn't want to run. He didn't want to reach the corner—ever. Halfway down the block he saw them; the oranges his sister had dropped. Most of them were in a little pile by the curb. But one was in the center of the sidewalk, near the corner.

66   Of a sudden, a man who had been part of the small crowd which seemed unable to leave the scene of the excitement, though there was nothing left to see… of a sudden a young man broke from the crowd and picked up the orange near the corner. He tested it in the palm of his hand, and, as if finding it acceptable, turned to walk up the street, away from the boy.

67   A neighbor, an old woman, noticed the boy and made a comforting gesture, a movement toward him. Seeing this, Nikos began to run, past the woman and the corner. In the middle of the next block he caught up with the young man who had picked up the orange. Without breaking stride, the boy leaped onto his back, his small fists flailing wildly. "That's my orange!" he screamed. " Give me my orange!"

1: CHARTING THE ACTIONS

The actions of any story, including "A Bag of Oranges," usually fit into one of five parts: (1) the presentation of the situation, (2) a difficulty or difficulties in the situation, (3) the *most* difficult or critical moment, (4) the withdrawal from the situation, and (5) the resolution (happy, unhappy, or both). Below is a list of most of the important actions of the story. Place them in the part of the story you think they best fit. With a classmate, compare where you placed each action of the story.

The Actions:

Model:

__1__ Stavro bargains with the strawberry seller.

_____ The father, Stavro, leaves to get a haircut.

_____ The oranges drop and roll down the bus aisle.

_____ The boy holds on to his father as they arrive home.

_____ On the bus, Stavro squeezes the hand of a man who caught one of the rolling oranges.

_____ Father (Stavro) and son (Nikos) sit in the coffeehouse together.

_____ Nikos sits alone with his mother in the kitchen after his father has left.

_____ Nikos chases the man who took the oranges Viki had dropped.

_____ Viki returns home and tells Nikos she saw her father lying in the street.

_____ Nikos brings in the trash cans from the street.

B. THE PROBLEM ITSELF

None of the actions stated above is a rare event. Every day people go to markets, shop, get haircuts, ride buses, and drop and pick up items of all kinds. Sadly, as in this story, people die every day in auto accidents. If these actions are not unusual, then why is this ordinary material the action of a short story?

2: WHAT'S THE PROBLEM?

State in one or two written sentences what seems to be the main problem of the story.

_____

_____

_____

ENTRANCES

Approaching the author's main concerns in the story, you will soon discover a room deep inside of "A Bag of Oranges" and will need to decide which entrance will take you to that room most efficiently, which aspect of the story will "open" the story most fully to you, and which elements will lead you smoothly from one part of the story to another part.

No one entrance will be a good one to follow for every story. Each story yields understanding according to its individual characteristics, just as different people can be appreciated from different perspectives. In this chapter, you will study some of the most typical entrances such as structure, character, language, images, and symbols, as well as some entrances new to you.

3: TAKE A VOTE

Which approach would most help readers begin to understand "A Bag of Oranges"? Each person should explain his or her reason for choosing a particular approach as the best, first entrance to the story and explain your reason for choosing that approach to the class.

C. ENTRANCE ONE: STRUCTURE

4: TRACING THE PATTERNS

"A Bag of Oranges" contains several clear contrasts which form patterns. Each one of these can be followed or traced, observing the movement from one point in the story, usually near the beginning, to another, usually near the end. Trace the two sample patterns described below. What directions does the story take to move from the first to the final word? What structural patterns can you find in "A Bag of Oranges"? How many patterns of your own can you find in the story?

Sample Pattern: From morning to late afternoon.
Sample Pattern: From the active life of the market in the morning to the quiet of
the home in the late afternoon.

Pattern 1

_____

_____

_____

Pattern 2

_____

_____

_____

Pattern 3

_____

_____

_____

5: SUBPLOT AND MAIN PLOT

In this chapter, as in "Feast" in Chapter Four, a subplot complements the main story. The subplot in "A Bag of Oranges" consists of only a very short scene in the coffee-house near the market. Stavro and Nikos, father and son, are there, but so are other characters who appear only in this scene. The sentences in the left column below are reproduced from this scene; those in the right column are reproduced from other sections of the story. The sentences on the left (from the subplot) contain ideas, feelings, or images that reinforce or support those on the right (from other sections of the story). Match each sentence on the left with the one it supports on the right. Discuss your reasons for matching the subplot and main plot items.

Subplot	Main Plot
Model:	
1. Stavro sat like a rock with his legs corralling the four brimming cloth sacks.	The boy's father finished his coffee in one long swallow and pushed himself up heavily. **1**
2. In the coffeehouse the boy sat on a corner of his father's chair.	"So it's *black* coffee is it; a man's drink."…He sipped. It was bitter, the price of being a man. —
3. "Michales is dying, you know."	The boy sat in his father's chair sipping the thick coffee; both had lost their warmth. —
4. The boy enjoyed the talk and sometimes felt he was being allowed to hear all the secrets of the world, and was only mildly frustrated by the mysteries he could not understand.	A neighbor, an old woman, noticed the boy and made a comforting gesture, a movement toward him. Seeing this, Nikos began to run, past the woman and the corner. —
5. "Old ladies, all of you. Gossiping old ladies."	"Then I saw Poppa. He wasn't bleeding. He looked okay. Like he was asleep." —

The Limits of Entrances

Each approach gives information about a story only to a certain point. To learn more, one must follow the chosen approach until it leads to the next approach that follows most directly. Concerning "A Bag of Oranges," where does the structural entrance lead? Where can one find the best possibility of answers to difficult structural questions?

D. ENTRANCE TWO: CHARACTER

Character can answer many questions raised by structure and so fulfills the promise structure offers. One way to understand character, to get a true sense of what is important to a particular character, what actions are typical of him or her, and how she or he interacts with other characters, is to ask yourself to which character you feel closest. To **feel something in common with** or **to identify with** means to understand the character well enough to sympathize with and even to imagine yourself as the character in his or her situation. For example, do you feel some of what Nikos Pappanoulos feels toward his father? On the other hand, can you imagine yourself feeling and acting toward your children as Stavro does? Perhaps you *identify* with both. Or do you immediately feel close to the mother and wife?

6: IDENTIFYING WITH A CHARACTER

Which character do you most identify with? Give at least two reasons why you can identify with him or her.

Model:

I identify with <u>Stavro</u> because he is a good father and because his son considers his father a stupid foreigner.

I identify with _____ because _____

_____

_____

_____

_____

_____

7: GROUPING THE CHARACTERS

You will find below a list of all the characters in "A Bag of Oranges." Some of them have more in common than others. Arrange the characters below in groups based on what they have in common. Who belongs most with whom and why? A character may belong to more than one group. A group may contain more than two characters. Create as many groups as there are relationships among characters.

The Characters: Stavro (father), mother, Nikos (son), Viki (daughter), Aphrodite ("aunt"), old Albanian, Peter Pappas (Stavro's brother), young man on the bus, Michales.

Model:

Nikos and the young man on the bus:

1. **To Nikos, they are both young American men, not foreigners.**

2. **To Nikos, they both hate and are embarrassed by stupid foreigners like his father.**

8: ROLE PLAYING

The father is obviously a very important person to everyone in the story: a husband, a parent and role model to the children, and a friendly countryman to the strawberry salesman in the market. His death is a central event in the story. How do the other characters feel about him? Choose one of the characters in the story and imagine you are that character. Then, *as that character,* be prepared to explain how you feel about Stavro.

E. ENTRANCE THREE: FAMILY DYNAMICS

People in fiction or in life rarely exist completely in isolation. Interaction among characters is usual, whether the characters are friends, family members, colleagues, or even, at times, strangers. In "A Bag of Oranges," the characters belong to that close-knit group we call "the family."

9: A FAMILY DIAGRAM

Consider your own family. Quickly (in five minutes) make a list of all your immediate family members. Then draw a diagram of the structure of the family as you know it. Who, for example, is the strongest member, the leader? Who is closest to whom? Who depends most on the others? Such questions will help you draw your family diagram.

Sample Family Diagram

1. Ages of the family members:

   Father **52**

   Mother **50**

   Sisters **26 22 21**

   Brothers

   Grandmother

   Grandfather

   Others

2. Name the person in your family closest to you: father, mother, brother, sister, or other, and explain why you are closest to him or her.

   eldest sister

   She understands what my parents cannot understand.

3. List in order the persons you consider strongest in your family. #1 indicates strongest, #2 next strongest, etc.

   1. **father**

   2. **mother**

   3. **eldest sister**

   4. **me**

   5. **two sisters**

4. Who makes the major decisions in your family about

   a. money   **mother**

   b. children's issues   **mother**

   c. division of responsibilities   **father**

5. Model diagram showing who is closest to whom in this family:

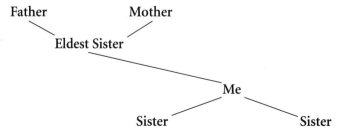

Explanation: The student who drew this diagram explained to the class that his father and mother are closest to his eldest sister. He is closer to his younger sisters than to either his eldest sister or his parents.

5. Now draw your own family diagram. Include all the members of the family in your diagram.

10: DISCUSSION

Briefly compare some of the habits of Stavro and Nikos. What led to the similarities and the differences between the father and son? How did these differences develop? Hint: If you have ever left your home and lived in another country, or if you are currently living in a "foreign" country, what changes did you notice or have you noticed in yourself?

F. ENTRANCE FOUR: RITUAL, MYTH, AND SYMBOL

RITUALS

As you grew up, you, like Nikos, experienced many mornings. What did you do when you woke up each morning? Do you still do some of the same things you did then?

11: YOUR DAILY RITUAL

Make a list of your usual daily morning activities.

_____

_____

_____

_____

_____

_____

Compare your list with your classmates' lists. Do you notice many common elements among your morning rituals? How do you explain these? What differences do you find among your morning activities? Are the differences or the similarities greater? Why?

Term: A **ritual** is a set of actions repeated so regularly by so many people in different times and lands that they are thought to be timeless and universal. Because of their repetition, the actions may **consciously or unconsciously** build up associations with people, events, or thoughts only indirectly related to the pattern of actions. For example, putting one's shoes away in a certain place before going to sleep each evening could be one person's ritual. Little by little, it may come to be associated with evening and sleep in the person's mind. A person or persons, such as a church congregation which prays each day at a certain hour and place, is also performing a ritual. This ritual reflects a certain belief.

12: ACTING OUT A RITUAL

With your partners in your group, choose one ritual you notice in "A Bag of Oranges." Without saying a word, act out the ritual for the class. Ask the class what ritual you have acted out. Taking turns, continue to act out one story ritual after another. Notice how many rituals the story contains.

13: LISTENING BREAK

Popular songs around the world often tell the story of rituals. Bring in a recording of a song from your country, have your fellow students listen to it, and briefly explain the ritual behind it. Some American songs with rituals are "Sunrise, Sunset," from the Broadway musical *Fiddler on the Roof*, "Try to Remember," from *The Fantastiks*, and Carly Simon's "Coming Round Again."

14: WRITING ABOUT RITUALS

Choose one ritual familiar to you. Think of all its parts and all the physical objects or details which belong to it. For example, the ritual of confirmation or coming of age in many religions includes a person studying certain books, saying certain prayers, and wearing certain religious clothes or symbols.

Write a five-paragraph account of the ritual you chose. The first paragraph should name and introduce the ritual. The second, third, and fourth paragraphs should each describe one part of the ritual, including all the materials or details used in that part. In the fifth paragraph, write your conclusion about the ritual. You may give your opinion of it or you may simply describe its usefulness or meaning to you.

MYTH AND SYMBOLS

The thoughts and actions which we call rituals often play an important part in myths. A myth may have its beginnings in some real, historical event, but is usually viewed as an imaginary—not a factual—story. A myth often reveals and explains the beliefs and activities of a people or culture. For example, in many ancient cultures, before people understood astronomy, the rising and setting of the sun and the seasons were often explained by a myth in which the sun was believed to be a person who traveled to and returned from another place each evening of the year and each winter, returning the following morning and spring, respectively.

15: SOME BASIC MYTHIC PATTERNS IN "A BAG OF ORANGES"

"A Bag of Oranges" contains several timeless and universal rituals. The patterns are as familiar as the rising and falling of the sun. In fact, the action begins in the morning and ends as "the late afternoon sun, subdued by the October mist, hung quietly just above the horizon." "It was getting dark earlier," the author points out. This pattern can be visualized as follows:

Beginning	End
Sun rising, bright colors of the market	Late afternoon sun, darkness coming on

Below are listed either the beginnings or the ends of other mythic patterns from the story. Write in the missing part, either beginning or end. Hint: Review the structural patterns you discovered in Activity 4.

	Boy jumping onto the back of the young man who took Viki's oranges.
Stavro runs his fingers through his thick, black hair.	
Discussion about Michales dying.	
The boy dislikes passing the chicken house, butcher shop, and fish market which "all reeked of death."	
	Harvest and October
	Father lying in the street as if he were asleep.

*In a ritual, some details may be more important than the others. Such details may appear over and over again in an account of a ritual. The detail may take on more and more meaning and may even become the most important detail of the story. Such a detail is often called a **symbol**. In the previous chapter, on Kate Chopin's "The Storm," you observed several examples of symbolic language. In the current chapter, the story's title may include the name of the symbol.*

16: THE CENTRAL SYMBOL

The oranges in "A Bag of Oranges" are more important than the other details. What kind of symbolic meaning do they hold?

G. SUMMING UP

When can a reader say she or he has "finished" a story? Reading the richest stories, such a moment never comes. It is always possible to reread and/or rethink the story and understand or appreciate something previously over-looked. Nevertheless , you may still feel the need to finish your study of the story, at least for the time being, with some final look at and statement of the story's overall meaning and impact—the **theme** of the story. Remember, a **theme** is a brief (usually one sentence) statement of the universal meaning or dominant idea of a literary work; each story may have many themes.

An effective statement of theme, while no substitute for the story or the experience of reading the story, may be a convenient and comfortable way to be sure of your understanding of the story.

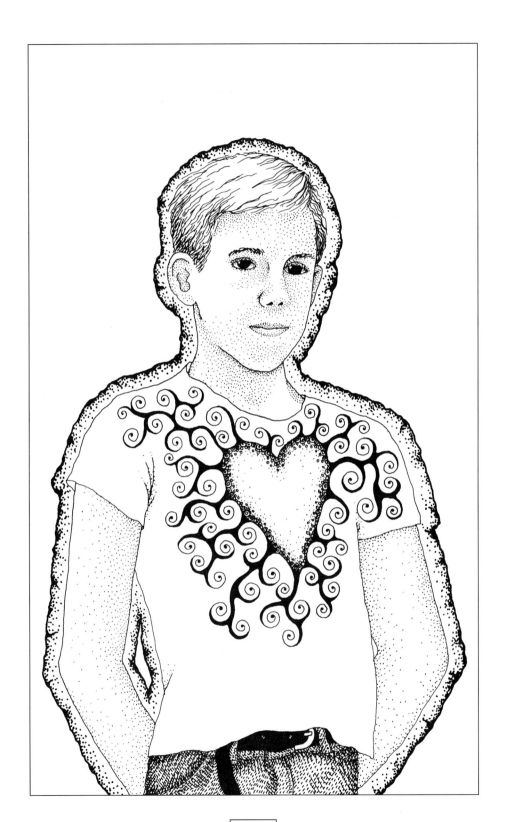

CHAPTER NINE
MID-JOURNEY

The goals for this chapter are:

    To locate the most useful elements for analyzing a story

    To review structure, character, theme, and symbol

In this chapter, you will read:

    "The Stone Boy" by Gina Berriault

"Were you and your brother good friends?"
What did he mean—good friends? Eugie was
his brother. That was different from a friend.

                            "The Stone Boy"

A. CRISIS

A moment of crisis, when we are forced to act or to make a very difficult decision quickly, brings out strong reactions in each of us. Sometimes, our reaction to a crisis reveals our fears, our needs, or even our family background. At other times, we respond in ways that don't seem like us at all. It is often difficult to know, as in the story you are about to read, which part of us we are expressing.

1: REACTING TO A CRISIS

Read the description of each potential emergency or crisis situation. What steps would you take in such situations? In what order would you take them?

Model: **If a six-year old child fell off a park toy and was bleeding badly from the head, first I would… Then, I would…**

Crises

1. Your six-year-old child falls off a park toy and is bleeding badly from the head.
2. The car you are driving suddenly loses its braking power as you are descending a hill.
3. In the evening, you and your friend are walking along a dark street in a mountain town. He is bitten by a stray dog.
4. At work one morning you are called and told a close friend of 30 years has died in a plane crash.
5. Your brother-in-law and his wife, who are visiting you, are having a violent fight. It appears he may hit her.
6. Your Hungarian doctor friend has just failed the qualifying test for overseas doctors for the third time. He calls you and threatens to commit suicide.
7. You are the chief of a construction company. You built a meeting hall with a faulty roof. Three people were badly injured when it fell.

Now explain to the group what you did to handle the crises and discuss the strengths and weaknesses of your actions.

2: ADDITIONAL CRISES

Answer with the first response that comes to your mind.

1. If you see a person on fire, you should…
2. If you see a car about to hit a child, you should…
3. If you lose your child in a city crowd, you should…
4. If you accidentally give your elderly parent an incorrect and dangerous medicine, you should…

B. THE PROBLEM

A work of fiction usually dramatizes one or more problems. As you read "The Stone Boy," you may notice more than one possible problem. Which one, however, is the central problem?

 # THE STONE BOY
Gina Berriault

1   Arnold drew his overalls and raveling gray sweater over his naked body. In the other narrow bed his brother Eugene went on sleeping, undisturbed by the alarm clock's rusty ring. Arnold, watching his brother sleeping, felt a peculiar dismay; he was nine, six years younger than Eugie, and in their waking hours it was he who was subordinate. To dispel emphatically his uneasy advantage over his sleeping brother, he threw himself on the hump of Eugie's body.

2   "Get up! Get up!" he cried.

3   Arnold felt his brother twist away and saw the blankets lifted in a great wing, and, all in an instant, he was lying on his back under the covers with only his face showing, like a baby, and Eugie was sprawled on top of him.

4   "Whassa matter with you?" asked Eugie in sleepy anger, his face hanging close.

5   "Get up," Arnold repeated. "You said you'd pick peas with me."

6   Stupidly, Eugie gazed around the room as if to see if morning had come into it yet. Arnold began to laugh derisively, making soft, snorting noises, and was thrown off the bed. He got up from the floor and went down the stairs, the laughter continuing, like hiccups, against his will. But when he opened the staircase door and entered the parlor, he hunched up his shoulders and was quiet because his parents slept in the bedroom downstairs.

7   Arnold lifted his .22-caliber rifle from the rack on the kitchen wall. It was an old lever-action Winchester that his father had given him because nobody else used it any more. On their way down to the garden he and Eugie would go by the lake, and if there were any ducks on it he'd take a shot at them. Standing on the stool before the cupboard, he searched on the top shelf in the confusion of medicines and ointments for man and beast and found a small yellow box of .22 cartridges. Then he sat down on the stool and began to load his gun.

8   It was cold in the kitchen so early, but later in the day, when his mother canned the peas, the heat from the wood stove would be almost unbearable. Yesterday she had finished preserving the huckleberries that the family had picked along the mountain, and before that she had canned all the cherries his father had brought from the warehouse in Corinth. Sometimes, on these summer days, Arnold would deliberately come out from the shade where he was playing and make himself as uncomfortable as his mother was in the kitchen by standing in the sun until the sweat ran down his body.

9   Eugie came clomping down the stairs and into the kitchen, his head drooping with sleepiness. From his perch on the stool Arnold watched Eugie slip on his green knit cap. Eugie didn't really need a cap; he hadn't had a haircut in a long time and his brown curls grew thick and matted, close around his ears and down his neck, tapering there to a small whorl. Eugie passed his left hand through his hair before he set his cap down with his right. The very way he slipped his cap on was an announcement of his status; almost everything he did was a reminder that he was eldest—first he, then Nora, then Arnold—and called attention to how tall he was (almost as tall as his father), how long his legs were, how small he was in the hips, and what a neat dip above his buttocks his thick-soled logger's boots gave him. Arnold never tired of watching Eugie offer silent praise unto himself. He wondered, as he sat enthralled, if when he got to be Eugie's age he would still be undersized and his hair still straight.

10 Eugie eyed the gun. "Don't you know this ain't duck-season?" he asked gruffly, as if he were the sheriff.

11 "No, I don't know," Arnold said with a snigger.

12 Eugie picked up the tin washtub for the peas, unbolted the door with his free hand and kicked it open. Then, lifting the tub to his head, he went clomping down the back steps. Arnold followed, closing the door behind him.

13 The sky was faintly gray, almost white. The mountains behind the farm made the sun climb a long way to show itself. Several miles to the south, where the range opened up, hung an orange mist, but the valley in which the farm lay was still cold and colorless.

14 Eugie opened the gate to the yard and the boys passed between the barn and the row of chicken houses, their feet stirring up the carpet of brown feathers dropped by the molting chickens. They paused before going down the slope to the lake. A fluky morning wind ran among the shocks of wheat that covered the slope. It sent a shimmer northward across the lake, gently moving the rushes that formed an island in the center. Killdeer, their white marking flashing, skimmed the water, crying their shrill, sweet cry. And there at the south end of the lake were four wild ducks, swimming out from the willows into open water.

15 Arnold followed Eugie down the slope, stealing, as his brother did, from one

shock of wheat to another. Eugie paused before climbing through the wire fence that divided the wheatfield from the marshy pasture around the lake. They were screened from the ducks by the willows along the lake's edge.

16 "If you hit your duck, you want me to go in after it?" Eugie said.

17 "If you want," Arnold said.

18 Eugie lowered his eyelids, leaving slits of mocking blue. "You'd drown 'fore you got to it, them legs of yours are so puny," he said.

19 He shoved the tub under the fence and, pressing down the center wire, climbed through into the pasture.

20 Arnold pressed down the bottom wire, thrust a leg through and leaned forward to bring the other leg after. His rifle caught on the wire and he jerked at it. The air was rocked by the sound of the shot. Feeling foolish, he lifted his face, baring it to an expected shower of derision from his brother. But Eugie did not turn around. Instead, from his crouching position, he fell to his knees and then pitched forward onto his face. The ducks rose up crying from the lake, cleared the mountain background and beat away northward across the pale sky.

21 Arnold squatted beside his brother. Eugie seemed to be climbing the earth, as if the earth ran up and down, and when he found he couldn't scale it he lay still.

22 "Eugie?"

23 Then Arnold saw it, under the tendril of hair at the nape of the neck—a slow rising of bright blood. It had an obnoxious movement, like that of a parasite.

24 "Hey, Eugie," he said again. He was feeling the same discomfort he had felt when he had watched Eugie sleeping; his brother didn't know that he was lying face down in the pasture.

25 Again he said, "Hey, Eugie," an anxious nudge in his voice. But Eugie was as still as the morning about them.

26 Arnold set his rifle on the ground and stood up. He picked up the tub and, dragging it behind him, walked along by the willows to the garden fence and climbed through. He went down on his knees among the tangled vines. The pods were cold with the night, but his hands were strange to him, and not until some time had passed did he realize that the pods were numbing his fingers. He picked from the top of the vine first, then lifted the vine to look underneath for pods and then moved on to the next.

27 It was the warmth on his back, like a large hand laid firmly there, that made him raise his head. Way up the slope the gray farmhouse was struck by the sun. While his head had been bent the land had grown bright around him.

28 When he got up his legs were so stiff that he had to go down on his knees again to ease the pain. Then, walking sideways, he dragged the tub, half full of peas, up the slope.

29   The kitchen was warm now; a fire was roaring in the stove with a closed-up, rushing sound. His mother was spooning eggs from a pot of boiling water and putting them into a bowl. Her short brown hair was uncombed and fell forward across her eyes as she bent her head. Nora was lifting a frying pan full of trout from the stove, holding the handle with a dish towel. His father had just come in from bringing the cows from the north pasture to the barn, and was sitting on the stool, unbuttoning his red plaid Mackinaw.

30   "Did you boys fill the tub?" his mother asked.

31   "They ought of by now," his father said. "They went out of the house an hour ago. Eugie woke me up comin' downstairs. I heard you shootin'—did you get a duck?"

32   "No," Arnold said. They would want to know why Eugie wasn't coming in for breakfast, he thought. "Eugie's dead," he told them.

33   They stared at him. The pitch cracked in the stove.

34   "You kids playin' a joke?" his father asked.

35   "Where's Eugene?" his mother asked scoldingly. She wanted, Arnold knew, to see his eyes, and when he had glanced at her she put the bowl and spoon down on the stove and walked past him. His father stood up and went out the door after her. Nora followed them with little skipping steps, as if afraid to be left alone.

36   Arnold went into the barn, down along the foddering passage past the cows waiting to be milked, and climbed into the loft. After a few minutes he heard a terrifying sound coming toward the house. His parents and Nora were returning from the willows, and sounds sharp as knives were rising from his mother's breast and carrying over the sloping fields. In a short while he heard his father go down the back steps, slam the car door and drive away.

37   Arnold lay still as a fugitive, listening to the cows eating close by. If his parents never called him he thought, he would stay up in the loft forever, out of the way. In the night he would sneak down for a drink of water from the faucet over the trough and whatever food they left for him by the barn.

38   The rattle of his father's car as it turned down the lane recalled him to the present. He heard voices of his Uncle Andy and Aunt Alice as they and his father went past the barn to the lake. He could feel the morning growing heavier with sun. Someone, probably Nora, had let the chickens out of their coops and they were cackling in the yard.

39   After a while another car turned down the road off the highway. The car drew to a stop and he heard the voices of strange men. The men also went past the barn and down to the lake. The undertakers, whom his father must have phoned from Uncle Andy's house, had arrived from Corinth. Then he heard everybody come back and heard the car turn around and leave.

40   "Arnold!" It was his father calling from the yard.

41   He climbed down the ladder and went out into the sun, picking wisps of hay from his overalls.

42   Corinth, nine miles away, was the county seat. Arnold sat in the front seat of the old Ford between his father, who was driving, and Uncle Andy; no one spoke. Uncle Andy was his mother's brother, and he had been fond of Eugie because Eugie had resembled him. Andy had taken Eugie hunting and had given him a knife and a lot of things, and now Andy, his eyes narrowed, sat tall and stiff beside Arnold.

43   Arnold's father parked the car before the courthouse. It was a two-story brick building with a lamp on each side of the bottom step. They went up the wide stone steps, Arnold and his father going first, and entered the darkly paneled hallway. The shirt-sleeved man in the sheriff's office said that the sheriff was at Carlson's Parlor examining the Curwing boy.

44   Andy went off to get the sheriff while Arnold and his father waited on a bench in the corridor. Arnold felt his father watching him, and he lifted his eyes with painful casualness to the announcement, on the opposite wall, of the Corinth County Annual Rodeo, and then to the clock with its loudly clucking pendulum. After he had come down from the loft his father and Uncle Andy had stood in the yard with him and asked him to tell them everything, and he had explained to them how the gun had caught on the wire. But when they had asked him why he hadn't run back to the house to tell his parents, he had had no answer—all he could say was that he had gone down into the garden to pick the peas. His father had stared at him in a pale, puzzled way, and it was then that he had felt his father and the others set their cold, turbulent silence against him. Arnold shifted on the bench, his only feeling a small one of compunction imposed by his father's eyes.

45   At a quarter past nine Andy and the sheriff came in. They all went into the sheriff's private office, and Arnold was sent forward to sit in the chair by the sheriff's desk; his father and Andy sat down on the bench against the wall.

46   The sheriff lumped down into his swivel chair and swung toward Arnold. He was an old man with white hair like wheat stubble. His restless green eyes made him seem not to be in his office but to be hurrying and bobbing around somewhere else.

47   "What did you say your name was?" the sheriff asked.

48   "Arnold," he replied; but he could not remember telling the sheriff his name before.

49   "Curwing?"

50   "Yes."

51   "What were you doing with a .22, Arnold?"

52   "It's mine," he said

53   "Okay. What were you going to shoot?"

54   "Some ducks," he replied.

55   "Out of season?"

56   He nodded.

57   "That's bad," said the sheriff. "Were you and your brother good friends?"

58   What did he mean—good friends? Eugie was his brother. That was different from a friend, Arnold thought. A best friend was your own age, but Eugie was almost a man. Eugie had had a way of looking at him, slyly and mockingly and yet confidentially, that had summed up how they both felt about being brothers. Arnold had wanted to be with Eugie more than with anybody else but he couldn't say they had been good friends.

59   "Did they ever quarrel?" the sheriff asked his father.

60   "Not that I know," his father replied. "It seemed to me that Arnold cared a lot for Eugie."

61   "Did you?" the sheriff asked Arnold.

62   If it seemed so to his father, then it was so. Arnold nodded.

63   "Were you mad at him this morning?"

64   "No."

65   "How did you happen to shoot him?"

66   "We was crawlin' through the fence."

67   "Yes?"

68   "An the gun got caught on the wire."

69   "Seems the hammer must of caught," his father put in.

70   "All right, that's what happened," said the sheriff. "But what I want you to tell me is this. Why didn't you go back to the house and tell your father right away? Why did you go and pick peas for an hour?"

71   Arnold gazed over his shoulder at his father, expecting his father to have an answer for this also. But his father's eyes, larger and even lighter blue than usual, were fixed upon him curiously. Arnold picked at a callus in his right palm. It seemed odd now that he had not run back to the house and wakened his father, but he could not remember why he had not. They were all waiting for him to answer.

72   "I come down to pick peas," he said.

73   "Didn't you think," asked the sheriff, stepping carefully from word to word, "that it was more important for you to go tell you parents what had happened?"

74   "The sun was gonna come up," Arnold said.

75   "What's that got to do with it?"

76   "It's better to pick peas while they're cool."

77   The sheriff swung away from him, laid both hands flat on his desk. "Well, all I can say is," he said across to Arnold's father and Uncle Andy, "he's either a moron or he's so reasonable that he's way ahead of us." He gave a challenging snort. "It's come to my notice that the most reasonable guys are mean ones. They don't feel nothing."

78   For a moment the three men sat still. Then the sheriff lifted his hand like a man taking an oath. "Take him home," he said.

79   Andy uncrossed his legs. "You don't want him?"

80   "Not now," replied the sheriff. "Maybe in a few years."

81   Arnold's father stood up. He held his hat against his chest. "The gun ain't his no more," he said wanly.

82   Arnold went first through the hallway, hearing behind him the heels of his father and Uncle Andy striking the floor boards. He went down the steps ahead of them and climbed into the back seat of the car. Andy paused as he was getting into the front seat and gazed back at Arnold, and Arnold saw that his uncle's eyes had absorbed the knowingness from the sheriff's eyes. Andy and his father and the sheriff had discovered what made him go down into the garden. It was because he was cruel, the sheriff had said, and didn't care about his brother. Was that the reason? Arnold lowered his eyelids meekly against his uncle's stare.

83   The rest of the day he did his tasks around the farm, keeping apart from the family. At evening, when he saw his father stomp tiredly into the house, Arnold did not put down his hammer and leave the chicken coop he was repairing. He was afraid that they did not want him to eat supper with them. But in a few minutes another fear that they would go to the trouble of calling him and that he would be made conspicuous by his tardiness made him follow his father into the house. As he went through the kitchen he saw the jars of peas standing in rows on the workbench, a reproach to him.

84   No one spoke at supper, and his mother, who sat next to him, leaned her head in her hand all through the meal, curving her fingers over her eyes so as not to see him. They were finishing their small, silent supper when the visitors began to arrive, knocking hard on the back door. The men were coming from their farms now that it was growing dark and they could not work any more.

85   Old Man Matthews, gray and stocky, came first, with his two sons, Orion, the elder, and Clint, who was Eugie's age. As the callers entered the parlor, where the family ate, Arnold sat down in a rocking chair. Even as he had been undecided before supper whether to remain outside or take his place at the table, he now thought that he should go upstairs, and yet he stayed to avoid being conspicuous by his absence. If he stayed, he thought, as he always stayed and listened when visitors came, they would see that he was only Arnold and not the person the sheriff thought he was. He sat with his arms crossed and his hands tucked into his armpits and did not lift his eyes.

86   The Matthews men had hardly settled down around the table, after Arnold's mother and Nora had cleared away the dishes, when another car rattled down the road and someone else rapped on the back door. This

time it was Sullivan, a spare and sandy man, so nimble of gesture and expression that Arnold had never been able to catch more than a few of his meanings. Sullivan, in dusty jeans, sat down in the other rocker, shot out his skinny legs and began to talk in his fast way, recalling everything that Eugene had ever said to him. The other men interrupted to tell of occasions they remembered, and after a time Clint's young voice, hoarse like Eugene's had been, broke in to tell about the time Eugene had beat him in a wrestling match.

87   Out in the kitchen the voices of Orion's wife and of Mrs. Sullivan mingled with Nora's voice but not, Arnold noticed, his mother's. Then dry little Mr. Cram came, leaving large Mrs. Cram in the kitchen, and there was no chair left for Mr. Cram to sit in. No one asked Arnold to get up and he was unable to rise. He knew that the story had got around to them during the day about how he had gone and picked peas after he had shot his brother, and he knew that although they were talking only about Eugie they were thinking about him and if he got up, if he moved even his foot, they would all be alerted. Then Uncle Andy arrived and leaned his tall, lanky body against the doorjamb and there were two men standing.

88   Presently Arnold was aware that the talk had stopped. He knew without looking up that the men were watching him.

89   "Not a tear in his eye," said Andy, and Arnold knew that it was his uncle who had gestured the men to attention.

90   "He don't give a hoot, is that how it goes?" asked Sullivan, trippingly.

91   "He's a reasonable fellow," Andy explained. "That's what the sheriff said. It's us who ain't reasonable. If we'd of shot our brother, we'd of come runnin' back to the house, cryin' like a baby. Well, we'd of been unreasonable. What would of been the use of actin' like that? If your brother is shot dead, he's shot dead. What's the use of gettin' emotional about it? The thing to do is go down to the garden and pick peas. Am I right?"

92   The men around the room shifted their heavy, satisfying weight of unreasonableness.

93   Matthews' son Orion said: "If I'd of done what he done, Pa would've hung my pelt by the side of that big coyote's in the barn."

94   Arnold sat in the rocker until the last man had filed out. While his family was out in the kitchen bidding the callers good night and the cars were driving away down the dirt lane to the highway, he picked up one of the kerosene lamps and slipped quickly up the stairs. In his room he undressed by lamplight, although he and Eugie had always undressed in the dark, and not until he was lying in his bed did he blow out the flame. He felt nothing, not any grief. There was only the same immense silence and crawling inside of him; it was the way the house and fields felt under a merciless sun.

95   He awoke suddenly. He knew that his father was out in the yard, closing the doors of the chicken houses so that the chickens could not roam out too early and fall prey to the coyotes that came down from the mountains at daybreak. The sound that had wakened him was the step of his father as he got up from the rocker and went down the back steps. And he knew that his mother was awake in her bed.

96   Throwing off the covers, he rose swiftly, went down the stairs and across the dark parlor to his parents' room. He rapped on the door.

97   "Mother?"

98   From the closed room her voice rose to him, a seeking and retreating voice. "Yes?"

99   "Mother?" he asked insistently. He had expected her to realize that he wanted to go down on his knees by her bed and tell her that Eugie was dead. She did not know it yet, nobody knew it, and yet she was sitting up in bed, waiting to be told, waiting for him to confirm her dread. He had expected her to tell him to come in, to allow him to dig his head into her blankets and tell her about the terror he had felt when he had knelt beside Eugie. He had come to clasp her in his arms and, in his terror, to pommel her breasts with his head. He put his hand upon the knob.

100   "Go back to bed, Arnold," she called sharply.

101   But he waited.

102   "Go back! Is night when you get afraid?"

103   At first he did not understand. Then, silently, he left the door and for a stricken moment stood by the rocker. Outside everything was still. The fences, the shocks of wheat seen through the window before him were so still it was as if they moved and breathed in the daytime and had fallen silent with the lateness of the hour. It was a silence that seemed to observe his father, a figure moving alone around the yard, his lantern casting a circle of light by his feet. In a few minutes his father would enter the dark house, the lantern still lighting his way.

104   Arnold was suddenly aware that he was naked. He had thrown off his blankets and come down the stairs to tell his mother how he felt about Eugie, but she had refused to listen to him and his nakedness had become unpardonable. At once he went back up the stairs, fleeing from his father's lantern.

105   At breakfast he kept his eyelids lowered as if to deny the humiliating night. Nora, sitting at his left, did not pass the pitcher of milk to him and he did not ask for it. He would never again, he vowed, ask them for anything, and he ate his fried eggs and potatoes only because everybody ate meals —cattle ate, and the cats; it was customary for everybody to eat.

106   "Nora, you gonna keep that pitcher for yourself?" his father asked.

107   Nora lowered her head unsurely.

108   "Pass it on to Arnold," his father said.

109   Nora put her hands in her lap.

110   His father picked up the metal pitcher and set it down at Arnold's plate.

111   Arnold, pretending to be deaf to the discord, did not glance up but relief rained over his shoulders at the thought that his parents recognized him again. They must have lain awake after his father had come in from the yard: had they realized together why he had come down the stairs and knocked at their door?

112   "Bessie's missin' this morning," his father called out to his mother, who had gone into the kitchen. "She went up the mountain last night and had her calf, most likely. Somebody's got to go up and find her 'fore the coyotes get the calf."

113   That had been Eugie's job, Arnold thought. Eugie would climb the cattle trails in search of a newborn calf and come down the mountain carrying the calf across his back, with the cow running down along behind him, mooing in alarm.

114   Arnold ate the few more forkfuls of his breakfast, put his hands on the edge of the table and pushed back his chair. If he went for the calf he'd be away from the farm all morning. He could switch the cow down the mountain slowly, and the calf would run along at its mother's side.

115   When he passed through the kitchen his mother was setting a kettle of water on the stove. "Where you going?" she asked awkwardly.

116   "Up to get the calf," he replied, averting his face.

117   "Arnold?"

118   At the door he paused reluctantly, his back to her, knowing that she was seeking him out, as his father was doing, and he called upon his pride to protect him from them.

119   "Was you knocking at my door last night?"

120   He looked over his shoulder at her, his eyes narrow and dry.

121   "What'd you want?" she asked humbly.

122   "I didn't want nothing," he said flatly.

123   Then he went out the door and down the back steps, his legs trembling from the fright his answer gave him.

3: PROBLEMS AND MORE PROBLEMS

Below are listed seven possible problems in "The Stone Boy." Arrange them from most important to least important. Number 1 represents the most important problem, number 7 the least important.

Arnold's family rejects him.

It was too hot to pick peas.

Arnold kills his brother.

The sheriff is considering accusing Arnold of murder.

The community judges and isolates Arnold.

Arnold feels guilty for murdering his brother.

Arnold doesn't feel close to his mother.

4: FINDING AN ENTRANCE

Which of the entrances listed below will help you most quickly appreciate and understand "The Stone Boy"?

Structure

Myth

Character

Symbol

Setting

Point of View

   Hint: If you don't understand some parts of the story, write down questions about these sections. To which entrances do these questions relate? These entrances may make a good place to start.

C. STRUCTURE

5: HOW IT'S PUT TOGETHER

List the actions of "The Stone Boy" in the order they occur.

   1. The boys wake up.

   2. _____

   3. _____

   4. _____

   5. _____

   6. _____

   7. _____

   8. _____

   9. _____

   10. _____

   11. _____

   12. _____

   13. _____

   14. _____

   15. _____

Now place the actions in the five sections of the story: (1) presentation of the situation; (2) difficulty or difficulties in the situation; (3) the most difficult moment of the situation; (4) the withdrawal or moving away from the situation; and, finally, (5) the resolution of the action.

I. **Presentation of the Situation**

    1. The boys wake up.

    2. _____

    3. _____

    4. _____

II. **Difficulty or Difficulties in the Situation**

    1. The boys are preparing to go duck hunting.

    2. _____

    3. _____

    4. _____

III. **The Most Difficult Moment of the Situation**

    1. Arnold's gun goes off, hitting and killing Eugene.

    2. _____

    3. _____

    4. _____

IV. **The Withdrawal or Moving Away from the Situation**

    1. The neighbors come to mourn Eugie.

    2. _____

    3. _____

    4. _____

V. **The Resolution of the Action**

    1. Arnold takes on Eugie's former job of finding the lost calf.

    2. _____

    3. _____

    4. _____

6: A QUESTION OF PROGRESSION

After Arnold tells his parents that Eugie is dead, several people ask Arnold questions about what happened. Put the list of the people who ask questions (below) in the right order.

Sheriff

The Neighbors

Uncle

Father and Mother

Is there any importance to this order of questioners?

D. CHARACTER

Although Eugene Curwing was killed by a bullet fired from his brother Arnold's gun, nobody actually accuses Arnold Curwing of planning to murder his brother. Nevertheless, his parents, his sister, his neighbors, and even the sheriff isolate him and act as if he committed a crime. Why? What do they believe he actually did wrong? What wrong do they believe Arnold is actually guilty of?

7: INTERVIEWING ARNOLD

Imagine you are a newspaper reporter assigned to write an article on the death of Eugene Curwing. You are given an opportunity to interview Arnold. What questions would you like to ask him? Prepare a list of questions you would ask him. What do you really want to know about the killing? About what happened after the killing? What do you believe will be the focus of the newspaper article that you write?

E. THEME

8: PREPARING TO STATE THE THEME

Answer the questions below. More than one answer may be correct. Discuss your answers with a classmate or as a group.

1. Eugie's death is

   A. the main event of the story.

   B. only the first event of the story.

   C. an event that leads to other, more important actions.

   D. not a very important event of the story.

2. The sheriff's attitude toward Arnold's killing of his brother is

   A. disbelief.

   B. suspicion.

   C. lack of interest.

   D. normal concern.

3. The neighbors' interest in Eugie's death is

   A. curiosity.

   B. distrust of someone as quiet and withdrawn as Arnold.

   C. anger.

   D. excitement because their lives are usually boring.

4. When the sheriff says "he's either a moron or he's so reasonable that he's way ahead of us," he means

   A. Arnold is abnormal because he didn't immediately try to get help for his brother.

   B. Eugie was dead, so there was nothing Arnold could do for him.

   C. Arnold logically planned to kill his brother because he was jealous of him.

   D. Arnold is too young to know the meaning of life and death.

5. At the end of the story, when his mother asks him what he wants, Arnold says "I didn't want nothing" because

   A. he knows his mother hates him because he killed his brother.

   B. he has rejected his parents because he considers them cold people who have rejected him because of an accident.

   C. he is ashamed of himself and doesn't want to ask for anything.

   D. he is still in shock after the killing the day before.

6. Arnold's father mentions the need to search for the newborn calf which is in danger because

   A. it used to be Eugie's job.

   B. the father wants to get rid of Arnold, get him out of the house.

   C. life must continue; the calf needs care.

   D. giving Arnold this job is the father's way of forgiving Arnold.

7. Arnold's Uncle Andy says "Not a tear in his eye" about Arnold because

    A. he cannot forgive Arnold for killing his favorite nephew.

    B. he himself is a very emotional man.

    C. he thinks people who don't cry don't have feelings.

    D. he is embarrassed because he himself cannot cry.

8. In the future Arnold will probably be

    A. very guilty because he killed his brother.

    B. a normal person who accidentally made a bad mistake.

    C. a bitter person who cannot love anybody.

    D. a very loving person who knows the importance of forgiveness.

9. Arnold's father and mother are

    A. typical, hard-working farm people who have little time for their children.

    B. sensitive parents.

    C. people who are afraid of feelings.

    D. practical people who judge everything by results.

10. As soon as Eugie is killed, Arnold doesn't run to get his parents because

    A. he knows he did something wrong and is afraid of punishment.

    B. he rejects his parents because they are cold people.

    C. he is ashamed of himself.

    D. he is in shock after the killing.

9: STATING THE THEME

Review your discussion of the theme questions in Activity 8. As a result of these discussions, has your idea of the theme changed? What are some other possible themes of this story? Write one sentence for each theme.

Theme:

_____

_____

_____

_____

Theme:

_____

_____

_____

_____

Theme:

_____

_____

_____

_____

F. SYMBOLISM

The strawberries in "The Strawberry Season," the mystery of the storm in Chopin's "The Storm," and the oranges in "A Bag of Oranges" are instances of symbolism and symbolic language. A symbol, however, need not be one object or person. Symbolism sometimes resides in two connected or opposing objects, situations, or conditions.

10: SYMBOLISM OF HOT AND COLD

In "The Stone Boy" hot and cold temperatures appear and reappear throughout the story. Below find two columns, one for hot and one for cold elements. List all the hot elements on the left and the cold on the right. What are the differences between the two kinds of elements? Is the meaning of hot always the same? Does the meaning of cold remain constant for the entire story?

Hot	Cold
Model: The Curwing kitchen in the morning.	The time when peas are best picked.

When you have completed listing all the hot and cold elements, can you say what associations cold has? What feelings are connected with hot? What meaning grows out of or accumulates from these associations and connections? What hot represents? What cold symbolizes?

G. STYLE

Understanding the structure, the symbolism, the theme, and the other aspects of a story is important in grasping a story's meaning. Still, understanding these aspects can never be sufficient in itself. Finally, a story is the sum of its sentences, phrases, words, syllables, and even individual sounds. All of these, in addition to other language components not mentioned here, make up an author's style. The more familiar and comfortable you become with an author's style, the better you will understand his or her overall meaning and nuances.

11: SAMPLE SHORT FICTION PASSAGE FOR ANALYSIS

Read the one paragraph below from "The Stone Boy" and notice the elements of the author's style, such as sentence length and structure, connections, and choice of words. In particular, do the following:

1. Count the words in each sentence. Decide how the sentence length affects the story's meaning.

2. Notice the many one-syllable words used. Consider why the author used so many monosyllabic words.

3. Underline the connections (*and, after,* etc.). Consider why the author chose these connections and how they affect the content of the story.

4. Evaluate the strength of the verbs used. Do they convey the energy of the action?

Andy went off to get the sheriff while Arnold and his father waited on a bench in the corridor. Arnold felt his father watching him, and he lifted his eyes with painful casualness to the announcement, on the opposite wall, of the Corinth County Annual Rodeo, and then to the clock with its loudly clucking pendulum. After he had come down from the loft his father and Uncle Andy had stood in the yard with him and asked him to tell them everything, and he had explained to them how the gun had caught on the wire. But when they had asked him why he hadn't run back to the house to tell his parents, he had had no answer—all he could say was that he had gone down into the garden to pick the peas. His father had stared at him in a pale, puzzled way, and it was then that he had felt his father and the others set their cold, turbulent silence against him. Arnold shifted on the bench, his only feeling a small one of compunction imposed by his father's eyes.

12: A DEBATE

"The Stone Boy" presents many issues which cannot easily be decided. A debate can help you to decide about your feelings and opinions on these topics. Debate one or more of the topics below.

Debate Topics

1. Arnold Curwing deliberately murdered his brother and felt no regret about the act, so he is lucky to have escaped punishment.

2. Arnold Curwing is an extremely sensitive child whose punishment is that he can never forget his accidental shooting of his brother.

3. Arnold Curwing is the only member of his family whose feelings still remain intact, but after this icy treatment by his family, the legal community, and the society, he will become like all the others—a stone person.

13: A WRITING OPPORTUNITY

Write a brief essay (two or three paragraphs) on one of the topics below. You may agree or disagree.

1. Every family has stronger and weaker members. Unfortunately, often the weaker members control the stronger.

2. You never know your true character until you are tested in an emergency.

3. There really is a generation gap. It is impossible for children and parents to understand each other.

Note: A film based on "The Stone Boy," directed by Christopher Cain and starring Glenn Close and Robert Duvall is available from CBS/Fox Video. Its length is 93 minutes and it is available in Beta or VHS format.

CHAPTER TEN
SOLO FLIGHT 1

The goals for this chapter are:

To understand and appreciate a story on your own using the elements learned in Chapters 1–9

In this chapter, you will read:

"Gerald's Song" by Philip F. O'Connor

People can love each other, it was in the hope of people loving each other that I picked pottery, pottery could let us know about other people....

"Gerald's Song"

This chapter gives you an opportunity to approach a story, "Gerald's Song," on your own, applying what you have learned. When necessary, review material from previous chapters to help you. Consider what approaches among those listed below will lead you most quickly and effectively into the story.

Selected List of Entrances

Structure

Character

Symbolism

Setting

Style

Add other entrances if necessary.

Some useful questions to ask about this story include:

1. What is the meaning of the title?
2. What are the main differences between Gerald and his mother?
3. Is there a conclusion to the story? If so, what is it?
4. Why is there a separation between the two parts of the story?

GERALD'S SONG
Philip F. O'Connor

1   My stocks have descended, my stocks are in pottery and my stocks have descended. The soldiers destroy all the pottery where they are fighting, my stocks are in the company that imports that pottery, other things are up but my stocks are down. Down because of the war in that country where there is pottery.

2   Once I said the boys are giving up their lives so I should not complain. I did not start the war, I did not like the war, I put my money in pottery not bullets, but I should not complain. The fighting boys have a right to complain but I should not complain. It didn't work.

3   I have my mother to think of. I live with her, I buy her things, she is tiny and pale and moves with a creak. She worries that I will have nothing when she dies. She says, *how is the pottery,* I say *down,* she bends and she whistles and she says, *O Gerald.*

4   The pottery looked good, the pottery had a future, the pottery was a sure

thing. I put all of my money, the money my father left me, in the pottery. The pottery has gone down to a dollar, has nearly vanished.

5   *O Gerald.*

6   *O Mother.*

7   I have wanted to do something, I have wanted to write to the stock exchange, I have wanted to write to the newspaper, I have wanted to write to the President. It is not good, this war, it is not good for any of us, but what can I do, what can I say, I can only fret and what does that change?

8   *O Mother.*

9   *O Gerald.*

10   People can love each other, it was in the hope of people loving each other that I picked pottery, pottery could let us know about other people, civilization is to be found in pottery, I was hopeful when I put my money into it, I thought of poor families eating better because of the market for their pottery. I did not invest solely to make a profit. He who does that would be sinful.

11   *O Gerald.*

12   *O Mother.*

13   We look in the shops on Sunday, my mother and I, we look in the windows and pick out things for each other. My mother does not walk well, I stop with her for tea, she says, *Gerald, you will look divine in that cravat.* O, my heart is heavy. O, my soul is heavy. Soon there will be no more cravats. *It's the war, Mother, I have put everything in pottery and now there is the war.*

14   *The war the war.*

15   *O Mother.*

16   The war is taking everything away.

17   I did not want to be a soldier, I could never have been a soldier. Her cousin helped us, he was on the draft board, it was not unfair, she was getting old, I could not go to the Army with my mother getting old, I did not go. I stayed home and we played chess. She said, *what are you going to do with your father's money?* I said, *put it in pottery.* She said, *are you sure that's wise?* I said, *pottery can't lose.*

18   O the war the war. What am I to do?

19   The President said we have to be there, I believed him, then the Secretary of State said we have to stay there, and I believed him, then out congressman said we have to bring this to a successful conclusion or we can't show our faces anywhere in the world, and I believed him. I believed them all. But the pottery is down and my mother is getting older.

20   *Gerald, you must do something.*

21   *What can I do?*

22   *You must do something. I will worry myself sick if you don't.*

23   *What can I do?*

24   *Don't let me down now.*

25   *What can I do?*

26   *O Gerald.*

27   *O Mother.*

28   She threw her teacup. It struck me on the forehead. *Do something, you stupid boy,* she said, *do something.*

29   I called our congressman and wired the Secretary of State and wrote a letter to the President. They all told me in one way or another that the war can't be stopped. I said to her, *they can't stop it.* I said, *once in it's hard to get out. I know that from the pottery.*

30   *You are as stupid as the government,* she said.

31   *No one could have predicted.*

32   *As stupid as the government.*

33   *I'm sorry, Mother.*

34   *What did you want with pottery anyway?*

35   *I wanted to help the people in other countries.*

36   *Let the sons-of-bitches help themselves.*

37   *I'm sorry, Mother.*

38   *In your father's day we let them help themselves. It was better.*

39   *Yes, Mother.*

40   *O Gerald, why can't they stop the stupid war?*

41   *I wish they would.*

42   *We'll be poor if they don't stop the war.*

43   *Yes, Mother.*

44   I went to my broker. I said, *what can I do?*

45   He said, *you shouldn't have invested in pottery.*

46   I said, *but you told me to.*

47   He said, *brokers make mistakes too. We are only human.*

48   I said, *do you have money in pottery?*

49   He said, *my money is in bullets. I was lucky.*

50   I said, *what can I do?*

51   He said, *wait and hope. When the pottery goes up we'll sell and put the money in bullets.*

52   The pottery didn't go up.

53   My mother kicked the coffee table. She said, *I have always lived well. I don't intend to live any other way now. I am old. My arthritis is acting up. How could you do this to me, Gerald?*

54   *I'm sorry, Mother.*

55   She spit at me. She wiggled her arms in the air. *How could anyone be so stupid?* She cursed and tried to get up. I think she was going to attack me. She fell back. She nearly fell to the floor.

56 *Take it easy, Mother.*

57 *Who can take it easy on the way to the poorhouse?*

58 *O Mother.*

59 *I am used to comfort, Gerald, and you are taking it from me.*

60 *O Mother.*

61 *O Gerald.*

62 They didn't stop the war, my pottery is down to thirty cents, I have taken to not coming straight home after my work at the library, I have taken to stopping for a drink, I have another drink and then another and then I worry that my mother has fallen off her chair and I go home. She is always awake, sitting, rigid, staring down my shirt front, saying *Gerald, you were always a dope.*

63 I can't bear the looks she gives me, that's why I drink, I didn't try to lose my money, I didn't ask for the war, it is too late to get my money out now, I feel I am going down, we are all going down, I don't want to go down, this is my life and I want to live it, I don't understand the war, politics bore me, speeches bore me, I want more interesting things, I like books, I read about pottery when it's not busy in the reference room, I used to enjoy reading about pottery, now it makes me sick, but it is my interest, I read about it, pottery is made all over the world, there are different kinds of pottery for different countries, pottery is one of the oldest things made, Mexican pottery is very pretty, my mother is old and dying, I didn't start this war, it was a happy country before the war, people could pursue their interests, pottery was mine, it still is, I don't enjoy it as much as I used to, the war makes it less interesting, the war makes my mother irritable, the war is taking my money away, we have a hard time getting page boys at the library, they are all going into the Army, why must they go, why must we fight, who knows why we are fighting, who knows what's important about that little country, what has happened that we don't know, what has happened that the congressman and the senator and the president can't help us, why is there war, who are those people we are fighting, what do they want with us. I would have gone on investing in their pottery, they could have made lots of money selling their pottery in this country, did they sell it in another country, is that why we are fighting them.

64 There is a war and I don't understand it, there is a war and I don't understand it, there is a war and I don't understand it.

65 *O Mother.*

66 *O Gerald.*

CHAPTER ELEVEN
SOLO FLIGHT II

The goals for this chapter are:

To have another opportunity to read, identify elements, and achieve maximum comprehension of a story on your own

In this chapter, you will read:

"Sunday in the Park" by Bel Kaufman

"My kid's got just as good right here as yours, and if he feels like throwing sand, he'll throw it, and if you don't like it, you can take your kid the hell out of here."

"Sunday in the Park"

This chapter gives you an additional opportunity, with a story very different from "Gerald's Song," to work on your own. Again, the emphasis is on finding approaches to the story that will make studying the story as pleasant as possible and yield as much understanding as possible in the shortest time. In addition to the Entrances approach, focus on the differences between the various characters as another convenient way to enter the story.

Some questions to help you move into the story follow.

COMPREHENSION AND STUDY QUESTIONS

1. Why does Joe's father emphasize this is a *public* sandbox?
2. What are "the funnies?"
3. What is Morton's profession? What characteristics do you associate with this work?
4. What does the phrase "You and who else?" mean?
5. Why does Morton's wife repeat this phrase at the end of the story?
6. What do you imagine will happen when Morton and his wife return home?
7. Is this story unique to the United States or could it happen anywhere? If it happened in your country, what differences might occur?

 # SUNDAY IN THE PARK
Bel Kaufman

1   It was still warm in the late-afternoon sun, and the city noises came muffled through the trees in the park. She put her book down on the bench, removed her sunglasses, and sighed contentedly. Morton was reading the *Times Magazine* section, one arm flung around her shoulder; their three-year-old son, Larry, was playing in the sandbox: a faint breeze fanned her hair softly against her cheek. It was five-thirty of a Sunday afternoon, and the small playground, tucked away in a corner of the park, was all but deserted. The swings and seesaws stood motionless and abandoned, the slides were empty, and only in the sandbox two little boys squatted diligently side by side. *How good this is,* she thought, and almost smiled at her sense of well-being. They must go out in the sun more often; Morton was so city-pale, cooped up all week inside the gray factorylike university. She squeezed his arm affectionately and glanced at Larry, delighting in the pointed little face frowning in

concentration over the tunnel he was digging. The other boy suddenly stood up and with a quick, deliberate swing of his chubby arm threw a spadeful of sand at Larry. It just missed his head. Larry continued digging; the boy remained standing, shovel raised, stolid and impassive.

2   "No, no, little boy." She shook her finger at him, her eyes searching for the child's mother or nurse. "We mustn't throw sand. It may get in some-one's eyes and hurt. We must play nicely in the nice sandbox." The boy looked at her in unblinking expectancy. He was about Larry's age but per-haps ten pounds heavier, a husky little boy with none of Larry's quickness and sensitivity in his face. Where was his mother? The only other people left in the playground were two women and a little girl on roller skates leav-ing now through the gate, and a man on a bench a few feet away. He was a big man, and he seemed to be taking up the whole bench as he held the Sunday comics close to his face. She supposed he was the child's father. He did not look up from his comics, but spat once deftly out of the corner of his mouth. She turned her eyes away.

3   At that moment, as swiftly as before, the fat little boy threw another spadeful of sand at Larry. This time some of it landed on his hair and fore-head. Larry looked up at his mother, his mouth tentative; her expression would tell him whether to cry or not.

4   Her first instinct was to rush to her son, brush the sand out of his hair, and punish the other child, but she controlled it. She always said that she wanted Larry to learn to fight his own battles.

5   "Don't do that, little boy," she said sharply, leaning forward on the bench. "You mustn't throw sand!"

6   The man on the bench moved his mouth as if to spit again, but instead he spoke. He did not look at her, but at the boy only.

7   "You go right ahead, Joe," he said loudly. "Throw all you want. This here is a *public* sandbox."

8   She felt a sudden weakness in her knees as she glanced at Morton. He had become aware of what was happening. He put his *Times* down carefully on his lap and turned his fine, lean face toward the man, smiling the shy, apolo-getic smile he might have offered a student in pointing out an error in his thinking. When he spoke to the man, it was with his usual reasonableness.

9   "You're quite right," he said pleasantly, "but just because this is a public place...."

10   The man lowered his funnies and looked at Morton. He looked at him from head to foot, slowly and deliberately. "Yeah?" His insolent voice was edged with menace. "My kid's got just as good right here as yours, and if he feels like throwing sand, he'll throw it, and if you don't like it, you can take your kid the hell out of here."

11   The children were listening, their eyes and mouths wide open, their spades forgotten in small fists. She noticed the muscle in Morton's jaw tighten. He was rarely angry; he seldom lost his temper. She was suffused with a tenderness for her husband and an impotent rage against the man for involving him in a situation so alien and so distasteful to him.

12   "Now, just a minute," Morton said courteously, "you must realize...."

13   "Aw, shut up," said the man.

14   Her heart began to pound. Morton half rose; the *Times* slid to the ground. Slowly the other man stood up. He took a couple of steps toward Morton, then stopped. He flexed his great arms, waiting. She pressed her trembling knees together. Would there be violence, fighting? How dreadful, how incredible.... She must do something, stop them, call for help. She wanted to put her hand on her husband's sleeve, to pull him down, but for some reason she didn't.

15   Morton adjusted his glasses. He was very pale. "This is ridiculous," he said unevenly. "I must ask you...."

16   "Oh, yeah?" said the man. He stood with his legs spread apart, rocking a little, looking at Morton with utter scorn. "You and who else?"

17   For a moment the two men looked at each other nakedly. Then Morton turned his back on the man and said quietly, "Come on, let's get out of here." He walked awkwardly, almost limping with self-consciousness, to the sandbox. He stooped and lifted Larry and his shovel out.

18   At once Larry came to life; his face lost its rapt expression and he began to kick and cry. "I don't *want* to go home, I want to play better, I don't *want* any supper, I don't *like* supper...." It became a chant as they walked, pulling their child between them, his feet dragging on the ground. In order to get to the exit gate they had to pass the bench where the man sat sprawling again. She was careful not to look at him. With all the dignity she could summon, she pulled Larry's sandy, perspiring little hand, while Morton pulled the other. Slowly and with head high she walked with her husband and child out of the playground.

19   Her first feelings was one of relief that a fight had been avoided, that no one was hurt. Yet beneath it there was a layer of something else, something heavy and inescapable. She sensed that it was more than just an unpleasant incident, more than defeat of reason by force. She felt dimly it had something to do with her and Morton, something acutely personal, familiar, and important.

20   Suddenly Morton spoke. "It wouldn't have proved anything."

21   "What?" she asked.

22   "A fight. It wouldn't have proved anything beyond the fact that he's bigger than I am."

23   "Of course," she said.

24   "The only possible outcome," he continued reasonably, "would have been—what? My glasses broken, perhaps a tooth or two replaced, a couple of days' work missed—and for what? For justice? For truth?"

25   "Of course," she repeated. She quickened her step. She wanted only to get home and to busy herself with her familiar tasks; perhaps then the feeling, glued like heavy plaster on her heart, would be gone. *Of all the stupid, despicable bullies,* she thought, pulling harder on Larry's hand. The child was still crying. Always before she had felt a tender pity for his defenseless little body, the frail arms, the narrow shoulders with sharp, winglike shoulder blades, the thin and unsure legs, but now her mouth tightened in resentment.

26   "Stop crying," she said sharply, "I'm ashamed of you!" She felt as if all three of them were tracking mud along the street. The child cried louder.

27   *If there had been an issue involved,* she thought, *if there had been something to fight for.... But what else could he possibly have done? Allow himself to be beaten? Attempt to educate the man? Call a policeman? "Officer, there's a man in the park who won't stop his child from throwing sand on mine...."* The whole thing was as silly as that, and not worth thinking about.

28   "Can't you keep him quiet, for Pete's sake?" Morton asked irritably.

29   "What do you suppose I've been trying to do?" she said.

30   Larry pulled back, dragging his feet.

31   "If you can't discipline this child, I will," Morton snapped, making a move toward the boy.

32   But her voice stopped him. She was shocked to hear it, thin and cold and penetrating with contempt. "Indeed?" she heard herself say. "You and who else?"

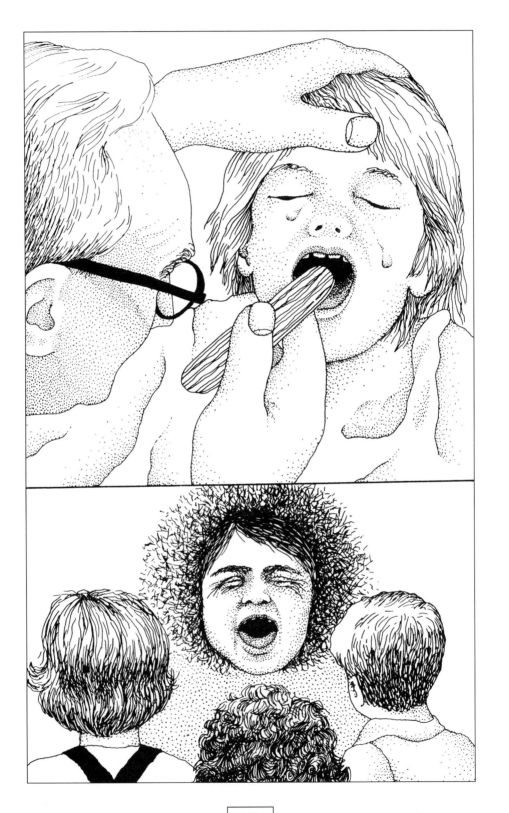

CHAPTER TWELVE
MANEUVERS I

The goals for this chapter are:

To study ordinary and extraordinary events in fiction

To re-examine point of view, character, language, and theme

In this chapter, you will read:

"The Use of Force" by William Carlos Williams

 Aren't you ashamed, the mother yelled at her.
Aren't you ashamed to act like that in front of
the doctor?

"The Use of Force"

A. THE ACTION

This far along in your fictional flight experience, you have read many stories, encountered many kinds of fiction, and learned many approaches with which to better enjoy and appreciate the stories. Even at this advanced moment, recall a basic of fiction: the **what** of the story.

Begin studying "The Use of Force" by locating the story's actions.

 # THE USE OF FORCE
William Carlos Williams

1   They were new patients to me, all I had was the name, Olson. Please come down as soon as you can, my daughter is very sick.

2   When I arrived I was met by the mother, a big startled-looking woman, very clean and apologetic who merely said, Is this the doctor? and let me in. In the back, she added, You must excuse us, doctor, we have her in the kitchen where it is warm. It is very damp here sometimes.

3   The child was fully dressed and sitting on her father's lap near the kitchen table. He tried to get up, but I motioned him not to bother, took off my overcoat and started to look things over. I could see that they were all very nervous, eyeing me up and down distrustfully. As often, in such cases, they weren't telling me more than they had to, it was up to me to tell them; that's why they were spending three dollars on me.

4   The child was fairly eating me up with her cold, steady eyes, and no expression to her face whatever. She did not move and seemed, inwardly, quiet; an unusually attractive little thing, and as strong as a heifer in appearance. But her face was flushed, she was breathing rapidly, and I realized that she had a high fever. She had magnificent blond hair, in profusion. One of those picture children often reproduced in advertising leaflets and the photogravure sections of the Sunday papers.

5   She's had a fever for three days, began the father and we don't know what it comes from. My wife has given her things, you know, like people do, but it don't do no good. And there's been a lot of sickness around. So we tho't you'd better look her over and tell us what is the matter.

6   As doctors often do I took a trial shot at it as a point of departure. Has she had a sore throat?

7   Both parents answered me together, No… No, she says her throat don't hurt her.

8   Does your throat hurt you? added the mother to the child. But the little girl's expression didn't change nor did she move her eyes from my face.

9   Have you looked?

10   I tried to, said the mother, but I couldn't see.

11   As it happens we had been having a number of cases of diphtheria in the school to which this child went during that month and we were all, quite apparently, thinking of that, though no one had as yet spoken of the thing.

12   Well, I said, suppose we take a look at the throat first. I smiled in my best professional manner and asking for the child's first name I said, come on, Mathilda, open your mouth and let's take a look at your throat.

13   Nothing doing.

14   Aw, come on, I coaxed, just open your mouth wide and let me take a look. Look, I said opening both hands wide, I haven't anything in my hands. Just open up and let me see.

15   Such a nice man, put in the mother. Look how kind he is to you. Come on, do what he tells you to. He won't hurt you.

16   At that I ground my teeth in disgust. If only they wouldn't use the word "hurt" I might be able to get somewhere. But I did not allow myself to be hurried or disturbed but speaking quietly and slowly I approached the child again.

17   As I moved my chair a little nearer suddenly with one cat-like movement both her hands clawed instinctively for my eyes and she almost reached them too. In fact she knocked my glasses flying and they fell, though unbroken, several feet away from me on the kitchen floor.

18   Both the mother and father almost turned themselves inside out in embarrassment and apology. You bad girl, said the mother, taking her and shaking her by one arm. Look what you've done. The nice man…

19   For heaven's sake, I broke in. Don't call me a nice man to her. I'm here to look at her throat on the chance that she might have diphtheria and possibly die of it. But that's nothing to her. Look here, I said to the child, we're going to look at your throat. You're old enough to understand what I'm saying. Will you open it now by yourself or shall we have to open it for you?

20   Not a move. Even her expression hadn't changed. Her breaths however were coming faster and faster. Then the battle began. I had to do it. I had to have a throat culture for her own protection. But first I told the parents that it was entirely up to them. I explained the danger but said that I would not insist on a throat examination so long as they would take the responsibility.

21   If you don't do what the doctor says you'll have to go to the hospital, the mother admonished her severely.

22   Oh yeah? I had to smile to myself. After all, I had already fallen in love with the savage brat, the parents were contemptible to me. In the ensuing

struggle they grew more and more abject, crushed, exhausted while she surely rose to magnificent heights of insane fury of effort bred of her terror of me.

23   The father tried his best, and he was a big man but the fact that she was his daughter, his shame at her behavior and his dread of hurting her made him release her just at the critical moment several times when I had almost achieved success, till I wanted to kill him. But his dread also that she might have diphtheria made him tell me to go on, go on though he himself was almost fainting, while the mother moved back and forth behind us raising and lowering her hands in an agony of apprehension.

24   Put her in front of you on your lap, I ordered, and hold both her wrists.

25   But as soon as he did the child let out a scream. Don't, you're hurting me. Let go of my hands. Let them go I tell you. Then she shrieked terrifyingly, hysterically. Stop it! Stop it! You're killing me!

26   Do you think she can stand it, doctor! said the mother.

27   You get out, said the husband to his wife. Do you want her to die of diphtheria?

28   Come on now, hold her, I said.

29   Then I grasped the child's head with my left hand and tried to get the wooden tongue depressor between her teeth. She fought, with clenched teeth, desperately! But now I also had grown furious—at a child. I tried to hold myself down but I couldn't. I know how to expose a throat for inspection. And I did my best. When finally I got the wooden spatula behind the last teeth and just the point of it into the mouth cavity, she opened up for an instant but before I could see anything she came down again and gripping the wooden blade between her molars she reduced it to splinters before I could get it out again.

30   Aren't you ashamed, the mother yelled at her. Aren't you ashamed to act like that in front of the doctor?

31   Get me a smooth-handled spoon of some sort, I told the mother. We're going through with this. The child's mouth was already bleeding. Her tongue was cut and she was screaming in wild hysterical shrieks. Perhaps I should have desisted and come back in an hour or more. No doubt it would have been better. But I have seen at least two children lying dead in bed of neglect in such cases, and feeling that I must get a diagnosis, now or never I went at it again. But the worst of it was that I too had got beyond reason. I could have torn the child apart in my own fury and enjoyed it. It was a pleasure to attack her. My face was burning with it.

32   The damned little brat must be protected against her own idiocy, one says to one's self at such times. Others must be protected against her. It is

social necessity. And all these things are true. But a blind fury, a feeling of adult shame, bred of a longing for muscular release are the operatives. One goes on to the end.

33   In a final unreasoning assault I overpowered the child's neck and jaws. I forced the heavy silver spoon back of her teeth and down her throat till she gagged. And there it was—both tonsils covered with membrane. She had fought valiantly to keep me from knowing her secret. She had been hiding that sore throat for three days at least and lying to her parents in order to escape just such a outcome as this.

34   Now truly she *was* furious. She had been on the defensive before but now she attacked. Tried to get off her father's lap and fly at me while tears of defeat blinded her eyes.

1A: SYNOPSIS

A **synopsis** is a brief oral or written account of the main events of a work. Sitting with your classmates in a circle, tell of one action that occurs in the story. You do not need to follow the order of the story, but only relate one event from the story. For example, Mathilda is a child in the Olson family.

1B: ORDINARY AND EXTRAORDINARY EVENTS

Review the action of the story. Did any of the actions surprise you? All fiction is composed of both the ordinary and the extraordinary matters of life. Divide the major events of "The Use of Force" into two lists, the ordinary and the unusual. List as many events as you can for each column.

Ordinary Actions	Unusual Actions
Model: A child is ill.	The doctor says he is in love with the child.

1._____

2._____

3._____

4._____

5._____

B. THE PROPER SUBJECT MATTER OF FICTION

Extraordinary actions are interesting both to an author and to his or her audience. Why are ordinary actions also attractive to readers of fiction? Why does an author include in his or her fiction actions that one experiences in daily life?

2: ORDINARY EVENTS IN OR OUT OF THE STORY?

As a class, choose three of the ordinary actions you listed above. Pretend you are an author. Would you include these actions in the story? Discuss with each other the reasons for or against including these actions.

Follow-up Discussion: Do you think fiction should include such ordinary events? Why or why not? Are there some ordinary events in your life about which you could write a story? Discuss these questions with your classmates.

C. POINT OF VIEW

Newspaper reporters are always told to emphasize the **who, what, when, where,** and, at times, the **why** in their news stories. For fiction writers the **who** is a major element, particularly for "The Use of Force."

In this story, one of the "who's" is the storyteller himself, the narrator. In many of the stories you have read, the narrator and the author are the same person. In "The Use of Force," however, this is not true.

When the author is not the narrator, examine the "what" of the story more closely. Certain character traits, such as the narrator's bad or selective memory, bias about what she or he is telling, or a personality habit may influence how she or he is telling the story. In other words, in such a case, the "who" and the "what" of the story are interconnected.

3: RETELLING THE STORY FROM ANOTHER POINT OF VIEW

You and other members of your assigned group will become one of the three other characters in the story: Mathilda, the mother, the father, or a character only mentioned, such as one of Mathilda's schoolmates. Imagine the events from your character's point of view, talking within your assigned group about your character's perception of the events. Then tell the story as you would tell it if you were that character. What events would you include or exclude? What events, characters, or comments would you add? With your group, narrate your version of the story to your classmates. Consider the changes in the story. What difference does the point of view make? What do you think about the doctor now?

D. CHARACTER MOTIVATION

4: WHAT A CHARACTER WANTS

To explore what a character wants, his or her motivation, complete the sentences below. Recall that motivation means the reason—conscious, unconscious, or a combination of the two—for one's actions or statements or what one wants or wishes to attain.

If I were _____ , I would like to…
              (character's name)

To complete the sentence for a particular character, first imagine what the character believes she or he wants and what you believe the character *really* wants. A difference between the two may exist if a character does not understand himself or herself very well. Write down as many sentences as you can for each character: (1) a mother, (2) a father, (3) the child, and (4) the doctor.

Model:
If I were <u>the doctor</u>, I would like <u>to help the child recover</u>.

5: CHARACTER AND CONFLICT

When two persons or characters have opposite goals or opposing ideas about how to reach those goals, we say they have a conflict. Make a chart of any opposing goals or ways to reach those goals you discover in the characters.

Model:
<u>The doctor</u> wants to examine the child, <u>but the child</u> doesn't want to be touched.

Write down and discuss some other character conflicts in the story.

E. LANGUAGE AND STYLE

"Oh yeah? I had to smile to myself. After all, I had already fallen in love with the savage brat, the parents were contemptible to me."

These are the words of the narrator of "The Use of Force." Because the narrator in this story is our only source of information, his words are important if we are to understand him. Even the mother's and father's words reach us through the doctor. He does not quote; he only paraphrases their thoughts in his words.

6: THE NARRATOR'S STYLE

Read the passages below, especially the words in capital letters. What do the word choices of the doctor tell you about him?

Passage 1 The child was fairly EATING ME UP with her cold, steady eyes, and no expression to her face whatever. She did not move and seemed, inwardly, quiet; AN UNUSUALLY ATTRACTIVE LITTLE THING, and as strong as a HEIFER in appearance. But her face was flushed, she was breathing rapidly, and I realized that she had a high fever. She had MAGNIFICENT blond hair, in profusion.

Passage 2 As I moved my chair a little nearer suddenly with one CAT-LIKE movement both her hands CLAWED instinctively for my eyes and she almost reached them too. In fact she knocked my glasses flying and they fell, though unbroken, several feet away from me on the kitchen floor.

Passage 3 Then I GRASPED the child's head with my left hand and tried to get the wooden tongue depressor between her teeth. She fought, WITH CLENCHED TEETH, desperately! But now I also had grown furious—at a child. I tried to HOLD MYSELF DOWN but I couldn't.

Passage 4 The DAMNED LITTLE BRAT must be PROTECTED against her own IDIOCY, one says to one's self at such times. Others must be PROTECTED against her. It is SOCIAL NECESSITY. And all these things are true. But a BLIND FURY, a feeling of ADULT SHAME, BRED of a longing for MUSCULAR RELEASE are the OPERATIVES.

7: SYNOPSIS (ONCE AGAIN)

The first time you gave a synopsis, you were deciding if the ordinary events of daily life were sufficient material for fiction. Now, having looked at the narrator, the language, and the characters of the story, discuss the meaning and importance of the story's actions. Are all of those actions essential? Can some of them be removed without harming the story? Make a list of the essential actions of the story and compare it with the class's first synopsis, noting what actions you cut.

F. THEMES AND ISSUES

Is the story only the sum of its parts? Is there something more to "The Use of Force" than the story of a doctor's visit to a sick child? In "Feast" you saw another instance in which a person was told by another person in authority to open her mouth. In Chapter Eight you explored the concept and an example of ritual. Can a doctor's visit also be a ritual? Why or why not?

THEME

8: DISCUSSING A THEME

With your classmates, discuss possible themes for this story.

A CRUCIAL ISSUE: ADULTS AND CHILDREN

9: ORAL REPORT

Prepare for class presentation an oral report on one aspect of parent-child relationships. Your report should be three to five minutes long and should consider one or more of the topics below.

Mutual Respect of Parent and Child

Knowledge Is Power

Financial Control Is Power

Parents' Needs

Children's Needs

Equality and Inequality

Manipulation of the Weaker by the Stronger

10: CONTINUING THE STORY

Write a new paragraph ending the story. You may continue in the voice of the doctor, you may change the narrator, or you may use dialogue. Read your new ending to the class and discuss your reasons for ending the story this way.

11: WRITING ACTIVITY

Write a composition on one of the topics below. Use your understanding of the story and your life experience to support your position.

Topic 1: The doctor in the story is a typical doctor, since he has no patience with the fears and desires of the patient or her family.

Topic 2: In every situation, one dominant person and one dominated person exist. Equality is impossible.

Topic 3: Control of language is one of the major tools of repression.

Topic 4: Every human being has both animal and human characteristics, and these two aspects are inseparable.

CHAPTER THIRTEEN

IN FLIGHT

The goals for this chapter are:

To explore symbolic language: Allusion, foreshadowing, and imagery

To recount events of a story from a different character's point of view

In this chapter, you will read:

"Guests of a Nation" by Frank O'Connor

"I never could make out what duty was myself," he said. *"I think you're all good lads, if that's what you mean."*

"Guests of the Nation"

A. THE CAMERA'S ANGLE

Most narrators want to tell the truth and think they are telling the truth. Nevertheless, narrators always present their "distortion" of events. In this sense, narratives are only partial truths.

 # GUESTS OF THE NATION
Frank O'Connor

I

1   At dusk the big Englishman, Belcher, would shift his long legs out of the ashes and say "Well, chums, what about it?" and Noble or me would say "All right, chum" (for we had picked up some of their curious expressions), and the little Englishman, Hawkins, would light the lamp and bring out the cards. Sometimes Jeremiah Donovan would come up and supervise the game and get excited over Hawkins's cards, which he always played badly, and shout at him as if he was one of our own "Ah, you divil, you, why didn't you play the tray?"

2   But ordinarily Jeremiah was a sober and contented poor devil like the big Englishman, Belcher, and was looked up to only because he was a fair hand at documents, though he was slow enough even with them. He wore a small cloth hat and big gaiters over his long pants, and you seldom saw him with his hands out of his pockets. He reddened when you talked to him, tilting from toe to heel and back, and looking down all the time at his big farmer's feet. Noble and me used to make fun of his broad accent, because we were from the town.

3   I couldn't at the time see the point of me and Noble guarding Belcher and Hawkins at all, for it was by belief that you could have planted that pair down anywhere from this to Claregalway and they'd have taken root there like native weed. I never in my short experience seen two men to take to the country as they did.

4   They were handed on to us by the Second Battalion when the search for them became too hot, and Noble and myself, being young, took over with a natural feeling of responsibility, but Hawkins made us look like fools when he showed that he knew the country better than we did.

5   "You're the bloke they calls Bonaparte," he says to me. "Mary Brigid

O'Connell told me to ask you what you done with the pair of her brother's socks you borrowed."

6   For it seemed, as they explained it, that the Second used to have little evenings, and some of the girls of the neighborhood turned in, and, seeing they were such decent chaps, our fellows couldn't leave the two Englishmen out of them. Hawkins learned to dance "The Walls of Limerick," "The Siege of Ennis," and the "Waves of Tory" as well as any of them, though, naturally, we couldn't return the compliment, because our lads at that time did not dance foreign dances on principle.

7   So whatever privileges Belcher and Hawkins had with the Second they just naturally took with us, and after the first day or two we gave up all pretense of keeping a close eye on them. Not that they could have got far, for they had accents you could cut with a knife and wore Khaki tunics and overcoats with civilian pants and boots.   But it's my belief that they never had any idea of escaping and were quite content to be where they were.

8   It was a treat to see how Belcher got off with the old woman of the house where we were staying. She was a great warrant to scold, and cranky even with us, but before ever she had a chance of giving our guests, as I may call them, a lick of her tongue, Belcher had made her his friend for life. She was breaking sticks, and Belcher, who hadn't been more than ten minutes in the house, jumped up from his seat and went over to her.

9   "Allow me, madam," he says, smiling his queer little smile, "please allow me"; and he takes the bloody hatchet. She was struck too paralytic to speak, and after that, Belcher would be at her heels, carrying a bucket, a basket, or a load of turf, as the case might be. As Noble said, he got into looking before she leapt, and hot water, or any little thing she wanted, Belcher would have it ready for her. For such a huge man (and though I am five foot ten myself I had to look up at him) he had an uncommon shortness —or should I say lack?—of speech. It took us some time to get used to him, walking in and out, like a ghost, without a word. Especially because Hawkins talked enough for a platoon, it was strange to hear big Belcher with his toes in the ashes come out with a solitary "Excuse me, chum," or "That's right, chum." His one and only passion was cards, and I will say for him that he was a good card-player. He could have fleeced myself and Noble, but whatever we lost to him Hawkins lost to us, and Hawkins played with the money Belcher gave him.

10   Hawkins lost to us because he had too much old gab, and we probably lost to Belcher for the same reason. Hawkins and Noble would spit at one another about religion into the early hours of the morning, and Hawkins worried the soul out of Noble, whose brother was a priest, with a string of questions that would puzzle a cardinal. To make it worse, even in treating of holy subjects, Hawkins had a deplorable tongue. I never in all my career

met a man who could mix such a variety of cursing and bad language into an argument. He was a terrible man, and a fright to argue. He never did a stroke of work, and when he had no one else to talk to, he got stuck in the old woman.

11   He met his match in her, for one day when he tried to get her to complain profanely of the drought, she gave him a great come-down by blaming it entirely on Jupiter Pluvius (a deity neither Hawkins nor I had ever heard of, though Noble said that among the pagans it was believed that he had something to do with the rain). Another day he was swearing at the capitalists for starting the German war when the old lady laid down her iron, puckered up her little crab's mouth, and said: "Mr. Hawkins, you can say what you like about the war, and think you'll deceive me because I'm only a simple poor countrywoman, but I know what started the war. It was the Italian Count that stole the heathen divinity out of the temple in Japan. Believe me, Mr. Hawkins, nothing but sorrow and want can follow the people that disturb the hidden powers."

12   A queer old girl, all right.

II

13   We had our tea one evening, and Hawkins lit the lamp and we all sat into cards. Jeremiah Donovan came in too, and sat down and watched us for a while, and it suddenly struck me that he had no great love for the two Englishmen. It came as a great surprise to me, because I hadn't noticed anything about him before.

14   Late in the evening a really terrible argument blew up between Hawkins and Noble, about capitalists and priests and love of your country.

15   "The capitalists," says Hawkins with an angry gulp, "pays the priests to tell you about the next world so as you won't notice what the bastards are up to in this."

16   "Nonsense, man!" says Noble, losing his temper. "Before ever a capitalist was thought of, people believed in the next world."

17   Hawkins stood up as though he was preaching a sermon.

18   "Oh, they did, did they?" he says with a sneer. "They believed all the things you believe, isn't that what you mean? And you believe that God created Adam, and Adam created Shem, and Shem created Jehoshophat. You believe all that silly old fairytale about Eve and Eden and the apple. Well, listen to me, chum. If you're entitled to hold a silly belief like that, I'm entitled to hold my silly belief—which is that the first thing your God created was a bleeding capitalist, with morality and Rolls-Royce complete. Am I right, chum?" he says to Belcher.

19   "You're right, chum," says Belcher with his amused smile, and got up from the table to stretch his long legs into the fire and stroke his mous-

tache. So, seeing that Jeremiah Donovan was going, and that there was no knowing when the argument about religion would be over, I went out with him. We strolled down to the village together, and then he stopped and started blushing and mumbling and saying I ought to be behind, keeping guard on the prisoners. I didn't like the tone he took with me, and anyway I was bored with life in the cottage, so I replied by asking him what the hell we wanted guarding them at all for. I told him I'd talked it over with Noble, and that we'd both rather be out with a fighting column.

20   "What use are those fellows to us?" says I.

21   He looked at me in surprise and said: "I thought you knew we were keeping them as hostages."

22   "Hostages?" I said.

23   "The enemy have prisoners belonging to us," he says, "and now they're talking of shooting them. If they shoot our prisoners, we'll shoot theirs."

24   "Shoot them?" I said.

25   "What else did you think we were keeping them for?" he says.

26   "Wasn't it very unforeseen of you not to warn Noble and myself of that in the beginning?" I said.

27   "How was it?" says he. "You might have known it."

28   "We couldn't know it, Jeremiah Donovan," says I. "How could we when they were on our hands so long?"

29   "The enemy have our prisoners as long and longer," says he.

30   "That's not the same thing at all," says I.

31   "What difference is there?" says he.

32   I couldn't tell him, because I knew he wouldn't understand. If it was only an old dog that was going to the vet's, you'd try and not get too fond of him, but Jeremiah Donovan wasn't a man that would ever be in danger of that.

33   "And when is this thing going to be decided?" says I.

34   "We might hear tonight," he says. "Or tomorrow or the next day at latest. So if it's only hanging around here that's a trouble to you, you'll be free soon enough."

35   It wasn't the hanging round that was a trouble to me at all by this time. I had worse things to worry about. When I got back to the cottage the argument was still on. Hawkins was holding forth in his best style, maintaining that there was no next world, and Noble was maintaining that there was; but I could see that Hawkins had had the best of it.

36   "Do you know what, chum?" he was saying with a saucy smile. "I think you're just as big a bleeding unbeliever as I am. You say you believe in the next world, and you know just as much about the next world as I do, which is sweet damn-all. What's heaven? You don't know. Where's heaven? You don't know. You know sweet damn-all! I ask you again, do they wear wings?"

37   "Very well, then," says Noble, "they do. Is that enough for you? They do wear wings."

38   "Where do they get them, then? Who makes them? Have they a factory for wings? Have they a sort of store where you hands in your chit and takes your bleeding wings?"

39   "You're an impossible man to argue with," says Noble. "Now, listen to me—" And they were off again.

40   It was long after midnight when we locked up and went to bed. As I blew out the candle I told Noble what Jeremiah Donovan was after telling me. Noble took it very quietly. When we'd been in bed about an hour he asked me did I think we ought to tell the Englishmen. I didn't think we should, because it was more than likely that the English wouldn't shoot our men, and even if they did, the brigade officers, who were always up and down with the Second Battalion and knew the Englishmen well, wouldn't be likely to want them plugged. "I think so too," says Noble. "It would be great cruelty to put the wind up them now."

41   "It was very unforeseen of Jeremiah Donovan anyhow," says I.

42   It was next morning that we found it so hard to face Belcher and Hawkins. We went about the house all day scarcely saying a word. Belcher didn't seem to notice; he was stretched into the ashes as usual, with his usual look of waiting in quietness for something unforeseen to happen, but Hawkins noticed and put it down to Noble's being beaten in the argument of the night before.

43   "Why can't you take a discussion in the proper spirit?" he says severely. "You and your Adam and Eve! I'm a Communist, that's what I am. Communist or anarchist, it all comes to much the same thing." And for hours he went round the house, muttering when the fit took him. "Adam and Eve! Adam and Eve! Nothing better to do with their time than picking bleeding apples!"

III

44   I don't know how we got through that day, but I was very glad when it was over, the tea things were cleared away, and Belcher said in his peaceable way: "Well, chums, what about it?" We sat round the table and Hawkins took out the cards, and just then I heard Jeremiah Donovan's footstep on the path and a dark presentiment crossed my mind. I rose from the table and caught him before he reached the door.

45   "What do you want?" I asked.

46   "I want those two soldier friends of your," he says, getting red.

47   "Is that the way, Jeremiah Donovan?" I asked

48   "That's the way. There were four of our lads shot this morning, one of them a boy of sixteen."

49   "That's bad," I said.

50   At that moment Noble followed me out, and the three of us walked

down the path together, talking in whispers. Feeney, the local intelligence officer, was standing by the gate.

51   "What are you going to do about it?" I asked Jeremiah Donovan.

52   "I want you and Noble to get them out; tell them they're being shifted again; that'll be the quietest way."

53   "Leave me out of that," says Noble under his breath.

54   Jeremiah Donovan looks at him hard.

55   "All right," he says. "You and Feeney get a few tools from the shed and dig a hole by the far end of the bog. Bonaparte and myself will be after you. Don't let anyone see you with the tools. I wouldn't like it to go beyond ourselves."

56   We saw Feeney and Noble go round to the shed and went in ourselves. I left Jeremiah Donovan to do the explanations. He told them that he had orders to send them back to the Second Battalion. Hawkins let out a mouthful of curses, and you could see that though Belcher didn't say anything, he was a bit upset too. The old woman was for having them stay in spite of us, and she didn't stop advising them until Jeremiah Donovan lost his temper and turned on her. He had a nasty temper, I noticed. It was pitch-dark in the cottage by this time, but no one thought of lighting a lamp, and in the darkness the two Englishmen fetched their topcoats and said good-bye to the old woman.

57   "Just as a man makes a home of a bleeding place, some bastard at headquarters thinks you're too cushy and shunts you off," says Hawkins, shaking her hand.

58   "A thousand thanks, madam," says Belcher. "A thousand thanks for everything"—as though he'd made it up.

59   We went round to the back of the house and down towards the bog. It was only then that Jeremiah Donovan told them. He was shaking with excitement.

60   "There were four of our fellows shot in Cork this morning and now you're to be shot as a reprisal."

61   "What are you talking about?" snaps Hawkins. "It's bad enough being mucked about as we are without having to put up with your funny jokes."

62   "It isn't a joke," says Donovan. "I'm sorry, Hawkins, but it's true," and begins on the usual rigmarole about duty and how unpleasant it is.

63   I never noticed that people who talk a lot about duty find it much of a trouble to them.

64   "Oh, cut it out!" says Hawkins.

65   "Ask Bonaparte," says Donovan, seeing that Hawkins isn't taking him seriously. "Isn't it true, Bonaparte?"

66   "It is," I say, and Hawkins stops.

67   "Ah, for Christ's sake, chum!"

68   "I mean it, chum," I say.

69   "You don't sound as if you meant it."

70   "If he doesn't mean it, I do," says Donovan, working himself up.

71   "What have you against me, Jeremiah Donovan?"

72   "I never said I had anything against you. But why did your people take out four of our prisoners and shoot them in cold blood?"

73   He took Hawkins by the arm and dragged him on, but it was impossible to make him understand that we were in earnest. I had the Smith and Wesson in my pocket and I kept fingering it and wondering what I'd do if they put up a fight for it or ran, and wishing to God they'd do one or the other. I knew if they did run for it, that I'd never fire on them. Hawkins wanted to know was Noble in it, and when we said yes, he asked us why Noble wanted to plug him. Why did any of us want to plug him? What had he done to us? Weren't we all chums? Didn't we understand him and didn't he understand us? Did we imagine for an instant that he'd shoot us for all the so-and-so officers in the so-and-so British Army?

74   By this time we'd reached the bog, and I was so sick I couldn't even answer him. We walked along the edge of it in the darkness, and every now and then Hawkins would call a halt and begin all over again, as if he was wound up, about our being chums, and I knew that nothing but the sight of the grave would convince him that we had to do it. And all the time I was hoping that something would happen; that they'd run for it or that Noble would take over the responsibility from me. I had the feeling that it was worse on Noble than on me.

IV

75   At last we saw the lantern in the distance and made towards it. Noble was carrying it, and Feeney was standing somewhere in the darkness behind him, and the picture of them so still and silent in the bogland brought it home to me that we were in earnest, and banished the last bit of hope I had.

76   Belcher, on recognizing Noble, said: "Hallo, chum," in his quiet way, but Hawkins flew at him at once, and the argument began all over again, only this time Noble had nothing to say for himself and stood with his head down, holding the lantern between his legs.

77   It was Jeremiah Donovan who did the answering. For the twentieth time, as though it was haunting his mind, Hawkins asked if anybody thought he'd shoot Noble.

78   "Yes, you would," says Jeremiah Donovan.

79   "No, I wouldn't, damn you!"

80   "You would, because you'd know you'd be shot for not doing it."

81   "I wouldn't, not if I was to be shot twenty times over. I wouldn't shoot a pal. And Belcher wouldn't—isn't that right, Belcher?"

82   "That's right, chum," Belcher said, but more by way of answering the

question than of joining in the argument. Belcher sounded as though whatever unforeseen thing he'd always been waiting for had come at last.

83   "Anyway, who says Noble would be shot if I wasn't? What do you think I'd do if I was in his place, out in the middle of a blasted bog?"

84   "What would you do?" asks Donovan.

85   "I'd go with him wherever he was going, of course. Share my last bob with him and stick by him through thick and thin. No one can ever say of me that I let down a pal."

86   "We had enough of this," says Jeremiah Donovan, cocking his revolver. "Is there any message you want to send?"

87   "No, there isn't."

88   "Do you want to say your prayers?"

89   Hawkins came out with a cold-blooded remark that even shocked me and turned on Noble again.

90   "Listen to me, Noble," he says. "You and me are chums. You can't come over to my side, so I'll come over to your side. That show you I mean what I say? Give me a rifle and I'll go along with you and the other lads."

91   Nobody answered him. We knew that was no way out.

92   "Hear what I'm saying?" he says. "I'm through with it. I'm a deserter or anything else you like. I don't believe in your stuff, but it's no worse than mine. That satisfy you?"

93   Noble raised his head, but Donovan began to speak and he lowered it again without replying.

94   "For the last time, have you any messages to send?" says Donovan in a cold, excited sort of voice.

95   "Shut up, Donovan! You don't understand me, but these lads do. They're not the sort to make a pal and kill a pal. They're not the tools of any capitalist."

96   I alone of the crowd saw Donovan raise his Webley to the back of Hawkins's neck, and as he did so I shut my eyes and tried to pray. Hawkins had begun to say something else when Donovan fired, and as I opened my eyes at the bang, I saw Hawkins stagger at the knees and lie out flat at Noble's feet, slowly and as quiet as a kid falling asleep, with the lantern-light on his lean legs and bright farmer's boots. We all stood very still, watching him settle out in the last agony.

97   Then Belcher took out a handkerchief and began to tie it about his own eyes (in our excitement we'd forgotten to do the same for Hawkins), and see-ing it wasn't big enough, turned and asked for the loan of mine. I gave it to him and he knotted the two together and pointed with his foot at Hawkins.

98   "He's not quite dead," he says. "Better give him another."

99   Sure enough, Hawkins's left knee is beginning to rise. I bend down and put my gun to his head; then, recollecting myself, I get up again. Belcher understands what's in my mind.

100   "Give him his first," he says. "I don't mind. Poor bastard, we don't know what's happening to him now."

101   I knelt and fired. By this time I didn't seem to know what I was doing. Belcher, who was fumbling a bit awkwardly with the handkerchiefs, came out with a laugh as he heard the shot. It was the first time I heard him laugh and it sent a shudder down my back; it sounded so unnatural.

102   "Poor bugger!" he said quietly. "And last night he was so curious about it all. It's very queer, chums, I always think. Now he knows as much about it as they'll ever let him know, and last night he was all in the dark."

103   Donovan helped him to tie the handkerchiefs about his eyes. "Thanks, chum," he said. Donovan asked if there were any messages he wanted sent.

104   "No, chum," he says. "Not for me. If any of you would like to write to Hawkins's mother, you'll find a letter from her in his pocket. He and his mother were great chums. But my missus left me eight years ago. Went away with another fellow and took the kid with her. I like the feeling of a home, as you may have noticed, but I couldn't start again after that."

105   It was an extraordinary thing, but in those few minutes Belcher said more than in all the weeks before. It was just as if the sound of the shot had started a flood of talk in him and he could go on the whole night like that, quite happily, talking about himself. We stood round like fools now that he couldn't see us any longer. Donovan looked at Noble, and Noble shook his head. Then Donovan raised his Webley, and at that moment Belcher gives his queer laugh again. He may have thought we were talking about him, or perhaps he noticed the same thing I'd noticed and couldn't understand it.

106   "Excuse me, chums," he says. "I feel I'm talking the hell of a lot, and so silly, about my being so handy about a house and things like that. But this thing came on me suddenly. You'll forgive me, I'm sure."

107   "You don't want to say a prayer?" asked Donovan.

108   "No, chum," he says. "I don't think it would help. I'm ready, and you boys want to get it over."

109   "You understand that we're only doing our duty?" says Donovan.

110   Belcher's head was raised like a blind man's, so that you could only see his chin and the tip of his nose in the lantern-light.

111   "I never could make out what duty was myself," he said. "I think you're all good lads, if that's what you mean. I'm not complaining."

112   Noble, just as if he couldn't bear any more of it, raised his fist at Donovan, and in a flash Donovan raised his gun and fired. The big man went over like a sack of meal, and this time there was no need of a second shot.

113   I don't remember much about the burying, but that it was worse than all the rest because we had to carry them to the grave. It was all mad lonely with nothing but a patch of lantern-light between ourselves and the dark, and birds hooting and screeching all round, disturbed by the guns. Noble

went through Hawkins's belongings to find the letter from his mother, and then joined his hands together. He did the same with Belcher. Then, when we'd filled in the grave, we separated from Jeremiah Donovan and Feeney and took our tools back to the shed. All the way we didn't speak a word. The kitchen was dark and cold as we'd left it, and the old woman was sitting over the hearth, saying her beads. We walked past her into the room, and Noble struck a match to light the lamp. She rose quietly and came to the doorway with all her cantankerousness gone.

114 "What did ye do with them?" she asked in a whisper, and Noble started so that the match went out in his hand.

115 "What's that?" he asked without turning round.

116 "I heard ye," she said.

117 "What did you hear?" asked Noble.

118 "I heard ye. Do ye think I didn't hear ye, putting the spade back in the houseen?"

119 Noble struck another match and this time the lamp lit for him.

120 "Was that what ye did to them?" she asked.

121 Then, by God, in the very doorway, she fell on her knees and began praying, and after looking at her for a minute or two Noble did the same by the fireplace. I pushed my way out past her and left them at it. I stood at the door, watching the stars and listening to the shrieking of the birds dying out over the bogs. It is so strange what you feel at times like that you can't describe it. Noble says he saw everything ten times the size, as though there were nothing in the whole world but that little patch of bog with the two Englishmen stiffening into it, but with me it was as if the patch of bog where the Englishmen were was a million miles away, and even Noble and the old woman, mumbling behind me, and the birds and the bloody stars were all far away, and I was somehow very small and very lost and lonely like a child astray in the snow. And anything that happened me afterwards, I never felt the same about again.

1: THE STORY FROM A DIFFERENT ANGLE

Fill in the blanks in the sentence below:

The narrator of "Guests of the Nation" is _____ , who is
                                              (name)

a/an _____ man in the _____ army.
       (Irish, British)   (Irish, British)

If another character, Belcher or Hawkins for example, were telling the story, their version, even their choice of words, would differ from Bonaparte's.

Choose one character from the story and retell the story in his or her words. Recount the main events as she or he sees them. Suit the word choice to the character. You do not need to write the story word for word. Write only the main events of the story from the point of view of the character you chose.

B. ENCOUNTER: HOBSON'S CHOICES

A **Hobson's Choice** is an idiom meaning a choice between two or more equally impossible or even horrible alternatives.

2: YOUR OWN HOBSON'S CHOICE

Write about an instance in your life when you felt you faced a Hobson's Choice decision. What decision did you make?

C. BACKGROUND AND ALLUSIONS

The conflict between the British and the Irish and their hatred for each other are well-known and long-standing. They continue, in the struggles of Northern Ireland, to this day. This story is set against this background and contains many allusions to Irish myth and history.

3: EXPLORING ALLUSIONS

In each sentence the allusions listed below refer to some aspect of Irish culture or history. See if you can discover their meanings in books about Ireland in your school or public library. Discuss the answers with your classmates.

Model:

Jupiter Pluvius is the name of

    A. the Old Testament God.

    B. an Irish sea town.

    C. a mythical Irish God in whom the old lady of the story believes.

1. "The Walls of Limerick," "The Siege of Ennis," and "The Waves of Tory" are names of

    A. Irish plays.

    B. Irish dances.

    C. British songs.

2. A Webley is the name of

    A. a type of horse.

    B. a type of car.

    C. a type of gun.

3. Claregalway is the name of

    A. a type of beer.

    B. a region of Ireland.

    C. an Irish god.

4. Cork is the name of

    A. an Irish county.

    B. a building material.

    C. a tool.

D. STRUCTURE AND FORESHADOWING

In a well-structured story, some of the actions which occur early in the story prepare the reader for later actions. This is called **foreshadowing**, an important aspect of "Guests of the Nation."

4: FORESHADOWING

Each action listed on the left foreshadows an action on the right which occurs later in the story. Connect the action on the left with the matching action on the right.

1. Hawkins and Noble debate religion and especially the afterlife.

    Hawkins offers to switch allegiance to the Irish to avoid being shot.

2. Donovan argues with Hawkins "as if he was one of our own."

    Bonaparte wishes Belcher and Hawkins would try to escape.

3. Hawkins and Belcher don't seem to have any idea of escaping.

Hawkins is killed and, as Belcher says, he knows as much as he'll ever know about the afterlife.

4. The Irish did not dance foreign dances on principle.

The two British soldiers are not killed for what they themselves have done but in retaliation for the British killing Irish soldiers.

E. STYLE: THE WAY IT'S SAID

Authors reveal some of their personality and intentions in their style—choice of words, phrases, clauses, and sentences. In the passages below from "Guests of the Nation," certain words have been removed. Without looking at the original passage, replace the missing words with your own choices. These two paragraphs are from different sections of the story.

5: CLOZE PASSAGE

Passage 1

_____ this time we'd reached the bog, _____ I was so
      (1)   (2)

sick I couldn't even answer him. We walked _____ the edge of
                                              (3)

it in the darkness, _____ every now and then Hawkins would call
                    (4)

a halt and begin all over again, _____ _____ he was
                              (5)   (6)

wound up, _____ our being chums, _____ I knew
           (7)   (8)

_____ nothing _____ the sight of the grave would
      (9)   (10)

convince him _____ we had to do it.
             (11)

Passage 2

I don't _____ much about the burying, but that it was worse
(1)

than all the _____ because we had to _____ them to
(2)   (3)

the grave. It was all mad lonely with _____ but a _____
(4)   (5)

of lantern-light between ourselves and the _____ , and birds
(6)

hooting and _____ all round, disturbed by the guns.
(7)

F. PACE

You probably noticed that your choice of words sped up or slowed down the reading of the text. That is, the pace (rate) of the writing changed. Pace in addition means how quickly or slowly the conflict in the story increases or decreases in strength.

Pace: the rate at which tension is injected into or released from the story.

6: NOTICING THE PACE

In "Guests of the Nation," O'Connor varies the pace from one section of the story to another. Label each section (I–IV) with one of the following terms:

S = slow; M = moderate; F = fast; VF = very fast

Can you explain the effect on the reader of the change of pace on the story? How does the tension increase or decrease because of the pace of the story?

7: CHARACTER SIMILARITY AND CONTRAST

Although "Guests of the Nation" tells of the men from the armies of two opposing nations, many similarities between the captors and captives surface. In the activity below some personality traits are listed. Next to the trait listed on the left write the names of the characters who share the trait.

Trait	Characters Who Share the Trait
Model:	
Sober, contented	Jeremiah Donovan and Belcher
City people	_____
Passion for religious discussion	_____
Young people	_____

Does the old woman have any similarity of personality to any character in the story?

G. IMAGERY

In "The Stone Boy" the opposites of hot and cold stood out. In "Guests of the Nation" another kind of contrast achieves the power of symbol and the strength of imagery. Look more closely at it in the activity below.

8: PINPOINTING IMAGERY AND SYMBOLISM

What kind of language do the quotations from the story below have in common?

1. "As I blew out the candle I told Noble what Jeremiah Donovan was after telling me."
2. "It was pitch-dark in the cottage by this time, but no one thought of lighting the lamp, and in the darkness the two Englishmen fetched their topcoats and said good-bye to the old woman."
3. "It was all mad lonely with nothing but a patch of lantern-light between ourselves and the dark, and birds hooting and screeching all round, disturbed by the guns."
4. "Noble struck another match and this time the lamp lit for him."
5. "I stood at the door, watching the stars and listening to the shrieking of the birds dying out over the bogs."

6. "'Poor bugger!'" he said quietly. "And last night he was so curious about it all. It's very queer, chums, I always think. Now he knows as much about it as they'll ever let him know, and last night he was all in the dark."

H. THEME

9: STATING THE THEMES

The sources of the story are in the intersection of the social, political, and religious conflicts of two countries. To what extent are these part of the story's theme? To what extent are they not important to the theme? The themes of "Guests of the Nation" are as follows (one sentence each):

1. _____

2. _____

3. _____

10: DEBATE

Prepare to debate one or more of the following issues related to "Guests of the Nation."

1. War is always more important than the value of human life. It has always been this way and always will be. It cannot be changed.

2. Life is worth losing if even one person (such as Bonaparte) can grow from and be altered by the experience.

3. It never makes any sense to fight a war.

4. Military leaders (such as Donovan) are never liked, but they benefit us because they do what we don't have the courage to do.

11: WRITING

Writing Topics

1. In a three-paragraph composition, defend Donovan's decision and actions.

2. In a three-paragraph composition, relate an experience that changed you and tell in what ways it changed you.

3. Argue for or against: It is always wrong to kill another human being.

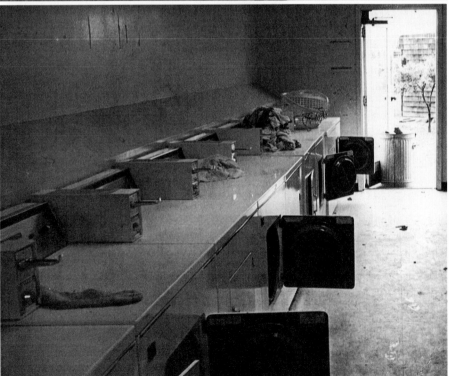

CHAPTER FOURTEEN

MANEUVERS II

The goals for this chapter are:

To discover how language choice reveals a character's personality

To explore the relationship between symbol and setting

In this chapter, you will read:

"The Other Launderette" by Helen Harris

*"It's more than a normal person can bear.
What with Their foreign coins jamming up
the machines and flooding and now a whole
house of Them opposite to cap it all, sometimes,
honestly, I just wish it would end."*

"The Other Launderette"

A. WARM-UP: DEALING WITH DIFFICULT PEOPLE AND/OR SITUATIONS

Have you heard that the American humorist Will Rogers (1879–1935) said "I never met a man I didn't like"? Most of us, however, have encountered plenty of people and situations we haven't liked. Meeting such people and situations is probably unavoidable, but we can all learn how to handle them better. Since "The Other Launderette" involves a situation and a person the narrator says he didn't particularly enjoy, begin this chapter by remembering some unpleasant people and situations.

1: THE SOUR SIDE OF LIFE

On a half-sheet of paper write down a brief account of an unpleasant situation and/or person you have met. Tell what happened and why the person and/or situation was unpleasant to you.

 # THE OTHER LAUNDERETTE
Helen Harris

1   Going to the launderette in the Place des Innocents was almost fun. I had switched my allegiance from a grubby little six-machine establishment at the end of the street when I found out that at the Place des Innocents there were nearly current issues of *Paris Match* and *Tours de France* and the woman who minded the washing-machines was svelte and soignée. The caretaker at the other launderette was, I am afraid to say, a most gruesome hag. No, not a hag, maybe; more a harpy, for she exuded a definitely lewd quality, despite her hideous appearance. A mat of dark, long hair flapped around her bloated face. She had mottled, swollen cheeks, which she sucked in and out obsessively. Her eyes flickered under thick, raw lids, which you could imagine being sold by weight in a charcuterie. She wore consistently a giant brown knitted cardigan over an old, flowery dress and, possibly most horribly of all, a pair of grubby, flirtatious little slippers, which seemed a mockery of her distended feet.

Paris Match, Tours de France: illustrated weekly magazines
svelte: slim
soignée: smart
charcuterie: a French shop selling cooked meats and a variety of sausages

2   She called me, "Meestur". My first visit to the launderette ought really to have been my last. But, in a silly way, one relishes these sordid experiences abroad, which one would not tolerate at home. I came in with my great bag of dirty washing and my accent, as I asked for a cup of detergent, informed her straight away that she had an Englishman on her hands. 'Ah Meestur,' she cried warmly, bustling forward. She sized up my recent haircut and reasonably good jacket and then waddled into her cubby-hole at the back to fetch the detergent. She stood over me as I loaded a machine, perhaps intentionally the one nearest the door, and seemed full of curiosity about my clothes. I was rather embarrassed. I had spent most of the last month settling down in the city and certainly hadn't given much thought before then to washing my clothes. They were pretty distasteful. But the caretaker did not seem concerned by all the grey collars and dubious socks. She bent forward and examined them frankly. 'What kind of collars are those?' she asked. 'That pullover, is it Shetland?' I bundled my things in as fast as I could and tried to hide the underpants inside the shirts. But my reticence did not discourage her and in her eagerness to see properly, she craned even closer. Then I noticed that she was none too fresh herself.

3   I sat down to wait and opened my book. Behind me, the caretaker had a mystifying conversation with another customer about her life. 'There are days,' I heard her say in an addled voice, 'when I wonder how I cope with it all, really I do. It's more than a normal person can bear. What with Their foreign coins jamming up the machines and flooding and now a whole house of Them opposite to cap it all, sometimes, honestly, I just wish it would end.'

4   When my machine finished, she was at the ready, with a plastic basket to transfer the clothes to a dryer. I took it from her rather promptly and protested, 'Non, non, madame, let me.' I tried to imply that I was doing it out of politeness but, of course, it was to avoid her fingers pawing my clothes. She beamed all over at being treated with such respect.

5   I cannot remember exactly when I came back for the second time. I am not all that keen on washing so let's say it was three or four weeks later. It would have been in the evening because the place was very full and I remember feeling relieved that the caretaker's attentions would be generally shared. The other customers were mainly Arabs, skinny, moustached labourers, staring mournfully at the turning drums. The air was blue with cheap cigarette smoke. The harpy was behaving atrociously. Through the steam and cigarette smoke, she was bellowing, apparently at no one in particular, 'Vile, that's what it is, vile. Maybe it's all right to carry on like that in some countries, but don't you dare try it here.' I couldn't quite understand what the matter was, but I assumed that someone had unhygienically broken some regulation of the launderette.

6   The woman was quite immense in her fury. Every now and then, she

would make an angry rush at one of the small men and almost jostle him, crying, 'Oh yes, go on, sit there, pretend it's nothing to do with you. You don't fool me, Mohammed, I know you're all the same.'

7   I put my clothes in as fast as possible and went out to walk around the evening. When I came back half an hour later, the launderette had cleared and the caretaker's rage seemed to have focused on one man. He was sitting rigidly straight at the end of the bench, self-righteously watching his clothes bump round and round in the suds, while, above him, the crazed figure hissed and squawked. She turned to me as I came in and cried, 'Ah, Meestur, tell this wretch how gentlemen behave in your country. They have such filthy habits where he comes from.' The Arab barely moved his head in my direction. He had clearly decided to submit to this persecution in silence, for the sake of clean clothes. I admired his tenacity.

8   'It's cold outside, isn't it?' I said rather feebly and burrowed into the dank drum to extract my washing. Behind me, the enraged caretaker gave a harsh laugh.

9   Then I came again in the daytime, on my day off. I had a newspaper, which I intended to hold up in front of my face, if necessary, like a screen. But the place was shut. An impromptu paper notice on the door said 'Closed Hour Due Circumstances'. I was walking back down the street, feeling displeased, when I heard a shriek behind me. I turned round to see the launderette woman, arms flailing extravagantly, beckoning to me from a café doorway. She called, 'It's all right, Meestur. We're opening right away. It's fine for you.' I hesitated. She darted back into the café and reappeared with a half-full glass of porto. She bobbed it at me explanatorily and then patted her cardigan pocket where, presumably, she kept her keys. Oh well, I thought limply, I'll get the chore over with. I started to go reluctantly back towards the launderette; I did not relish the prospect of half an hour's intimacy with the harpy. When I reached the café doorway, she cackled placatingly and, to my dismay, actually suggested I came in for a drink too. 'I'm in a hurry,' I said rather brusquely, 'I haven't got time.' 'Ah bon, ah bon,' the woman said good-humouredly and, causing me slight guilt, she downed her glass, returned it to the bar and came hobbling up the street with me to her launderette.

10   That time, I came close to abandoning the horrid place. In the steamy gloom—she did not bother to switch on all the lights just for me—there was a melancholic atmosphere, which provoked the miserable woman to confide in me. (Was that glass of porto her first?) She sat down beside me on the long bench and, for a minute, just watched my clothes turn sympathetically, as if they were whimsical fish frolicking in an aquarium. 'They're pretty, aren't they?' she said, 'all those sleeves hugging each other.'

11   'Well now, I'd better do my shopping,' I said and she placed her hand, briefly, on my knee.

12   'You cook for yourself, do you?' she asked tenderly. 'Dinner for one?'

13   My life in the city had never struck me as pathetic till then; I rather enjoyed the ritual of cooking on my single gas ring, going down to the market to choose fruit and cheese. But there was something so ghastly behind her maudlin inquiry that I suddenly felt desperate. I had a vision of myself eating a meal on my own, all off the one plate, with a book in front of me, that horrified me by its nightmarish solitude.

14   'It's not always easy on one's own, is it?' she went on, 'I know all about it, believe me. I've been through it all since my husband died.'

15   'Yes,' I said, standing up, 'I have to buy some dinner.' I added brutally, 'I've invited friends.'

16   I came back half an hour later with a loaded bag of groceries. I had missed the moment to unload my clothes and they were already rotating in the dryer. The caretaker welcomed me back with approval. 'You're a good boy,' she said primly, 'you keep your clothes nice and clean, I see.'

17   I blenched, but she did not seem inclined to continue the theme. She was smoking, with one elbow propped on a washing-machine, and she appeared uncharacteristically placid. I topped up the dryer with one-franc pieces and opened my paper. Behind me, the woman stubbed out her cigarette with a nasty grinding noise and began on some launderette job. There was a fair bit of dragging and sighing, which I resolutely ignored. Then she appeared momentously in front of me with an armful of dirty washing. 'You keep your clothes nice and clean,' she repeated, unfolding her bundle, 'Not like some people.' And, to my utter disgust, she started to display the inner crevices of the clothes, dismally encrusted with filth and grime. 'Sickening,' she said. 'Isn't it? Vile.'

18   I could only stammer, 'Who—whose are they?'

19   She swelled triumphantly as she said, 'Theirs. They're all as bad as each other when it comes to cleanliness, you know, those Arabs.'

20   After this, needless to say, I more than dreaded the place. I did go again, once or twice, before the dénouement, but nothing memorable happened. Visits to the launderette hardly constitute events in the normal course of affairs. I was leading a full, rich life in the city and I certainly didn't look to the launderette for any sleazy thrill.

21   Then, about six months ago, I went there for the last time. The woman wasn't in the launderette, but the door was open when I arrived so I went in and put my clothes in to wash. It was a relief to find the place empty. I sat down in front of my machine, lit a cigarette and stretched my legs. After maybe ten minutes, I noticed a lopsided couple approaching along the opposite side of the street; a teetering female balloon and a minute male. It was not until they were nearly opposite and turning to cross the road that I actually registered what my vision held. It was the caretaker, arm in arm

with one of the Arabs. I stayed rooted to the bench, unable to react for surprise and shock. They crossed the street and came up to the door of the launderette. To my amazement, I recognized the little man whom the harpy had abused so viciously in the launderette that night a few months previously. They came in cosily and we said 'Bonjour.' The woman looked pink and very pleased with herself, her little slippers clopped on the tiles. I had stood up, expecting some sort of confrontation, but she seemed quite unembarrassed by my presence.

22   'Bonjour Meestur,' she trilled, 'All O.K. with the machine? No problems?' The Arab eyed me sullenly and I answered brightly, 'Oh no, oh no. I think it's almost finished.' They went through into the little cubby-hole at the back and then the woman came out again with a scrap of paper in her hand. She grinned at me unspeakably and up went that tatty sign again, 'Closed Hour Due Circumstances'.

23   I hurried to finish. I was overcome with such revulsion for the place, I could hardly wait to leave it. I was a naive idiot, I told myself; if ever there was a den of vice, this was it. The caretaker treated me like a regular. She padded cosily around her establishment, letting down the Venetian blinds, turning out the lights, until I felt I was becoming involved in their foul act. She even asked me to join them for an aperitif.

24   I banged the glass door behind me and, having found a better launderette, I never went back. There had been preliminary giggles from the cubby-hole as I fumed in front of the dryer and, twice, the small Arab had come out and glared at me.

25   I felt resentful. That revelation had shown me that, in certain respects, I was still a callow English public schoolboy, with stale socks. I loathed the place which had proved it and, in what is, I suppose, a classic act of revenge, I decided to write about it. In time, my indignation was moderated by pity. What a wretched, debased world they inhabited.

26   The smart supervisor and the magazines at the Place des Innocents were all very fine. But I could not help feeling sometimes, as I sat under the blown-up photographs of Alpine meadows, that I was dodging the issue by coming here and that the other launderette was real life.

B. THE TITLE AND ITS MEANINGS

2: IDIOMS WITH THE WORD "OTHER"

The title of this story itself is interesting. What are the two elements of the title?
Try to think of some idioms with the word "other." Write down at least three.
Model:

The "other" woman

1. _____

2. _____

3. _____

C. SETTING: THE POWER OF PLACE

The other part of the title is the launderette itself, which is the setting or location
of the story. As part of the title, it is obviously an important part of the story.

3: DECORATING THE LAUNDERETTE

Imagine you are in the launderette, which is the setting of the story. Although some
of the details about the launderette are given, many are not. What do you see, smell,
hear, touch, even taste in the launderette? If you can draw, make a sketch of the
launderette in the space below or on a separate piece of paper. Include as many
details as possible. If you prefer, make a list in the same space of what is actually in
the launderette: on the wall, on the floor, in the back room, in the window, and the
like. Bring the launderette as closely as possible to our senses.

4: A PLACE THAT HAS INFLUENCED ME

Many writers and artists are able to bring out the sense of a place so vividly that we feel we are there. Describe such a place you know.

Recall this place (a room, natural view, or the like) and explain orally why that place had the power to affect you. As part of your explanation, describe many of the details which made it a special place for you. The place may be one you have seen only once (on vacation, perhaps) or one you see regularly (a barber or hairdresser's shop, department store, etc.).

D. THE LAUNDERETTE AS SYMBOL

5: THE MEANINGS OF THE LAUNDERETTE

For the narrator, the laundromat was more than a place; it "was real life." Read the passages below. What does each passage reveal about the narrator's attitude toward the launderette? What meanings does the launderette have for the narrator?

Model:
The other customers were mainly Arabs, skinny, mustached labourers, staring mournfully at the turning drums.

The narrator sees himself as different from—better than—the other persons in the laundromat. He imagines other places more fitting to his class and education. At the same time, the depressed atmosphere he associates with this launderette matches the reality of his single life—eating alone while reading in a small apartment.

1. That time, I came close to abandoning the horrid place. In the steamy gloom—she did not bother to switch on all the lights just for me—there was a melancholic atmosphere, which provoked the miserable woman to confide in me.

   _____

   _____

   _____

   _____

   _____

2. I was overcome with such revulsion for the place, I could hardly wait to leave it. I was a naive idiot, I told myself; if ever there was a den of vice, this was it.

_____

_____

_____

_____

_____

3. That revelation had shown me that, in certain respects, I was still a callow English public schoolboy, with stale socks. I loathed the place which had proved it and, in what is, I suppose, a classic act of revenge, I decided to write about it. In time, my indignation was moderated by pity. What a wretched, debased world they inhabited.

_____

_____

_____

_____

_____

4. I had switched my allegiance from a grubby little six-machine establishment at the end of the street....

_____

_____

_____

_____

_____

5. But the place was shut. An impromptu paper notice on the door said 'Closed Hour Due Circumstances'.

_____

_____

_____

_____

_____

E. GETTING TO KNOW YOU THROUGH WORDS

To know a character in a story is usually to observe his or her words, thoughts, and actions, including interactions with other characters. Of these possibilities, words are one of the most important clues to a character's personality.

6: YOU ARE WHAT YOU SAY

Pick out *one* word that reveals some aspect of one of the characters in the story. Study that word carefully, including its etymology (origin), sound, definition, associations, syllables, synonyms and antonyms, and any other aspect you can think of or your teacher can suggest. Then prepare a full report on the relationship of that word to one of the characters in the story, and present it to your class.

F. STYLE

While one word may reveal much about character, one sentence may reveal much about the style of the story. Since the narrator is the sole reporter of the action, except for the quoted words of the manager of the launderette, you are observing the *narrator's* style in this story.

7: THE STYLE IS THE MAN OR WOMAN

Pick out one sentence of the story that you consider important. Analyze its structure, word choice, important grammatical elements, length, punctuation, and other important elements. What does this sentence reveal about the narrator? What does it contribute to the entire story?

G. POINT OF VIEW

You may find it useful in understanding the narrator of "The Other Launderette" to compare the narrator to the narrators of other stories in this book, for example, the narrator of "Guests of the Nation." One way to do so is to imagine what they do with their time when they are not telling their stories to you or to the public.

8: MY NINE-TO-FIVE DAY

Choose one of the following activities:

1. Imagine a "normal" or typical day in the lives of either the narrator or the manager of the launderette. Using the first person, write a diary of what he or she ("I") does during the day. Be as specific as possible. Base your activities on what you know and imagine about them.

2. Describe an imagined meeting between the two characters ten years after the story ended. Do they remember each other? What will they say to each other? Make part of the description a dialogue using some of the actual words you imagine they would say. What have you learned about them through this activity?

H. CHARACTER CHANGE

The central character of the story, the narrator, is upset by what he has experienced in the launderette, upset enough to remember and to recount the events. Would he like you to help him if you could? Decide how you can help.

9: PSYCHOLOGIST AND PATIENT

Pretend you are a psychologist and the narrator has come to you for advice. Write a dialogue in which he explains his problem to you. How would you advise him? What would you say to him?

I. CONFLICTS IN FICTION

Most stories present a conflict which is developed and, in some cases, resolved by the end of the story. In the writing exercise below, you will be writing about the conflicts in this story.

10: AN ESSAY ON CONFLICT

Write a four paragraph essay on conflict. Follow the guidelines below.

Paragraph 1: State briefly and clearly the conflict of the story. State whose conflict it is.

Paragraph 2: Explain one side of the conflict, giving examples.

Paragraph 3: Explain the other side of the conflict, giving examples.

Paragraph 4: Offer a resolution to the conflict and/or explain why the person with the conflict has difficulty resolving it. Give examples.

The essay should contain at least 350 words.

CHAPTER FIFTEEN
SOLO FLIGHT III

The goals for this chapter are:

To read and understand a more complex story on your own with confidence

In this chapter, you will read:

"Rope" by Katherine Anne Porter

The question was, when both of them were working on their own time, was there going to be a division of housework, or wasn't there? She merely wanted to know, she had to make her plans.

"Rope"

Having studied "The Use of Force," "Guests of the Nation," and "The Other Launderette," all of which required you to apply your understanding of many different areas of fiction, you are now at an advanced stage of reading fiction. Feel confident, therefore, to decide what approaches will lead you most directly and most profitably into this story by Katherine Anne Porter, "Rope." Read it on your own.

Pay attention to the following:

- Subtle variations in point of view
- Style, especially sentence structure
- Symbolism, especially the title symbol
- Word choice and language in general
- Psychological rather than physical action
- Tone or overall feeling of the story

This story, unlike the others in this book, seems to have little action. What actually happens in this story? Is there a change in the main characters from the start to the end of the story?

 # ROPE
Katherine Anne Porter

1   On the third day after they moved to the country he came walking back from the village carrying a basket of groceries and a twenty-four-yard coil of rope. She came out to meet him, wiping her hands on her green smock. Her hair was tumbled, her nose was scarlet with sunburn; he told her that already she looked like a born country woman. His gray flannel shirt stuck to him, his heavy shoes were dusty. She assured him he looked like a rural character in a play.

2   Had he brought the coffee? She had been waiting all day long for coffee. They had forgot it when they ordered at the store the first day.

3   Gosh, no, he hadn't. Lord, now he'd have to go back. Yes, he would if it killed him. He thought, though, he had everything else. She reminded him it was only because he didn't drink coffee himself. If he did he would remember it quick enough. Suppose they ran out of cigarettes? Then she saw the rope. What was that for? Well, he thought it might do to hang clothes on, or something. Naturally she asked him if he thought they were going to run a laundry? They already had a fifty-foot line hanging right

before his eyes? Why, hadn't he noticed it, really? It was a blot on the land-scape to her.

4   He thought there were a lot of things a rope might come in handy for. She wanted to know what, for instance. He thought a few seconds, but nothing occurred. They could wait and see, couldn't they? You need all sorts of strange odds and ends around a place in the country. She said, yes, that was so; but she thought just at that time when every penny counted, it seemed funny to buy more rope. That was all. She hadn't meant anything else. She hadn't just seen, not at first, why he felt it was necessary.

5   Well, thunder, he had bought it because he wanted to, and that was all there was to it. She thought that was reason enough, and couldn't under-stand why he hadn't said so, at first. Undoubtedly it would be useful, twen-ty-four yards of rope, there were hundreds of things, she couldn't think of any at the moment, but it would come in. Of course. As he had said, things always did in the country.

6   But she was a little disappointed about the coffee, and oh, look, look, look at the eggs! Oh, my, they're all running! What had he put on top of them? Hadn't he known eggs mustn't be squeezed? Squeezed, who squeezed them, he wanted to know. What a silly thing to say. He had sim-ply brought them along in the basket with the other things. If they got broke it was the grocer's fault. He should know better than to put heavy things on top of eggs.

7   She believed it was the rope. That was the heaviest thing in the pack, she saw him plainly when he came in from the road, the rope was a big package on top of everything. He desired the whole wide world to witness that this was not a fact. He had carried the rope in one hand and the basket in the other, and what was the use of her having eyes if that was the best they could do for her?

8   Well, anyhow, she could see one thing plain: no eggs for breakfast. They'd have to scramble them now, for supper. It was too damned bad. She had planned to have steak for supper. No ice, meat wouldn't keep. He wanted to know why she couldn't finish breaking the eggs in a bowl and set them in a cool place.

9   Cool place! if he could find one for her, she'd be glad to set them there. Well, then, it seemed to him they might very well cook the meat at the same time they cooked the eggs and then warm up the meat for tomorrow. The idea simply choked her. Warmed-over meat, when they might as well have had it fresh. Second best and scraps and makeshifts, even to the meat! He rubbed her shoulder a little. It doesn't really matter so much, does it, darling? Sometimes when they were playful, he would rub her shoulder and she would arch and purr. This time she hissed and clawed. He was getting ready to say that they could surely manage somehow when

she turned to him and said, if he told her they could manage somehow she would certainly slap his face.

10   He swallowed the words red hot, his face burned. He picked up the rope and started to put it on the top shelf. She would not have it on the top shelf, the jars and tins belonged there; positively she would not have the top shelf cluttered up with a lot of rope. She had borne all the clutter she meant to bear in the flat in town, there was space here at least and she meant to keep things in order.

11   Well, in that case, he wanted to know what the hammer and nails were doing up there? And why had she put them there when she knew very well he needed that hammer and those nails upstairs to fix the window sashes? She simply slowed down everything and made double work on the place with her insane habit of changing things around and hiding them.

12   She was sure she begged his pardon, and if she had any reason to believe he was going to fix the sashes this summer she would have left the hammer and nails right where he put them; in the middle of the bedroom floor where they could step on them in the dark. And now if he didn't clear the whole mess out of there she would throw them down the well.

13   Oh, all right, all right—could he put them in the closet? Naturally not, there were brooms and mops and dustpans in the closet, and why couldn't he find a place for his rope outside her kitchen? Had he stopped to consider there were seven God-forsaken rooms in the house, and only one kitchen?

14   He wanted to know what of it? And did she realize that she was making a complete fool of herself? And what did she take him for, a three-year-old idiot? The whole trouble with her was she needed something weaker than she was to heckle and tyrannize over. He wished to God now they had a couple of children she could take it out on. Maybe he'd get some rest.

15   Her face changed at this, she reminded him he had forgot the coffee and had bought a worthless piece of rope. And when she thought of all the things they actually needed to make the place even decently fit to live in, well, she could cry, that was all. She looked so forlorn, so lost and despairing he couldn't believe it was only a piece of rope that was causing all the racket. What *was* the matter, for God's sake?

16   Oh, would he please hush and go away, and *stay* away, if he could, for five minutes? By all means, yes, he would. He'd stay away indefinitely if she wished. Lord, yes, there was nothing he'd like better than to clear out and never come back. She couldn't for the life of her see what was holding him, then. It was a swell time. Here she was, stuck, miles from a railroad, with a half-empty house on her hands, and not a penny in her pocket, and everything on earth to do; it seemed the God-sent moment for him to get out from under. She was surprised he hadn't stayed in town as it was until she had come out and done the work and got things straightened out. It was his usual trick.

17   It appeared to him that this was going a little far. Just a touch out of bounds, if she didn't mind his saying so. Why the hell had he stayed in town the summer before? To do a half-dozen extra jobs to get the money he had sent her. That was it. She knew perfectly well they couldn't have done it otherwise. She had agreed with him at the time. And that was the only time so help him he had ever left her to do anything by herself.

18   Oh, he could tell that to his great-grandmother. She had her notion of what had kept him in town. Considerably more than a notion, if he wanted to know. So, she was going to bring all that up again, was she? Well, she could just think what she pleased. He was tired of explaining. It may have looked funny but he had simply got hooked in, and what could he do? It was impossible to believe that she was going to take it seriously. Yes, yes, she knew how it was with a man: if he was left by himself a minute, some woman was certain to kidnap him. And naturally he couldn't hurt her feelings by refusing!

19   Well, what was she raving about? Did she forget she had told him those two weeks alone in the country were happiest she had known for four years? And how long had they been married when she said that? All right, shut up! If she thought that hadn't stuck in his craw.

20   She hadn't meant she was happy because she was away from him. She meant she was happy getting the devilish house nice and ready for him. That was what she had meant, and now look! Bringing up something she said a year ago simply to justify himself for forgetting her coffee and breaking the eggs and buying a wretched piece of rope they couldn't afford. She really thought it was time to drop the subject, and now she wanted only two things in the world. She wanted him to get that rope from underfoot, and go back to the village and get her coffee, and if he could remember it, he might bring a metal mitt for the skillets, and two more curtain rods, and if there were any rubber gloves in the village, her hands were simply raw, and a bottle of milk of magnesia from the drugstore.

21   He looked out at the dark blue afternoon, sweltering on the slopes, and mopped his forehead and sighed heavily and said, if only she could wait a minute for *anything,* he was going back. He had said so, hadn't he, the very instant they found he had overlooked it?

22   Oh, yes well…run along. She was going to wash the windows. The country was so beautiful! She doubted they'd have a moment to enjoy it. He meant to go, but he could not until he had said that if she wasn't such a hopeless melancholiac she might see that this was only for a few days. Couldn't she remember anything pleasant about the other summers? Hadn't they ever had any fun? She hadn't time to talk about it, and now would he please not leave the rope lying around for her to trip on? He picked it up, somehow it had toppled off the table, and walked out with it under his arm.

23   Was he going this minute? He certainly was. She thought so. Sometimes it seemed to her he had second sight about the precisely perfect moment to leave her ditched. She had meant to put the mattresses out to sun, if they put them out this minute they would get at least three hours, he must have heard her say that morning she meant to put them out. So of course he would walk off and leave her to it. She supposed he thought the exercise would do her good.

24   Well, he was merely going to get her coffee. A four-mile walk for two pounds of coffee was ridiculous, but he was perfectly willing to do it. The habit was making a wreck of her, but if she wanted to wreck herself there was nothing he could do about it. If he thought it was coffee that was making a wreck of her, she congratulated him: he must have a damned easy conscience.

25   Conscience or no conscience, he didn't see why the mattresses couldn't very well wait until tomorrow. And anyhow, for God's sake, were they living *in* the house, or were they going to let the house ride them to death? She paled at this, her face grew livid about the mouth, she looked quite dangerous, and reminded him that housekeeping was no more her work than it was his: she had other work to do as well, and when did he think she was going to find time to do it at this rate?

26   Was she going to start on that again? She knew as well as he did that his work brought in the regular money, hers was only occasional, if they depended on what *she* made—and she might as well get straight on this question once for all!

27   That was positively not the point. The question was, when both of them were working on their own time, was there going to be a division of housework, or wasn't there? She merely wanted to know, she had to make her plans. Why, he thought that was all arranged. It was understood that he was to help. Hadn't he always, in the summers?

28   Hadn't he, though? Oh, just hadn't he? And when, and where, and doing what? Lord, what an uproarious joke!

29   It was such a very uproarious joke that her face turned slightly purple, and she screamed with laughter. She laughed so hard she had to sit down, and finally a rush of tears spurted from her eyes and poured down into the lifted corners of her mouth. He dashed towards her and dragged her up to her feet and tried to pour water on her head. The dipper hung by a string on a nail and he broke it loose. Then he tried to pump water with one hand while she struggled in the other. So he gave it up and shook her instead.

30   She wrenched away, crying out for him to take his rope and go to hell, she had simply given him up: and ran. He heard her high-heeled bedroom slippers clattering and stumbling on the stairs.

31   He went out around the house and into the lane; he suddenly realized he had a blister on his heel and his shirt felt as if it were on fire. Things broke so

suddenly you didn't know where you were. She would work herself into a fury about simply nothing. She was terrible, damn it: not an ounce of reason. You might as well talk to a sieve as that woman when she got going. Damned if he'd spend his life humoring her! Well, what to do now? He would take back the rope and exchange it for something else. Things accumulated, things were mountainous, you couldn't move them or sort them out or get rid of them. They just lay and rotted around. He'd take it back. Hell, why should he? He wanted it. What was it anyhow? A piece of rope. Imagine anybody caring more about a piece of rope than about a man's feelings. What earthly right had she to say a word about it? He remembered all the useless, meaningless things she bought for herself: Why? because I wanted it, that's why! He stopped and selected a large stone by the road. He would put the rope behind it. He would put it in the tool-box when he got back. He'd heard enough about it to last him a life-time.

32   When he came back she was leaning against the post box beside the road waiting. It was pretty late, the smell of broiled steak floated nose high in the cooling air. Her face was young and smooth and fresh-looking. Her unmanageable funny black hair was all on end. She called out that supper was ready and waiting, was he starved?

33   You bet he was starved. Here was the coffee. He waved it at her. She looked at his other hand. What was that he had there?

34   Well, it was the rope again. He stopped short. He had meant to exchange it but forgot. She wanted to know why he should exchange it, if it was something he really wanted. Wasn't the air sweet now, and wasn't it fine to be here?

35   She walked beside him with one hand hooked into his leather belt. She pulled and jostled him a little as he walked, and leaned against him. He put his arm clear around her and patted her stomach. They exchanged wary smiles. Coffee, coffee for the Ootsum-Wootsoms! He felt as if he were bringing her a beautiful present.

36   He was a love, she firmly believed, and if she had had her coffee in the morning, she wouldn't have behaved so funny... There was a whippoorwill still coming back, imagine, clear out of season, sitting in the crab-apple tree calling all by himself. Maybe his girl stood him up. Maybe she did. She hoped to hear him once more, she loved whippoorwills... He knew how she was, didn't he?

37   Sure, he knew how she was.

CHAPTER SIXTEEN
MANEUVERS III

The goals for this chapter are:

To explore recurring patterns through characters, plot, and setting

To learn about epiphanies or moments of instant importance, in fiction

In this chapter, you will read:

"The Boarding House" by James Joyce

It was a bright Sunday morning of early summer, promising heat, but with a fresh breeze blowing. All the windows of the boardinghouse were open and the lace curtains ballooned gently towards the street beneath the raised sashes.

"The Boarding House"

A. THE WORLD OF THE BOARDING HOUSE

In many places, including Dublin, Ireland, where this story is set, students and young single people often live temporarily in boarding houses. A boarding house, a unique living situation, was very popular in the first half of this century because it offered an inexpensive, convenient, and friendly living arrangement. Meals were prepared for the boarders and taken together. Each boarder had his or her own space but had the convenience of nearby friendship. For the landlord or landlady, the income earned from the boarders was often a necessity. Moreover, the work, although sometimes difficult, was rarely impossible to handle.

THE BOARDING HOUSE
James Joyce

1   Mrs. Mooney was a butcher's daughter. She was a woman who was quite able to keep things to herself: a determined woman. She had married her father's foreman and opened a butcher's shop near Spring Gardens. But as soon as his father-in-law was dead Mr. Mooney began to go to the devil. He drank, plundered the till, ran headlong into debt. It was no use making him take the pledge: he was sure to break out again a few days after. By fighting his wife in the presence of customers and by buying bad meat he ruined his business. One night he went for his wife with the cleaver and she had to sleep in a neighbor's house.

2   After that they lived apart. She went to the priest and got a separation from him with care of the children. She would give him neither money nor food nor house-room; and so he was obliged to enlist himself as a sheriff's man. He was a shabby stooped little drunkard with a white face and a white mustache and white eyebrows, penciled above his little eyes, which were pink-veined and raw; and all day long he sat in the bailiff's room, waiting to be put on a job. Mrs. Mooney, who had taken what remained of her money out of the butcher business and set up a boarding house in Hardwicke Street, was a big imposing woman. Her house had a floating population made up of tourists from Liverpool and the Isle of Man and, occasionally, *artistes* from the music halls. Its resident population was made up of clerks from the city. She governed the house cunningly and firmly, knew when to give credit, when to be stern and when to let things pass. All the resident young men spoke of her as *The Madam*.

3   Mrs. Mooney's young men paid fifteen shillings a week for board and lodgings (beer or stout at dinner excluded). They shared in common tastes and occupations and for this reason they were very chummy with one another. They discussed with one another the chances of favorites and outsiders. Jack Mooney, the Madam's son, who was clerk to a commission agent in Fleet Street, had the reputation of being a hard case. He was fond of using soldiers' obscenities: usually he came home in the small hours. When he met his friends he had always a good one to tell them and he was always sure to be on to a good thing—that is to say, a likely horse or a likely *artiste*. He was also handy with the mits and sang comic songs. On Sunday nights there would often be a reunion in Mrs. Mooney's front drawing room. The music-hall *artistes* would oblige; and Sheridan played waltzes and polkas and vamped accompaniments. Polly Mooney, the Madam's daughter, would also sing. She sang:

> "I'm a...naughty girl.
> You needn't sham:
> You know I am."

4   Polly was a slim girl of nineteen; she had light soft hair and a small full mouth. Her eyes, which were gray with a shade of green through them, had a habit of glancing upwards when she spoke with anyone, which made her look like a little perverse madonna. Mrs. Mooney had first sent her daughter to be a typist in a corn factor's office but, as a disreputable sheriff's man used to come every other day to the office, asking to be allowed to say a word to his daughter, she had taken her daughter home again and set her to do housework. As Polly was very lively the intention was to give her the run of the young men. Besides, young men like to feel that there is a young woman not very far away. Polly, of course, flirted with the young men but Mrs. Mooney, who was a shrewd judge, knew that the young men were only passing the time away: none of them meant business. Things went on so for a long time and Mrs. Mooney began to think of sending Polly back to typewriting when she noticed that something was going on between Polly and one of the young men. She watched the pair and kept her own counsel.

5   Polly knew that she was being watched, but still her mother's persistent silence could not be misunderstood. There had been no open complicity between mother and daughter, no open understanding but, though people in the house began to talk of the affair, still Mrs. Mooney did not intervene. Polly began to grow a little strange in her manner and the young man was evidently perturbed. At last, when she judged it to be the right moment, Mrs. Mooney intervened. She dealt with moral problems as a cleaver deals with meat: and in this case she had made up her mind.

6 It was a bright Sunday morning of early summer, promising heat, but with a fresh breeze blowing. All the windows of the boardinghouse were open and the lace curtains ballooned gently towards the street beneath the raised sashes. The belfry of George's Church sent out constant peals and worshipers, singly or in groups, traversed the little circus before the church, revealing their purpose by their self-contained demeanor no less than by the little volumes in their gloved hands. Breakfast was over in the board-inghouse and the table of the breakfast room was covered with plates on which lay yellow streaks of eggs with morsels of bacon fat and bacon rind. Mrs. Mooney sat in the straw armchair and watched the servant Mary remove the breakfast things. She made Mary collect the crusts and pieces of broken bread to help to make Tuesday's bread-pudding. When the table was cleared, the broken bread collected, the sugar and butter safe under lock and key, she began to reconstruct the interview which she had had the night before with Polly. Things were as she had suspected: she had been frank in her questions and Polly had been frank in her answers. Both had been somewhat awkward, of course. She had been made awkward by her not wishing to receive the news in too cavalier a fashion or to seem to have connived and Polly had been made awkward not merely because allusions of that kind always made her awkward but also because she did not wish it to be thought that in her wise innocence she had divined the intention behind her mother's tolerance.

7 Mrs. Mooney glanced instinctively at the little gilt clock on the mantel-piece as soon as she had become aware through her revery that the bells of George's Church had stopped ringing. It was seventeen minutes past eleven: she would have lots of time to have the matter out with Mr. Doran and then catch short twelve at Marlborough Street. She was sure she would win. To begin with she had all the weight of social opinion on her side: she was an outraged mother. She had allowed him to live beneath her roof, assuming that he was a man of honor, and he had simply abused her hospitality. He was thirty-four or thirty-five years of age, so that youth could not be pleaded as his excuse; nor could ignorance be his excuse since he was a man who had seen something of the world. He had simply taken advantage of Polly's youth and inexperience: that was evident. The ques-tion was: What reparation would he make?

8 There must be reparation made in such case. It is all very well for the man: he can go his ways as if nothing had happened, having had his moment of pleasure, but the girl has to bear the brunt. Some mothers would be content to patch up such an affair for a sum of money; she had known cases of it. But she would not do so. For her only one reparation could make up for the loss of her daughter's honor: marriage.

9 She counted all her cards again before sending Mary up to Mr. Doran's

room to say that she wished to speak with him. She felt sure she would win. He was a serious young man, not rakish or loud-voiced like the others. If it had been Mr. Sheridan or Mr. Meade or Bantam Lyons her task would have been much harder. She did not think he would face publicity. All the lodgers in the house knew something of the affair; details had been invented by some. Besides, he had been employed for thirteen years in a great Catholic wine merchant's office and publicity would mean for him, perhaps, the loss of his job. Whereas if he agreed all might be well. She knew he had a good screw for one thing and she suspected he had a bit of stuff put by.

10   Nearly the half-hour! She stood up and surveyed herself in the pier glass. The decisive expression of her great florid face satisfied her and she thought of some mothers she knew who could not get their daughters off their hands.

11   Mr. Doran was very anxious indeed this Sunday morning. He had made two attempts to shave but his hand had been so unsteady that he had been obliged to desist. Three days' reddish beard fringed his jaws and every two or three minutes a mist gathered on his glasses so that he had to take them off and polish them with his pocket handkerchief. The recollection of his confession of the night before was a cause of acute pain to him; the priest had drawn out every ridiculous detail of the affair and in the end had so magnified his sin that he was almost thankful at being afforded a loophole of reparation. The harm was done. What could he do now but marry her or run away? He could not brazen it out. The affair would be sure to be talked of and his employer would be certain to hear of it. Dublin is such a small city: everyone knows everyone else's business. He felt his heart leap warmly in his throat as he heard in his excited imagination old Mr. Leonard calling out in his rasping voice: "Send Mr. Doran here, please."

12   All his long years of service gone for nothing! All his industry and diligence thrown away! As a young man he had sown his wild oats, of course; he had boasted of his free thinking and denied the existence of God to his companions in public houses. But that was all passed and done with…nearly. He still bought a copy of Reynolds's Newspaper every week but he attended to his religious duties and for nine-tenths of the year lived a regular life. He had money enough to settle down on; it was not that. But the family would look down on her. First of all there was her disreputable father and then her mother's boarding house was beginning to get a certain fame. He had a notion that he was being had. He could imagine his friends talking of the affair and laughing. She *was* a little vulgar; sometimes she said "I seen" and "If I had've known." But what would grammar matter if he really loved her? He could not make up his mind whether to like her or despise her for what she had done. Of course, he had done it too. His instinct urged him to remain free, not to marry. Once you are married you are done for, it said.

13   While he was sitting helplessly on the side of the bed in shirt and trousers she tapped lightly at his door and entered. She told him all, that she had made a clean breast of it to her mother and that her mother would speak with him that morning. She cried and threw her arms round his neck, saying:

14   "O, Bob! Bob! What am I to do? What am I to do at all?"

15   She would put an end to herself, she said.

16   He comforted her feebly, telling her not to cry, that it would be all right never fear. He felt against his shirt the agitation of her bosom.

17   It was not altogether his fault that it had happened. He remembered well, with the curious patient memory of the celibate, the first casual caresses her dress, her breath, her fingers had given him. Then late one night as he was undressing for bed she had tapped at his door, timidly. She wanted to relight her candle at his for hers had been blown out by a gust. It was her bath night. She wore a loose open combing-jacket of printed flannel. Her white instep shone in the opening of her furry slippers and the blood glowed warmly behind her perfumed skin. From her hands and wrists too as she lit and steadied her candle a faint perfume arose.

18   On nights when he came in very late it was she who warmed up his dinner. He scarcely knew what he was eating, feeling her beside him alone, at night, in the sleeping house. And her thoughtfulness! If the night was anyway cold or wet or windy there was sure to be a little tumbler of punch ready for him. Perhaps they could be happy together....

19   They used to go upstairs together on tiptoe, each with a candle, and on the third landing exchange reluctant good nights. They used to kiss. He remembered well her eyes, the touch of her hand and his delirium....

20   But delirium passes. He echoed her phrase, applying it to himself: *"What am I to do?"* The instinct of the celibate warned him to hold back. But the sin was there; even his sense of honor told him that reparation must be made for such a sin.

21   While he was sitting with her on the side of the bed Mary came to the door and said that the missus wanted to see him in the parlor. He stood up to put on his coat and waistcoat, more helpless than ever. When he was dressed he went over to her to comfort her. It would be all right, never fear. He left her crying on the bed and moaning softly: *"Oh my God!"*

22   Going down the stairs his glasses became so dimmed with moisture that he had to take them off and polish them. He longed to ascend through the roof and fly away to another country where he would never hear again of his trouble, and yet a force pushed him downstairs step by step. The implacable faces of his employer and of the Madam stared upon his discomfiture. On the last flight of stairs he passed Jack Mooney who was coming up from the pantry nursing two bottles of *Bass*. They saluted coldly; and the lover's eyes rested for a second or two on a thick bulldog face and a

pair of thick short arms. When he reached the foot of the staircase he glanced up and saw Jack regarding him from the door of the return-room.

23   Suddenly he remembered the night when one of the music-hall *artistes*, a little blond Londoner, had made a rather free allusion to Polly. The reunion had been almost broken up on account of Jack's violence. Everyone tried to quiet him. The music-hall *artiste*, a little paler than usual, kept smiling and saying that there was no harm meant; but Jack kept shouting at him that if any fellow tried that sort of a game on with *his* sister he'd bloody well put his teeth down his throat, so he would.

24   Polly sat for a little time on the side of the bed, crying. Then she dried her eyes and went over to the looking glass. She dipped the end of the towel in the water jug and refreshed her eyes with the cool water. She looked at herself in profile and readjusted a hairpin above her ear. Then she went back to the bed again and sat at the foot. She regarded the pillows for a long time and the sight of them awakened in her mind secret amiable memories. She rested the nape of her neck against the cool iron bed rail and fell into a revery. There was no longer any perturbation visible on her face.

25   She waited on patiently, almost cheerfully, without alarm, her memories gradually giving place to hopes and visions of the future. Her hopes and visions were so intricate that she no longer saw the white pillows on which her gaze was fixed or remembered that she was waiting for anything.

26   At last she heard her mother calling. She started to her feet and ran to the banisters.

27   "Polly! Polly!"

28   "Yes, mamma?"

29   "Come down, dear. Mr. Doran wants to speak to you."

30   Then she remembered what she had been waiting for.

1: RENTING OR RENTING OUT A ROOM

Choose one of the following possibilities. Whichever possibility you choose, be as specific as possible.

1. You are the manager of a boarding house. Write a newspaper advertisement (50 words only) describing a room you wish to rent. Describe not only the condition of the room itself but the neighborhood and the social environment of the house.

2. You wish to rent a room in a boarding house. Write a 50-word description of the kind of room you wish to rent. Describe your requirements for the room and the social environment you desire.

B. NARRATION AND DESCRIPTION

2: NARRATIVE AND DESCRIPTIVE DETAIL

Narration and description, the heart of fiction, are present in folk and fairy tales and even in complex stories such as "The Boarding House."

The passages below from "The Boarding House" are not difficult, yet each advances the story in some important way. Explain how the action or the description in the passage adds to the story.

Model:

Her house had a floating population made up of tourists from Liverpool and the Isle of Man and, occasionally, *artistes* from the music halls. Its resident population was made up of clerks from the city.

Comment:

This passage describes the two kinds of boarders Mrs. Mooney took in: responsible workers from the city and temporary types from all areas and fields, even performing artists. This combination gave the Mooney boarding house a shaky reputation, forcing her to struggle to keep up the name of her house and family. Mrs. Mooney has learned how to get the most benefits for herself from both types of boarders, something she demonstrates to Mr. Doran.

1. He [Mr. Mooney] was a shabby stooped little drunkard with a white face and a white mustache and white eyebrows, penciled above his little eyes, which were pink-veined and raw;…"

_____

_____

_____

_____

_____

_____

2. Polly was a slim girl of nineteen; she had light soft hair and a small full mouth. Her eyes, which were gray with a shade of green through them, had a habit of glancing upwards when she spoke with anyone, which made her look like a perverse madonna.

_____

_____

_____

_____

_____

_____

3. Mrs. Mooney glanced instinctively at the little gilt clock in the mantelpiece as soon as she had become aware through her revery that the bells of George's Church had stopped ringing. It was seventeen minutes past eleven: she would have lots of time to have the matter out with Mr. Doran and then catch short twelve at Marlborough Street.

_____

_____

_____

_____

_____

_____

4. The recollection of his [Mr. Doran's] confession the night before was a cause of acute pain to him; the priest had drawn out every ridiculous detail of the affair and in the end had so magnified his sin that he was almost thankful at being afforded a loophole of reparation.

_____

_____

_____

_____

_____

5. Then one late night as he was undressing for bed she had tapped at his door, timidly. She wanted to relight her candle at his for hers had been blown out by a gust. It was her bath night. She wore a loose open combing-jacket of printed flannel. Her white instep shone in the opening of her furry slippers and the blood glowed warmly behind her perfumed skin. From her hands and wrists too as she lit and steadied her candle a faint perfume arose.

_____

_____

_____

_____

_____

_____

6. On the last flight of stairs he passed Jack Mooney who was coming up from the pantry nursing two bottles of *Bass*. They saluted coldly; and the lover's eyes rested for a second or two on a thick bulldog face and a pair of thick short arms. When he reached the foot of the staircase he glanced up and saw Jack regarding him from the door of the return-room.

_____

_____

_____

_____

_____

_____

C. CHARACTER AND THE STORY

Words can move the action of a story forward. They can also reveal some dimension of a character's personality which can be overlooked by observing his or her actions.

4: FROM WORDS TO CHARACTER

In the passages below, the words or phrases in boldface reveal the personality of one of the characters. Explain how they do so. Notice particularly the background and the motivation (desires and/or needs) of the character.

Model:

He [Mr. Doran] could not **brazen** it out.

Comment:

Brazen is most often used as an adjective meaning outspoken or bold. By using it as a verb, Joyce shows that Mr. Doran is not just soft-spoken but is paralyzed, incapable of acting for his own self-interest.

1. They saluted coldly; and the lover's eyes rested for a second or two on a thick **bulldog face.…"** (Jack Mooney)

2. Her eyes, which were gray with a shade of green through them, had a habit of glancing upwards when she spoke with anyone, which made her look like a **little perverse madonna.** (Polly Mooney)

3. He was a shabby stooped little drunkard with a white face and a white mustache and white eyebrows, penciled above his little eyes, which were **pink-veined and raw.** (Mr. Mooney)

4. Mrs. Mooney, who had taken what remained of her money out of the butcher business and set up a boardinghouse in Hardwicke Street, was a **big imposing woman.** (Mrs. Mooney)

D. OTHER ROUTES TO CHARACTER

Your imagination does not have to be limited by the characters, the actions, or the words in a particular story. In fact, you may learn even more about a story by creating imaginary characters not in the story.

5: YOUR CHARACTERS AND MR. JOYCE'S CHARACTERS

Write a dialogue between one character that appears in "The Boarding House" and one that you invent. You can use Joyce's suggestion for this "new" character or you can make up one of your own. For example, in "The Boarding House" Joyce mentions Mr. Doran's employer. This person never appears in the story. Imagine that Mr. Doran refused to accept Mrs. Mooney's "offer," and Mrs. Mooney actually visited Mr. Doran's employer. What might they say? Imagine such a conversation and write a dialogue between them.

Write at least a 12-part dialogue (one in which each character speaks at least six times). Practice your dialogue and read it aloud to the class.

E. ALLUSIONS

An **allusion** is an informal reference in a poem, play, or story to a famous literary or historical event or person. Allusions may be single words, phrases, clauses, full sentences, even paragraphs or longer.

6: ALLUSIONS FOR PRACTICE

a. Increase your knowledge of this story by discovering the meanings of the following allusions.

1. All the resident young men spoke of her as **The Madam.**

2. It was seventeen minutes past eleven: she would have lots of time to have the matter out with Mr. Doran and then catch **short twelve** at Marlborough Street.

3. But his sin was there; even his sense of honor told him that **reparation** must be made for such a sin.

5. They discussed with one another the chances of **favorites and outsiders.**

b. Now find five additional allusions to study and discuss. What does each add to the story? Where do you have to look to discover the meaning of these allusions? What can you say about the nature of allusions in fiction? What are some of the similarities and differences among the allusions you discussed?

7: ALLUSIONS AND SYMBOLS

A symbol sometimes accumulates so much meaning that it takes on more importance than a single allusion. It begins to take on the significance and power of a symbol. Choose one allusion that takes on such a symbolic dimension. Look into it fully. Then present an oral or written report about this symbol.

F. CONGRUENT PATTERNS

In geometry, congruent shapes are those that while not the same size are identical in shape.

A **congruent shape** in fiction means a pattern that recurs. That is, while two or more actions in the same story may differ from each other, they have similar shapes which reinforce each other. They create a series of echoes. In "The Boarding House" important ways of looking at objects and people recur. For example, Mrs. Mooney glances at the clock to calculate the time it requires to speak to Mr. Doran and get to church. Mr. Doran cannot see because his glasses fog up with moisture. Polly looks at herself in the mirror. These glances and others have similar congruent shapes.

8: WRITING ABOUT THE ECHOES OF YOUR LIFE OR YOUR COUNTRY'S HISTORY

Think first about the echoes in your own life or in the life of your country. Are there events that occurred to you in earlier years that echo in later, more recent events of your life? Are there congruent events in your country's history that you can follow? For example, does your country repeat a certain cultural pattern in different circumstances and times? Trace three separate echo patterns and see how they are similar (though not identical).

Explain your understanding of one of these echo patterns, either in your life or the life of your country, in a five paragraph composition.

Paragraph 1: Introduce the organization you will follow and explain the general connection among the events in the echo chain.

Paragraph 2: Explain one event of the echo chain.

Paragraph 3: Explain the second event of the echo chain.

Paragraph 4: Explain the third event of the echo chain.

Paragraph 5: Write a conclusion.

G. STRUCTURE

9: IDENTIFYING FORESHADOWING AND FLASHBACKS

When characters, actions, or scenes suggest earlier parts of a story, a **flashback** to an earlier action has occurred. The earlier character, action, or scene may foreshadow a later one. Both foreshadowing and flashbacks occur in "The Boarding House.

Complete the following sentences with the action, scene, or character which is a foreshadowing of or a flashback to an earlier one. Use a quotation from the story if it helps you to answer.

Model:

"Mrs. Mooney was a butcher's daughter" foreshadows her **ability to handle the Doran transaction as simply another bit of disagreeable business. "She dealt with moral problems as a cleaver deals with meat."**

1. Jack Mooney's skill as a boxer foreshadows _____

    _____

    _____

    _____

2. The mist gathering on Mr. Doran's glasses so that he could not see foreshadows

    _____

    _____

    _____

3. While sitting in his room on Sunday morning, Mr. Doran has a flashback to the time when _____

    _____

    _____

    _____

4. While going down the stairs, Mr. Doran has a flashback to a time when, during a music-hall evening, _____

    _____

    _____

    _____

H. EPIPHANIES

Echoes, foreshadowings, and flashbacks depend primarily on earlier or later effects for their power. On the other hand, actions, words, and people that are of instant importance and do not depend as much on other events Joyce called epiphanies—significant single moments of speech, action, or vision.

10: IDENTIFYING EPIPHANIES

Try to locate a few such important moments in "The Boarding House." In preparation, think of the other stories you have read, for example, "The Strawberry Season," and identify the epiphanies in these stories.

11: I WOULD IF I COULD

In "The Boarding House," as in much other 20th-century short fiction, the characters want to do many more things than they can actually do.

To reveal these two sides of a character, what they want to do and what they can do, complete the three blanks below for each character. Then discuss the results with your classmates.

I would _____ if I could, but because of

_____ I cannot. You can help me

by _____ .

12: PRESS CONFERENCE WITH THE CHARACTERS

Become a character in "The Boarding House." Take your turn sitting in front of the room. The class, like newspaper reporters at a press conference, will then take turns asking you questions about your background, actions, future plans, and other important issues in the story.

13: INTERVIEW WITH THE AUTHOR

Does the author of a work understand as much about his or her own story as you do? Many people like to imagine what the author wanted or intended to say in his or her story.

Two or three volunteers in your class will pretend to be the author of "The Boarding House." Ask the "authors" the questions you have about the story. See if you can find out more about the themes of "The Boarding House."

Ann Petry.

CHAPTER SEVENTEEN
ADVANCED SOLO

The goals for this chapter are:

To review the more complex elements for understanding fiction, learned in Chapters 12–16

In this chapter, you will read:

"Like a Winding Sheet" by Ann Petry

He stuck his pay envelope in his pants' pocket and followed the line of workers heading for the subway in a slow-moving stream. He glanced up at the sky. It was a nice night, the sky looked packed full to running over with stars. And he thought if he and Mae would go right to bed when they got home from work they'd catch a few hours of darkness for sleeping.

"Like a Winding Sheet"

Ann Petry's "Like a Winding Sheet," concerns the ordinary events of daily life: a man's work, a couple at home, an argument, violence. The way the author presents the material, however, is far from ordinary. Use the list of entrances to understand the story and answer the questions that follow.

Possible Entrance Points

1. Style, including

    Sentence structure and length

    Word choice

    Imagery

2. Structure, including

    Foreshadowing

    Echoes

3. Pace

4. Tone

5. Character

6. Symbolism

QUESTIONS FOR ANALYSIS AND DISCUSSION

1. What is a winding sheet?

2. Why does Johnson get angry at Mrs. Scott, his supervisor?

3. Why does Johnson get angry at the white girl in the coffee shop?

4. Why does Johnson beat his wife?

5. What is the importance of lipstick in the story?

6. Describe the relationship between Johnson and his wife Mae.

7. What is the theme of "Like a Winding Sheet"?

LIKE A WINDING SHEET
Ann Petry

1   He had planned to get up before Mae did and surprise her by fixing breakfast. Instead he went back to sleep and she got out of bed so quietly he didn't know she wasn't there beside him until he woke up and heard the queer soft gurgle of water running out of the sink in the bathroom.

2   He knew he ought to get up but instead he put his arms across his forehead to shut the afternoon sunlight out of his eyes, pulled his legs up close to his body, testing them to see if the ache was still in them.

3   Mae had finished in the bathroom. He could tell because she never closed the door when she was in there and now the sweet smell of talcum powder was drifting down the hall and into the bedroom. Then he heard her coming down the hall.

4   "Hi, babe," she said affectionately.

5   "Hum," he grunted, and moved his arms away from his head, opened one eye.

6   "It's a nice morning."

7   "Yeah." He rolled over and the sheet twisted around him, outlining his thighs, his chest. "You mean afternoon, don't ya?"

8   Mae looked at the twisted sheet and giggled. "Looks like a winding sheet," she said. "A shroud—" Laughter tangled with her words and she had to pause for a moment before she could continue. "You look like a huckleberry—in a winding sheet—"

9   "That's no way to talk. Early in the day like this," he protested.

10   He looked at his arms silhouetted against the white of the sheets. They were inky black by contrast and he had to smile in spite of himself and he lay there smiling and savoring the sweet sound of Mae's giggling.

11   "Early?" She pointed a finger at the alarm clock on the table near the bed and giggled again. "It's almost four o'clock. And if you don't spring up out of there, you're going to be late again."

12   "What do you mean 'again'?"

13   "Twice last week. Three times the week before. And once the week before and—"

14   "I can't get used to sleeping in the daytime," he said fretfully. He pushed his legs out from under the covers experimentally. Some of the ache had gone out of them but they weren't really rested yet. "It's too light for good sleeping. And all that standing beats the hell out of my legs."

15   "After two years you oughta be used to it," Mae said.

16   He watched her as she fixed her hair, powdered her face, slipped into a pair of blue denim overalls. She moved quickly and yet she didn't seem to hurry.

17   "You look like you'd had plenty of sleep," he said lazily. He had to get up but he kept putting the moment off, not wanting to move, yet he didn't dare let his legs go completely limp because if he did he'd go back to sleep. It was getting later and later but the thought of putting his weight on his legs kept him lying there.

18   When he finally got up he had to hurry, and he gulped his breakfast so fast that he wondered if his stomach could possibly use food thrown at it at such a rate of speed. He was still wondering about it as he and Mae were putting their coats on in the hall.

19   Mae paused to look at the calendar. "It's the thirteenth," she said. Then a faint excitement in her voice, "Why, it's Friday the thirteenth." She had one arm in her coat sleeve and she held it there while she stared at the calendar. "I oughta stay home," she said. "I shouldn't go outa the house."

20   "Aw, don't be a fool," he said. "Today's payday. And payday is a good luck day everywhere, any way you look at it." And as she stood hesitating he said, "Aw, come on."

21   And he was late for work again because they spent fifteen minutes arguing before he could convince her she ought to go to work just the same. He had to talk persuasively, urging her gently, and it took time. But he couldn't bring himself to talk to her roughly or threaten to strike her like a lot of men might have done. He wasn't made that way.

22   So when he reached the plant he was late and he had to wait to punch the time clock because the day-shift workers were streaming out in long lines, in groups and bunches that impeded his progress.

23   Even now just starting his workday his legs ached. He had to force himself to struggle past the outgoing workers, punch the time clock, and get the little cart he pushed around all night, because he kept toying with the idea of going home and getting back in bed.

24   He pushed the cart out on the concrete floor, thinking that if this was his plant he'd make a lot of changes in it. There were too many standing-up jobs for one thing. He'd figure out some way most of 'em could be done sitting down and he'd put a lot more benches around. And this job he had —this job that forced him to walk ten hours a night, pushing this little cart, well, he'd turn it into a sitting-down job. One of those little trucks they used around the railroad stations would be good for a job like this. Guys sat on a seat and the thing moved easily, taking up little room and turning in hardly any space at all, like on a dime.

25   He pushed the cart near the foreman. He never could remember to refer to her as the forelady even in his mind. It was funny to have a white woman for a boss in a plant like this one.

26   She was sore about something. He could tell by the way her face was red and her eyes were half-shut until they were slits. Probably been out late and didn't get enough sleep. He avoided looking at her and hurried a little, head down, as he passed her though he couldn't resist stealing a glance at her out of the corner of his eye. He saw the edge of the light-colored slacks she wore and the tip end of a big tan shoe.

27   "Hey, Johnson!" the woman said.

28   The machines had started full blast. The whirr and the grinding made the building shake, made it impossible to hear conversations. The men and women at the machines talked to each other but looking at them from just a little distance away, they appeared to be simply moving their lips because you couldn't hear what they were saying. Yet the woman's voice cut across the machine sounds—harsh, angry.

29   He turned his head slowly. "Good evenin', Mrs. Scott," he said and waited.

30   "You're late again."

31   "That's right. My legs were bothering me."

32   The woman's face grew redder, angrier looking. "Half this shift comes in late," she said. "And you're the worst one of all. You're always late. Whatsa matter with ya?"

33   "It's my legs," he said. "Somehow they don't ever get rested. I don't seem to get used to sleeping days. And I just can't get started."

34   "Excuses. You guys always got excuses," her anger grew and spread. "Every guy comes in here late always has an excuse. His wife's sick or his grandmother died or somebody in the family had to go to the hospital." she paused, drew a deep breath. "And the niggers is the worse. I don't care what's wrong with your legs. You get in here on time. I'm sick of you niggers—"

35   "You got the right to get mad," he interrupted softly. "You got the right to cuss me fourways to Sunday but I ain't letting nobody call me a nigger."

36   He stepped closer to her. His fists were doubled. His lips were drawn back in a thin narrow line. A vein in his forehead stood out swollen, thick.

37   And the woman backed away from him, not hurriedly but slowly—two, three steps back.

38   "Aw, forget it," she said. "I didn't mean nothing by it. It slipped out. It was an accident." The red of her face deepened until the small blood vessels in her cheeks were purple. "Go on and get to work," she urged. And she took three more slow backward steps.

39   He stood motionless for a moment and then turned away from the sight of the red lipstick on her mouth that made him remember that the foreman was a woman. And he couldn't bring himself to hit a woman. He felt a curious tingling in his fingers and he looked down at his hands. They were clenched tight, hard, ready to smash some of those small purple veins in her face.

40   He pushed the cart ahead of him, walking slowly. When he turned his head, she was staring in his direction, mopping her forehead with a dark blue handkerchief. Their eyes met and then they both looked away.

41   He didn't glance in her direction again but moved past the long work benches, carefully collecting the finished parts, going slowly and steadily up and down, and back and forth the length of the building, and as he walked he forced himself to swallow his anger, get rid of it.

42   And he succeeded so that he was able to think about what had happened without getting upset about it. An hour went by but the tension stayed in his hands. They were clenched and knotted on the handles of the cart as though ready to aim a blow.

43   And he thought he should have hit her anyway, smacked her hard in the face, felt the soft flesh of her face give under the hardness of his hands. He tried to make his hands relax by offering them a description of what it would have been like to strike her because he had the queer feeling that his hands were not exactly a part of him anymore—they had developed a separate life of their own over which he had no control. So he dwelt on the pleasure his hands would have felt—both of them cracking at her, first one and then the other. If he had done that his hands would have felt good now—relaxed, rested.

44   And he decided that even if he'd lost his job for it, he should have let her have it and it would have been along time, maybe the rest of her life, before she called anybody else a nigger.

45   The only trouble was he couldn't hit a woman. A woman couldn't hit back the same way a man did. But it would have been a deeply satisfying thing to have cracked her narrow lips wide open with just one blow, beautifully timed and with all his weight in back of it. That way he would have gotten rid of all the energy and tension his anger had created in him. He kept remembering how his heart had started pumping blood so fast he had felt it tingle even in the tips of his fingers.

46   With the approach of night, fatigue nibbled at him. The corners of his mouth drooped, the frown between his eyes deepened, his shoulders sagged; but his hands stayed tight and tense. As the hours dragged by he noticed that the women workers had started to snap and snarl at each

other. He couldn't hear what they said because of the sound of machines but he could see the quick lip movements that sent words tumbling from the sides of their mouths. They gestured irritably with their hands and scowled as their mouths moved.

47   Their violent jerky motions told him that it was getting close on to quitting time but somehow he felt that the night still stretched ahead of him, composed of endless hours of steady walking on his aching legs. When the whistle finally blew he went on pushing the cart, unable to believe that it had sounded. The whirring of the machines died away to a murmur and he knew then that he'd really heard the whistle. He stood still for a moment, filled with a relief that made him sigh.

48   Then he moved briskly, putting the cart in the storeroom, hurrying to take his place in the line forming before the paymaster. That was another thing he'd change, he thought. He'd have the pay envelopes handed to the people right at their benches so there wouldn't be ten or fifteen minutes lost waiting for the pay. He always got home about fifteen minutes late on payday. They did it better in the plant where Mae worked, brought the money right to them at their benches.

49   He stuck his pay envelope in his pants' pocket and followed the line of workers heading for the subway in a slow-moving stream. He glanced up at the sky. It was a nice night, the sky looked packed full to running over with stars. And he thought if he and Mae would go right to bed when they got home from work they'd catch a few hours of darkness for sleeping. But they never did. They fooled around—cooking and eating and listening to the radio and he always stayed in a big chair in the living room and went almost but not quite to sleep and when they finally got to bed it was five or six in the morning and daylight was already seeping around the edges of the sky.

50   He walked slowly, putting off the moment when he would have to plunge into the crowd hurrying toward the subway. It was a long ride to Harlem and tonight the thought of it appalled him. He paused outside an all-night restaurant to kill time, so that some of the first rush of workers would be gone when he reached the subway.

51   The lights in the restaurant were brilliant, enticing. There was life and motion inside. And as he looked through the window he thought that everything within range of his eyes gleamed—the long imitation marble counter, the tall stools, the white porcelain-topped tables and especially the big metal coffee urn right near the window. Steam issued from its top and a gas flame flickered under it—a lively, dancing, blue flame.

52   A lot of the workers from his shift—men and women—were lining up near the coffee urn. He watched them walk to the porcelain-topped tables

carrying steaming cups of coffee and he saw that just the smell of the coffee lessened the fatigue lines in their faces. After the first sip their faces softened, they smiled, they began to talk and laugh.

53   On a sudden impulse he shoved the door open and joined the line in front of the coffee urn. The line moved slowly. And as he stood there the smell of the coffee, the sound of the laughter and of the voices, helped dull the sharp ache in his legs.

54   He didn't pay any attention to the white girl who was serving the coffee at the urn. He kept looking at the cups in the hands of the men who had been ahead of him. Each time a man stepped out of the line with one of the thick white cups the fragrant steam got in his nostrils. He saw that they walked carefully so as not to spill a single drop. There was a froth of bubbles at the top of each cup and he thought about how he would let the bubbles break against his lips before he actually took a big deep swallow.

55   Then it was his turn. "A cup of coffee," he said, just as he heard the others say.

56   The white girl looked past him, put her hands up to her head and gently lifted her hair away from the back of her neck, tossing her head back a little. "No more coffee for a while," she said.

57   He wasn't certain he'd heard her correctly and he said "What?" blankly.

58   "No more coffee for a while," she repeated.

59   There was silence behind him and then uneasy movement. He thought someone would say something, ask why or protest, but there was only silence and then a faint shuffling sound as though the men standing behind him had simultaneously shifted their weight from one foot to the other.

60   He looked at the girl without saying anything. He felt his hands begin to tingle and the tingling went all the way down to his finger tips so that he glanced down at them. They were clenched tight, hard, into fists. Then he looked at the girl again. What he wanted to do was hit her so hard that the scarlet lipstick on her mouth would smear and spread over her nose, her chin, out toward her cheeks, so hard that she would never toss her head again and refuse a man a cup of coffee because he was black.

61   He estimated the distance across the counter and reached forward, balancing his weight on the balls of his feet, ready to let the blow go. And then his hands fell back down to his sides because he forced himself to lower them, to unclench them and make them dangle loose. The effort took his breath away because his hands fought against him. But he couldn't hit her. He couldn't even now bring himself to hit a woman, not even this one, who had refused him a cup of coffee with a toss of her

head. He kept seeing the gesture with which she had lifted the length of her blond hair from the back of her neck as expressive of her contempt for him.

62   When he went out the door he didn't look back. If he had he would have seen the flickering blue flame under the shiny coffee urn being extinguished. The line of men who had stood behind him lingered a moment to watch the people drinking coffee at the tables and then they left just as he had without having had the coffee they wanted so badly. The girl behind the counter poured water in the urn and swabbed it out and as she waited for the water to run out, she lifted her hair gently from the back of her neck and tossed her head before she began making a fresh lot of coffee.

63   But he had walked away without a backward look, his head down, his hands in his pockets, raging at himself and whatever it was inside of him that had forced him to stand quiet and still when he wanted to strike out.

64   The subway was crowded and he had to stand. He tried grasping an overhead strap and his hands were too tense to grip it. So he moved near the train door and stood there swaying back and forth with the rocking of the train. The roar of the train beat inside his head, making it ache and throb, and the pain in his legs clawed up into his groin so that he seemed to be bursting with pain and he told himself that it was due to all that anger-born energy that had piled up in him and not been used and so it had spread through him like a poison—from his feet and legs all the way up to his head.

65   Mae was in the house before he was. He knew she was home before he put the key in the door of the apartment. The radio was going. She had it tuned up loud and she was singing along with it.

66   "Hello, babe," she called out, as soon as he opened the door.

67   He tried to say "hello" and it came out half grunt and half sigh.

68   "You sure sound cheerful," she said.

69   She was in the bedroom and he went and leaned against the doorjamb. The denim overalls she wore to work were carefully draped over the back of a chair by the bed. She was standing in front of the dresser, tying the sash of a yellow housecoat around her waist and chewing gum vigorously as she admired her reflection in the mirror over the dresser.

70   "Whatsa matter?" she said. "You get bawled out by the boss or somep'n?"

71   "Just tired," he said slowly. "For God's sake, do you have to crack that gum like that?"

72   "You don't have to lissen to me," she said complacently. She patted a curl in place near the side of her head and then lifted her hair away from the back of her neck, ducking her head forward and then back.

73   He winced away from the gesture. "What you got to be always fooling with your hair for?" he protested.

74   "Say, what's the matter with you anyway?" She turned away from the mirror to face him, put her hands on her hips. "You ain't been in the house two minutes and you're picking on me."

75   He didn't answer her because her eyes were angry and he didn't want to quarrel with her. They'd been married too long and got along too well and so he walked all the way into the room and sat down in the chair by the bed and stretched his legs out in front of him, putting his weight on the heels of his shoes, leaning way back in the chair, not saying anything.

76   "Lissen," she said sharply. "I've got to wear those overalls again tomorrow. You're going to get them all wrinkled up leaning against them like that."

77   He didn't move. He was too tired and his legs were throbbing now that he had sat down. Besides the overalls were already wrinkled and dirty, he thought. They couldn't help but be for she'd worn them all week. He leaned further back in the chair.

78   "Come on, get up," she ordered.

79   "Oh, what the hell," he said wearily, and got up from the chair. "I'd just as soon live in a subway. There'd be just as much place to sit down."

80   He saw that her sense of humor was struggling with her anger. But her sense of humor won because she giggled.

81   "Aw, come on and eat," she said. There was a coaxing note in her voice. "You're nothing but an old hungry nigger trying to act tough and—" she paused to giggle and then continued, "You—"

82   He had always found her giggling pleasant and deliberately said things that might amuse her and then waited, listening for the delicate sound to emerge from her throat. This time he didn't even hear the giggle. He didn't let her finish what she was saying. She was standing close to him and that funny tingling started in his finger tips, went fast up his arms and sent his fist shooting straight for her face.

83   There was the smacking sound of soft flesh being struck by a hard object and it wasn't until she screamed that he realized he had hit her in the mouth—so hard that the dark red lipstick had blurred and spread over her full lips, reaching up toward the tip of her nose, down toward her chin, out toward her cheeks.

84   The knowledge that he had struck her seeped through him slowly and he was appalled but he couldn't drag his hands away from her face. He kept striking her and he thought with horror that something inside him was holding him, binding him to this act, wrapping and twisting about him so that he had to continue it. He had lost all control over his hands. And he groped for a phrase, a word, something to describe what this thing was like that was happening to him and he thought it was like being enmeshed in a winding sheet—that was it—like a winding sheet. And even as the thought formed in his mind, his hands reached for her face again and yet again.

INNER MARKER

Universal Timeless Challenges

Since more or less the middle of this book, mid-journey, you have moved more and more deeply into the world of fiction. In that world you found stories of a child, after an accidental crisis, facing adult judgment ("The Stone Boy"); of adults, mother and grown-up son ("Gerald's Song"); of fathers from very different backgrounds ("Sunday in the Park") in conflict; of soldiers from one army forced by circumstances to take the lives of men from the other army who had become their friends ("Guests of the Nation"); of a quiet conflict between a man and a woman ("Rope"); and of social conflict and adjustment ("The Boarding House"). These and the other stories were not reported to you briefly as facts and ended. Rather, the authors tried to bring out the joy and pain of the struggles in each situation. To do so, they pressed the language to carry as much meaning as possible (word choice and images), they sought universal and timeless patterns to carry their stories (myth and symbols), they tried to compress the story into a strong, unified package (echoes, motifs, foreshadowing, and flashbacks), they brought the real world into the story (allusions), and they chose places (settings) and people (point of view) which could best carry their stories.

CHAPTER EIGHTEEN

THE TERRITORY AHEAD

The goals for this chapter are:

To understand longer fiction, using the elements previously learned for shorter fiction in this text

In this chapter, you will read:

"The Open Boat" by Stephen Crane

A singular disadvantage of the sea lies in the fact that after successfully surmounting one wave you discover that there is another behind it just as important and just as nervously anxious to do something effective in the way of swamping boats.

"The Open Boat"

241

▲·▲

A. THE WORLD OF LONGER FICTION

You have now made your way through many short stories in English, yet there is still more territory ahead to explore. Interestingly, it may be territory you have traveled in your own language: the longer short story and the novel.

Stephen Crane, author of "The Open Boat," wrote many shorter pieces that you can look at *before* you read this long story. In fact, he wrote many very short poems which contain some of the same themes as his short stories and novels. Read and discuss both of the poems below as an entrance into his longer fiction.

XXIV

A man said to the universe:
"Sir, I exist!"
"However," replied the universe,
"The fact has not created in me
"A sense of obligation."

LVI

A man feared that he might find an assassin;
Another that he might find a victim.
One was more wise than the other.

▲·▲·▲·▲·▲·▲·▲·▲·▲·▲·▲·▲·▲·▲·▲·▲·▲·▲·▲·▲

B. THE AUTHOR'S BACKGROUND

An advantage of reading a novel is that the work you are reading is long enough for you to spend more time studying it in class. This will give you more opportunity to look into the author's life, for example, where the author lived, what he did during his lifetime, and with whom he associated. Since Crane wrote a news story based on his own experience in a shipwreck, as you study "The Open Boat" you have a rather rare opportunity to directly compare art and life, usually seen as opposites,

Two news stories as well as Crane's own news account of the shipwreck appeared in newspapers in New York and Florida. They can be conveniently read in *Stephen Crane: Stories and Tales* edited by Robert W. Stallman (New York: Random House, 1955).

THE OPEN BOAT
Stephen Crane

A Tale intended to be after the fact. Being the Experience of Four Men from the Sunk Steamer "Commodore"

I

1   None of them knew the color of the sky. Their eyes glanced level, and were fastened upon the waves that swept toward them. These waves were of the hue of slate, save for the tops, which were of foaming white, and all of the men knew the colors of the sea. The horizon narrowed and widened, and dipped and rose, and at all times its edge was jagged with waves that seemed thrust up in points like rocks.

2   Many a man ought to have a bath-tub larger than the boat which here rode upon the sea. These waves were most wrongfully and barbarously abrupt and tall, and each froth-top was a problem in small boat navigation.

3   The cook squatted in the bottom and looked with both eyes at the six inches of gunwale which separated him from the ocean. His sleeves were rolled over his fat forearms, and the two flaps of his unbuttoned vest dangled as he bent to bail out the boat. Often he said: "Gawd! That was a narrow clip." As he remarked it he invariably gazed eastward over the broken sea.

4   The oiler, steering with one of the two oars in the boat, sometimes raised himself suddenly to keep clear of water that swirled in over the stern. It was a thin little oar and it seemed often ready to snap.

5   The correspondent, pulling at the other oar, watched the waves and wondered why he was there.

6   The injured captain, lying in the bow, was at this time buried in that profound dejection and indifference which comes temporarily at least, to even the bravest and most enduring when, willy nilly, the firm fails, the army loses, the ship goes down. The mind of the master of a vessel is rooted deep in the timbers of her, though he command for a day or a decade, and this captain had on him the stern impression of a scene in the grays of dawn of seven turned faces, and later a stump of a top-mast with a white ball on it that slashed to and fro at the waves, went low and lower, and down. Thereafter there was something strange in his voice. Although steady, it was deep with mourning, and of a quality beyond oration or tears.

7   "Keep 'er a little more south, Billie," said he.

8   " 'A little more south,' sir," said the oiler in the stern.

9   A seat in this boat was not unlike a seat upon a bucking broncho, and, by the same token, a broncho is not much smaller. The craft pranced and

reared, and plunged like an animal. As each wave came, and she rose for it, she seemed like a horse making at a fence outrageously high. The manner of her scramble over these walls of water is a mystic thing, and, moreover, at the top of them were ordinarily these problems in white water, the foam racing down from the summit of each wave, requiring a new leap, and a leap from the air. Then, after scornfully bumping a crest, she would slide, and race, and splash down a long incline, and arrive bobbing and nodding in front of the next menace.

10   A singular disadvantage of the sea lies in the fact that after successfully surmounting one wave you discover that there is another behind it just as important and just as nervously anxious to do something effective in the way of swamping boats. In a ten-foot dingey one can get an idea of the resources of the sea in the line of waves that is not probable to the average experience which is never at sea in a dingey. As each slaty wall of water approached, it shut all else from the view of the men in the boat, and it was not difficult to imagine that this particular wave was the final outburst of the ocean, the last effort of the grim water. There was a terrible grace in the move of the waves, and they came in silence, save for the snarling of the crests.

11   In the wan of light, the faces of the men must have been gray. Their eyes must have glinted in strange ways as they gazed steadily astern. Viewed from a balcony, the whole thing would doubtless have been weirdly picturesque. But the men in the boat had no time to see it, and if they had had leisure there were other things to occupy their minds. The sun swung steadily up the sky, and they knew it was broad day because the color of the sea changed from slate to emerald-green, streaked with amber lights, and the foam was like tumbling snow. The process of the breaking day was unknown to them. They were aware only of this effect upon the color of the waves that rolled toward them.

12   In disjointed sentences the cook and the correspondent argued as to the difference between a life-saving station and a house of refuge. The cook had said: "There's a house of refuge just north of the Mosquito Inlet Light, and as soon as they see us, they'll come off in their boats and pick us up."

13   "As soon as who see us?" said the correspondent.

14   "The crew," said the cook.

15   "Houses of refuge don't have crews," said the correspondent. "As I understand them, they are only places where clothes and grub are stored for the benefit of shipwrecked people. They don't carry crews."

16   "Oh, yes, they do," said the cook.

17   "No, they don't," said the correspondent.

18   "Well, we're not there yet, anyhow," said the oiler, in the stern.

19   "Well," said the cook, "perhaps it's not a house of refuge that I'm thinking of as being near Mosquito Inlet Light. Perhaps it's a life-saving station."

20   "We're not there yet," said the oiler, in the stern.

II

21   As the boat bounced from the top of each wave, the wind tore through the hair of the hatless men, and as the craft plopped her stern down again the spray splashed past them. The crest of each of these waves was a hill, from the top of which the men surveyed, for a moment, a broad tumultuous expanse, shining and wind-riven. It was probably splendid. It was probably glorious, this play of the free sea, wild with lights of emerald and white and amber.

22   "Bully good thing it's an on-shore wind," said the cook. "If not, where would we be? Wouldn't have a show."

23   "That's right," said the correspondent.

24   The busy oiler nodded his assent.

25   Then the captain, in the bow, chuckled in a way that expressed humor, contempt, tragedy, all in one. "Do you think we've got much of a show now, boys?" said he.

26   Whereupon the three were silent, save for a trifle of hemming and hawing. To express any particular optimism at this time they felt to be childish and stupid, but they all doubtless possessed this sense of the situation in their mind. A young man thinks doggedly at such times. On the other hand, the ethics of their condition was decidedly against any open suggestion of hopefulness. So they were silent.

27   "Oh, well," said the captain, soothing his children, "we'll get ashore all right."

28   But there was that in his tone which made them think, so the oiler quoth: "Yes! If this wind holds!"

29   The cook was bailing: "Yes! If we don't catch hell in the surf."

30   Canton flannel gulls flew near and far. Sometimes they sat down on the sea, near patches of brown seaweed that rolled over the waves with a movement like carpets on a line in a gale. The birds sat comfortably in groups, and there were envied by some in the dingey, for the wrath of the sea was no more to them than it was to a covey of prairie chickens a thousand miles inland. Often they came very close and stared at the men with black bead-like eyes. At these times they were uncanny and sinister in their unblinking scrutiny, and the men hooted angrily at them, telling them to be gone. One came, and evidently decided to alight on the top of the captain's head. The bird flew parallel to the boat and did not circle, but made short sidelong jumps in the air in chicken-fashion. His black eyes were wistfully fixed upon the captain's head. "Ugly brute," said the oiler to the bird. "You look as if you were made with a jack-knife." The cook and the correspon-

dent swore darkly at the creature. The captain naturally wished to knock it away with the end of the heavy painter; but he did not dare do it, because anything resembling an emphatic gesture would have capsized this freighted boat, and so with his open hand, the captain gently and carefully waved the gull away. After it had been discouraged from the pursuit the captain breathed easier on account of his hair, and others breathed easier because the bird struck their minds at this time as being somehow gruesome and ominous.

31   In the meantime the oiler and the correspondent rowed. And also they rowed.

32   They sat together in the same seat, and each rowed an oar. Then the oiler took both oars; then the correspondent took both oars; then the oiler; then the correspondent. They rowed and they rowed. The very ticklish part of the business was when the time came for the reclining one in the stern to take his turn at the oars. By the very last star of truth, it is easier to steal eggs from under a hen than it was to change seats in the dingey. First the man in the stern slid his hand along the thwart and moved with care, as if he were of Sèvres. Then the man in the rowing seat slid his hand along the other thwart. It was all done with the most extraordinary care. As the two sidled past each other, the whole party kept watchful eyes on the coming wave, and the captain cried: "Look out now! Steady there!"

33   The brown mats of seaweed that appeared from time to time were like islands, bits of earth. They were traveling, apparently, neither one way nor the other. They were, to all intents, stationary. They informed the men in the boat that it was making progress slowly toward the land.

34   The captain, rearing cautiously in the bow, after the dingey soared on a great swell, said that he had seen the lighthouse at Mosquito Inlet. Presently the cook remarked that he had seen it. The correspondent was at the oars then, and for some reason he too wished to look at the lighthouse, but his back was toward the far shore and the waves were important, and for some time he could not seize an opportunity to turn his head. But at last there came a wave more gentle than the others, and when at the crest of it he swiftly scoured the western horizon.

35   "See it?" said the captain.

36   "No," said the correspondent slowly. "I didn't see anything."

37   "Look again," said the captain. He pointed. "It's exactly in that direction."

38   At the top of another wave, the correspondent did as he was bid, and this time his eyes chanced on a small still thing on the edge of the swaying horizon. It was precisely like the point of a pin. It took an anxious eye to find a lighthouse so tiny.

39   "Think we'll make it, captain?"

40   "If this wind holds and the boat don't swamp, we can't do much else," said the captain.

41   The little boat, lifted by each towering sea, and splashed viciously by the crests, made progress that in the absence of seaweed was not apparent to those in her. She seemed just a wee thing wallowing, miraculously top up, at the mercy of five oceans. Occasionally, a great spread of water, like white flames, swarmed into her.

42   "Bail her, cook," said the captain serenely.

43   "All right, captain," said the cheerful cook.

III

44   It would be difficult to describe the subtle brotherhood of men that was here established on the seas. No one said that it was so. No one mentioned it. But it dwelt in the boat, and each man felt it warm him. They were a captain, an oiler, a cook, and a correspondent, and they were friends, friends in a more curiously iron-bound degree than may be common. The hurt captain, lying against the water-jar in the bow, spoke always in a low voice and calmly, but he could never command a more ready and swiftly obedient crew than the motley three of the dingey. It was more than a mere recognition of what was best for the common safety. There was surely in it a quality that was personal and heartfelt. And after this devotion to the commander of the boat there was this comradeship that the correspondent, for instance, who had been taught to be cynical of men, knew even at the time was the best experience of his life. But no one said that it was so. No one mentioned it.

45   "I wish we had a sail," remarked the captain. "We might try my overcoat on the end of an oar and give you two boys a chance to rest." So the cook and the correspondent held the mast and spread wide the overcoat. The oiler steered, and the little boat made good way with her new rig. Sometimes the oiler had to scull sharply to keep a sea from breaking into the boat, but otherwise sailing was a success.

46   Meanwhile the lighthouse had been growing slowly larger. It has now almost assumed color, and appeared like a little gray shadow on the sky. The man at the oars could not be prevented from turning his head rather often to try for a glimpse of this little gray shadow.

47   At last, from the top of each wave the men in the tossing boat could see land. Even as the lighthouse was an upright shadow on the sky, this land seemed but a long black shadow on the sea. It certainly was thinner than paper. "We must be about opposite New Smyrna," said the cook, who had coasted this shore often in schooners. "Captain, by the way, I believe they abandoned that life-saving station there about a year ago."

48   "Did they?" said the captain.

49   The wind slowly died away. The cook and the correspondent were not now obliged to slave in order to hold high the oar. But the waves continued their old impetuous swooping at the dingey, and the little craft, no longer under way, struggled woundily over them. The oiler or the correspondent took the oars again.

50   Shipwrecks are apropos of nothing. If men could only train for them and have them occur when the men had reached pink condition, there would be less drowning at sea. Of the four in the dingey none had slept any time worth mentioning for two days and two nights previous to embarking in the dingey, and in the excitement of clambering about the deck of a foundering ship they had also forgotten to eat heartily.

51   For these reasons, and for others, neither the oiler nor the correspondent was fond of rowing at this time. The correspondent wondered ingenuously how in the name of all that was sane could there be people who thought it amusing to row a boat. It was not an amusement; it was a diabolical punishment, and even a genius of mental aberrations could never conclude that it was anything but a horror to the muscles and a crime against the back. He mentioned to the boat in general how the amusement of rowing struck him, and the weary-faced oiler smiled in full sympathy. Previously to the foundering, by the way, the oiler had worked double-watch in the engine-room of the ship.

52   "Take her easy, now, boys," said the captain. "Don't spend yourselves. If we have to run a surf you'll need all your strength, because we'll sure have to swim for it. Take your time."

53   Slowly the land arose from the sea. From a black line it became a line of black and a line of white, trees and sand. Finally, the captain said that he could make out a house on the shore. "That's the house of refuge, sure," said the cook. "They'll see us before long, and come out after us."

54   The distant lighthouse reared high. "The keeper ought to be able to make us out now, if he's looking through a glass," said the captain. "He'll notify the life-saving people."

55   "None of those other boats could have got ashore to give word of the wreck," said the oiler, in a low voice. "Else the life-boat would be out hunting us."

56   Slowly and beautifully the land loomed out of the sea. The wind came again. It had veered from the north-east to the south-east. Finally, a new sound struck the ears of the men in the boat. It was the low thunder of the surf on the shore. "We'll never be able to make the lighthouse now," said the captain. "Swing her head a little more north, Billie."

57   " 'A little more north,' sir," said the oiler.

58   Whereupon the little boat turned her nose once more down the wind, and all but the oarsman watched the shore grow. Under the influence of this

expansion doubt and direful apprehension was leaving the minds of the men. The management of the boat was still most absorbing, but it could not prevent a quiet cheerfulness. In an hour, perhaps, they would be ashore.

59 Their backbones had become thoroughly used to balancing in the boat, and they now rode this wild colt of a dingey like circus men. The correspondent thought that he had been drenched to the skin, but happening to feel in the top pocket of his coat, he found therein eight cigars. Four of them were soaked with sea-water; four were perfectly scatheless. After a search, somebody produced three dry matches, and thereupon the four waifs rode in their little boat, and with an assurance of an impending rescue shining in their eyes, puffed at the big cigars and judged well and ill of all men. Everybody took a drink of water.

IV

60 "Cook," remarked the captain, "there don't seem to be any signs of life about your house of refuge."

61 "No," replied the cook. "Funny they don't see us!"

62 A broad stretch of lowly coast lay before the eyes of the men. It was of low dunes topped with dark vegetation. The roar of the surf was plain, and sometimes they could see the white lip of a wave as it spun up the beach. A tiny house was blocked out black upon the sky. Southward, the slim lighthouse lifted its little gray length.

63 Tide, wind, and waves were swinging the dingey northward. "Funny they don't see us," said the men.

64 The surf's roar was here dulled, but its tone was, nevertheless, thunderous and mighty. As the boat swam over the great rollers, the men sat listening to this roar. "We'll swamp sure," said everybody.

65 It is fair to say here that there was not a life-saving station within twenty miles in either direction, but the men did not know this fact, and in consequence they made dark and opprobrious remarks concerning the eyesight of the nation's life-savers. Four scowling men sat in the dingey and surpassed records in the invention of epithets.

66 "Funny they don't see us."

67 The light-heartedness of a former time had completely faded. To their sharpened minds it was easy to conjure pictures of all kinds of incompetency and blindness and, indeed, cowardice. There was the shore of the populous land, and it was bitter and bitter to them that from it came no sign.

68 "Well," said the captain, ultimately, "I suppose we'll have to make a try for ourselves. If we stay out here too long, we'll none of us have strength left to swim after the boat swamps.

69 And so the oiler, who was at the oars, turned the boat straight for the shore. There was a sudden tightening of muscles. There was some thinking.

70   "If we don't all get ashore—" said the captain. "If we don't all get ashore, I suppose you fellows know where to send news of my finish?"

71   They then briefly exchanged some addresses and admonitions. As for the reflections of the men, there was a great deal of rage in them. Perchance they might be formulated thus: "If I am going to be drowned—if I am going to be drowned—if I am going to be drowned, why, in the name of the seven mad gods who rule the sea, was I allowed to come thus far and contemplate sand and trees? Was I brought here merely to have my nose dragged away as I was about to nibble the sacred cheese of life? It is preposterous. If this old ninny-woman, Fate, cannot do better than this, she should be deprived of the management of men's fortunes. She is an old hen who knows not her intention. If she has decided to drown me, why did she not do it in the beginning and save me all this trouble? The whole affair is absurd. …But no, she cannot mean to drown me. She dare not drown me. She cannot drown me. Not after all this work." Afterward the man might have had an impulse to shake his fist at the clouds: "Just you drown me, now, and then hear what I call you!"

72   The billows that came at this time were more formidable. They seemed always just about to break and roll over the little boat in a turmoil of foam. There was a preparatory and long growl in the speech of them. No mind unused to the sea would have concluded that the dingey could ascend these sheer heights in time. The shore was still afar. The oiler was a wily surfman. "Boys," he said swiftly, "she won't live three minutes more, and we're too far out to swim. Shall I take her to sea again, captain?"

73   "Yes! Go ahead!" said the captain.

74   This oiler, by a series of quick miracles, and fast and steady oarsmanship, turned the boat in the middle of the surf and took her safely to sea again.

75   There was a considerable silence as the boat bumped over the furrowed sea to deeper water. Then somebody in gloom spoke. "Well, anyhow, they must have seen us from the shore by now."

76   The gulls went in slanting flight up the wind toward the gray desolate east. A squall, marked by dingy clouds, and clouds brick-red, like smoke from a burning building, appeared from the south-east.

77   "What do you think of those life-saving people? Ain't they peaches?"

78   "Funny they haven't seen us."

79   "Maybe they think we're out here for sport! Maybe they think we're fishin'. Maybe they think we're damned fools."

80   It was a long afternoon. A changed tide tried to force them southward, but wind and wave said northward. Far ahead, where coastline, sea, and sky formed their mighty angle, there were little dots which seemed to indicate a city on the shore.

81   "St. Augustine?"

82   The captain shook his head. "Too near Mosquito Inlet."

83   And the oiler rowed, and then the correspondent rowed. Then the oiler rowed. It was a weary business. The human back can become the seat of more aches and pains than are registered in books for the composite anatomy of a regiment. It is a limited area, but it can become the theater of innumerable muscular conflicts, tangles, wrenches, knots, and other comforts.

84   "Did you ever like to row, Billie?" asked the correspondent.

85   "No," said the oiler. "Hang it!"

86   When one exchanged the rowing-seat for a place in the bottom of the boat, he suffered a bodily depression that caused him to be careless of everything save an obligation to wiggle one finger. There was cold seawater swashing to and fro in the boat, and he lay in it. His head, pillowed on a thwart, was within an inch of the swirl of a wave crest, and sometimes a particularly obstreperous sea came inboard and drenched him once more. But these matters did not annoy him. It is almost certain that if the boat had capsized he would have tumbled comfortably out upon the ocean as if he felt sure that it was a great soft mattress.

87   "Look! There's a man on the shore!"

88   "Where?"

89   "There! See 'im? See 'im?"

90   "Yes, sure! He's walking along."

91   "Now he's stopped. Look! He's facing us!"

92   "He's waving at us!"

93   "So he is! By thunder!"

94   "Ah, now we're all right! Now we're all right! There'll be a boat out here for us in half an hour."

95   "He's going on. He's running. He's going up to that house there."

96   The remote beach seemed lower than the sea, and it required a searching glance to discern the little black figure. The captain saw a floating stick and they rowed to it. A bath-towel was by some weird chance in the boat, and tying this on the stick, the captain waved it. The oarsman did not dare turn his head, so he was obliged to ask questions.

97   "What's he doing now?"

98   "He's standing still again. He's looking. I think… There he goes again. Toward the house… Now he's stopped again."

99   "Is he waving at us?"

100   "No, not now! he was, though."

101   "Look! There comes another man!"

102   "He's running."

103   "Look at him go, would you."

104   "Why, he's on a bicycle. Now he's met the other man. They're both waving at us. Look!"

105   "There comes something up the beach."

106   "What the devil is that thing?"

107   "Why, it looks like a boat."

108   "Why, certainly it's a boat."

109   "No, it's on wheels."

110   "Yes, so it is. Well, that must be the life-boat. They drag them along shore on a wagon."

111   "That's the life-boat, sure."

112   "No, by—, it's—it's an omnibus."

113   "I tell you it's a life-boat."

114   "It is not! It's an omnibus. I can see it plain. See? One of these big hotel omnibuses."

115   "By thunder, you're right. It's an omnibus, sure as fate. What do you suppose they are doing with an omnibus? Maybe they are going around collecting the life-crew, hey?"

116   "That's it, likely. Look! There's a fellow waving a little black flag. He's standing on the steps of the omnibus. There come those other two fellows. Now they're all talking together. Look at the fellow with the flag. Maybe he ain't waving it."

117   "That ain't a flag, is it? That's his coat. Why, certainly, that's his coat."

118   "So it is. It's his coat. He's taken it off and is waving it around his head. But would you look at him swing it."

119   "Oh, say, there isn't any life-saving station there. That's just a winter resort hotel omnibus that has brought over some of the boarders to see us drown."

120   "What's that idiot with the coat mean? What's he signaling, anyhow?"

121   "It looks as if he were trying to tell us to go north. There must be a life-saving station up there."

122   "No! He thinks we're fishing. Just giving us a merry hand. See? Ah, there, Willie."

123   "Well, I wish I could make something out of those signals. What do you suppose he means?"

124   "He don't mean anything. He's just playing."

125   "Well, if he'd just signal us to try the surf again, or to go to sea and wait, or go north, or go south, or go to hell—there would be some reason in it. But look at him. He just stands there and keeps his coat revolving like a wheel. The ass!"

126   "There come more people."

127   "Now there's quite a mob. Look! Isn't that a boat?"

128   "Where? Oh, I see where you mean. No, that's no boat."

129   "That fellow is still waving his coat."

130   "He must think we like to see him do that. Why don't he quit it? It don't mean anything."

131   "I don't know. I think he is trying to make us go north. It must be that there's a life-saving station there somewhere."

132   "Say, he ain't tired yet. Look at 'im wave."

133   "Wonder how long he can keep that up. He's been revolving his coat ever since he caught sight of us. He's an idiot. Why aren't they getting men to bring a boat out? A fishing boat—one of those big yawls—could come out here all right. Why don't he do something?"

134   "Oh, it's all right, now."

135   "They'll have a boat out here for us in less than no time, now that they've seen us."

136   A faint yellow tone came into the sky over the low land. The shadows on the sea slowly deepened. The wind bore coldness with in, and the men began to shiver.

137   "Holy smoke!" said one, allowing his voice to express his impious mood, "if we keep on monkeying out here! If we've got to flounder out here all night!"

138   "Oh, we'll never have to stay here all night! Don't you worry. They've seen us now, and it won't be long before they'll come chasing out after us."

139   The shore grew dusky. The man waving a coat blended gradually into this gloom, and it swallowed in the same manner the omnibus and the group of people. The spray, when it dashed uproariously over the side, made the voyagers shrink and swear like men who were being branded.

140   "I'd like to catch the chump who waved the coat. I feel like soaking him one, just for luck."

141   "Why? What did he do?"

142   "Oh, nothing, but then he seemed so damned cheerful."

143   In the meantime the oiler rowed, and then the correspondent rowed, and then the oiler rowed. Gray-faced and bowed forward, they mechanically, turn by turn, plied the leaden oars. The form of the lighthouse had vanished from the southern horizon, but finally a pale star appeared, just lifting from the sea. The streaked saffron in the west passed before all-merging darkness, and the sea to the east was black. The land had vanished, and was expressed only by the low and drear thunder of the surf.

144   "If I am going to be drowned—if I am going to be drowned—if I am going to be drowned, why, in the name of the seven mad gods who rule the sea, was I allowed to come thus far and contemplate sand and trees? Was I brought here merely to have my nose dragged away as I was about to nibble the sacred cheese of life?"

145   The patient captain, drooped over the water-jar, was sometimes obliged to speak to the oarsman.

146   "Keep her head up! Keep her head up!"

147   " 'Keep her head up,' sir." The voices were weary and low.

148   This was surely a quiet evening. All save the oarsman lay heavily and listlessly in the boat's bottom. As for him, his eyes were just capable of noting the tall black waves that swept forward in a most sinister silence, save for an occasional subdued growl of a crest.

149   The cook's head was on a thwart, and he looked without interest at the water under his nose. He was deep in other scenes. Finally, he spoke. "Billie," he murmured, dreamily, "what kind of pie do you like best?"

V

150   "Pie," said the oiler and the correspondent, agitatedly. "Don't talk about those things, blast you!"

151   "Well," said the cook, "I was just thinking about ham sandwiches, and—"

152   A night on the sea in an open boat is a long night. As darkness settled finally, the shine of the light, lifting from the sea in the south, changed to full gold. On the northern horizon a new light appeared, a small bluish gleam on the edge of the waters. These two lights were the furniture of the world. Otherwise there was nothing but waves.

153   Two men huddled in the stern, and distances were so magnificent in the dingey that the rower was enabled to keep his feet partly warmed by thrusting them under his companions. Their legs indeed extended far under the rowing-seat until they touched the feet of the captain forward. Sometimes, despite the efforts of the tired oarsman, a wave came piling

into the boat, an icy wave of the night, and the chilling water soaked them anew. They would twist their bodies for a moment and groan, and sleep the dead sleep once more, while the water in the boat gurgled about them as the craft rocked.

154 The plan of the oiler and the correspondent was for one to row until he lost the ability, and then arouse the other from his sea-water couch in the bottom of the boat.

155 The oiler plied the oars until his head drooped forward, and the overpowering sleep blinded him. And he rowed yet afterward. Then he touched a man in the bottom of the boat, and called his name. "Will you spell me for a little while?" he said, meekly.

156 "Sure, Billie," said the correspondent, awakening and dragging himself to a sitting position. They exchanged places carefully, and the oiler, cuddling down in the sea-water at the cook's side, seemed to go to sleep instantly.

157 The particular violence of the sea had ceased. The waves came without snarling. The obligation of the man at the oars was to keep the boat headed so that the tilt of the rollers would not capsize her, and to preserve her from filling when the crests rushed past. The black waves were silent and hard to be seen in the darkness. Often one was almost upon the boat before the oarsman was aware.

158 In a low voice the correspondent addressed the captain. He was not sure that the captain was awake, although this iron man seemed to be always awake. "Captain, shall I keep her making for that light north, sir?"

159 The same steady voice answered him. "Yes. Keep it about two points off the port bow."

160 The cook had tied a life-belt around himself in order to get even the warmth which this clumsy cork contrivance could donate, and he seemed almost stove-like when a rower, whose teeth invariably chattered wildly as soon as he ceased his labor, dropped down to sleep.

161 The correspondent, as he rowed, looked down at the two men sleeping underfoot. The cook's arm was around the oiler's shoulders, and, with their fragmentary clothing and haggard faces, they were the babes of the sea, a grotesque rendering of the old babes in the wood.

162 Later he must have grown stupid at his work, for suddenly there was a growling of water, and a crest came with a roar and a swash into the boat, and it was a wonder that it did not set the cook afloat in his life-belt. The cook continued to sleep, but the oiler sat up, blinking his eyes and shaking with the new cold.

163 "Oh, I'm awful sorry, Billie," said the correspondent, contritely.

164 "That's all right, old boy," said the oiler, and lay down again and was asleep.

165   Presently it seemed that even the captain dozed, and the correspondent thought that he was the one man afloat on all the oceans. The wind had a voice as it came over the waves, and it was sadder than the end.

166   There was a long, loud swishing astern of the boat, and a gleaming trail of phosphorescence, like blue flame, was furrowed on the black waters. It might have been made by a monstrous knife.

167   Then there came a stillness, while the correspondent breathed with the open mouth and looked at the sea.

168   Suddenly there was another swish and another long flash of bluish light, and this time it was alongside the boat, and might almost have been reached with an oar. The correspondent saw an enormous fin speed like a shadow through the water, hurling the crystalline spray and leaving the long glowing trail.

169   The correspondent looked over his shoulder at the captain. His face was hidden, and he seemed to be asleep. He looked at the babes of the sea. They certainly were asleep. So, being bereft of sympathy, he leaned a little way to one side and swore softly into the sea.

170   But the thing did not then leave the vicinity of the boat. Ahead or astern, on one side or the other, at intervals long or short, fled the long sparkling streak, and there was to be heard the whiroo of the dark fin. The speed and power of the thing was greatly to be admired. It cut the water like a gigantic and keen projectile.

171   The presence of this biding thing did not affect the man with the same horror that it would have if he had been a picnicker. He simply looked at the sea dully and swore in an undertone.

172   Nevertheless, it is true that he did not wish to be alone. He wished one of his companions to awaken by chance and keep him company with it. But the captain hung motionless over the water-jar, and the oiler and cook in the bottom of the boat were plunged in slumber.

VI

173   "If I am going to be drowned—if I am going to be drowned—if I am going to be drowned, why, in the name of the seven mad gods who rule the sea, was I allowed to come thus far and contemplate sand and trees?"

174   During this dismal night, it may be remarked that a man would conclude that it was really the intention of the seven mad gods to drown him, despite the abominable injustice of it. For it was certainly an abominable injustice to drown a man who had worked so hard, so hard. The man felt it would be a crime most unnatural. Other people had drowned at sea since galleys swarmed with painted sails, but still—

175   When it occurs to a man that nature does not regard him as important, and that she feels she would not maim the universe by disposing of him, he

at first wishes to throw bricks at the temple, and he hates deeply the fact that there are no bricks and no temples. Any visible expression of nature would surely be pelleted with his jeers.

176   Then, if there be no tangible thing to hoot he feels, perhaps, the desire to confront a personification and indulge in pleas, bowed to one knee, and with hands supplicant, saying: "Yes, but I love myself."

177   A high cold star on a winter's night is the word he feels that she says to him. Thereafter he knows the pathos of his situation.

178   The men in the dingey had not discussed these matters, but each had, no doubt, reflected upon them in silence and according to his mind. There was seldom any expression upon their faces save the general one of complete weariness. Speech was devoted to the business of the boat.

179   To chime the notes of his emotion, a verse mysteriously entered the correspondent's head. He had even forgotten that he had forgotten this verse, but it suddenly was in his mind.

> "A soldier of the Legion lay dying in Algiers,
> There was lack of woman's nursing, there was dearth of woman's tears;
> But a comrade stood beside him, and he took that comrade's hand,
> And he said: 'I shall never see my own, my native land.' "

180   In his childhood, the correspondent had been made acquainted with the fact that a soldier of the Legion lay dying in Algiers, but he had never regarded the fact as important. Myriads of his school-fellows had informed him of the soldier's plight, but the dinning had naturally ended by making him perfectly indifferent. He had never considered it his affair that a soldier of the Legion lay dying in Algiers, nor had it appeared to him as a matter for sorrow. It was less to him than the breaking of a pencil's point.

181   Now, however, it quaintly came to him as a human, living thing. It was no longer merely a picture of a few throes in the breast of a poet, meanwhile drinking tea and warming his feet at the grate; it was an actuality—stern, mournful, and fine.

182   The correspondent plainly saw the soldier. He lay on the sand with his feet out straight and still. While his pale left hand was upon his chest in an attempt to thwart the going of his life, the blood came between his fingers. In the far Algerian distance, a city of low square forms was set against a sky that was faint with the last sunset hues. The correspondent, plying the oars and dreaming of the slow and slower movements of the lips of the soldier, was moved by a profound and perfectly impersonal comprehension. He was sorry for the soldier of the Legion who lay dying in Algiers.

183   The thing which had followed the boat and waited had evidently grown bored at the delay. There was no longer to be heard the slash of the cut water, and there was no longer the flame of the long trail. The light in the

north still glimmered, but it was apparently no nearer to the boat. Sometimes the boom of the surf rang in the correspondent's ears, and he turned the craft seaward then and rowed harder. Southward, someone had evidently built a watch-fire on the beach. It was too low and too far to be seen, but it made a shimmering, roseate reflection upon the bluff back of it, and this could be discerned from the boat. The wind came stronger, and sometimes a wave suddenly raged out like a mountain-cat, and there was to be seen the sheen and sparkle of a broken crest.

184   The captain, in the bow, moved on his water-jar and sat erect. "Pretty long night," he observed to the correspondent. He looked at the shore. "Those life-saving people take their time."

185   "Did you see that shark playing around?"

186   "Yes, I saw him. He was a big fellow, all right."

187   "Wish I had known you were awake."

188   Later the correspondent spoke into the bottom of the boat.

189   "Billie!" There was a slow and gradual disentanglement. "Billie, will you spell me?"

190   "Sure," said the oiler.

191   As soon as the correspondent touched the cold comfortable sea-water in the bottom of the boat, and had huddled close to the cook's life-belt he was deep in sleep, despite the fact that his teeth played all the popular airs. This sleep was so good to him that it was but a moment before he heard a voice call his name in a tone that demonstrated the last stages of exhaustion. "Will you please spell me?"

192   "Sure, Billie."

193   The light in the north had mysteriously vanished, but the correspondent took his course from the wide-awake captain.

194   Later in the night they took the boat farther out to sea, and the captain directed the cook to take one oar at the stern and keep the boat facing the seas. He was to call out if he should hear the thunder of the surf. This plan enabled the oiler and the correspondent to get respite together. "We'll give those boys a chance to get into shape again," said the captain. They curled down and, after a few preliminary chatterings and trembles, slept once more the dead sleep. Neither knew they had bequeathed to the cook the company of another shark, or perhaps the same shark.

195   As the boat caroused on the waves, spray occasionally bumped over the side and gave them a fresh soaking, but this had no power to break their repose. The ominous slash of the wind and the water affected them as it would have affected mummies.

196   "Boys," said the cook, with the notes of every reluctance in his voice, "she's drifted in pretty close. I guess one of you had better take her to sea again." The correspondent aroused, heard the crash of the toppled crests.

197   As he was rowing, the captain gave him some whiskey-and-water, and this steadied the chills out of him. "If I ever get ashore and anybody shows me even a photograph of an oar—"

198   At last there was a short conversation.

199   "Billie…Billie, will you spell me?"

200   "Sure," said the oiler.

VII

201   When the correspondent again opened his eyes, the sea and the sky were each of the gray hue of the dawning. Later, carmine and gold was painted upon the waters. The morning appeared finally, in its splendor, with a sky of pure blue, and the sunlight flamed on the tips of the waves.

202   On the distant dunes were set many little black cottages, and a tall white windmill reared above them. No man, nor dog, nor bicycle appeared on the beach. The cottages might have formed a deserted village.

203   The voyagers scanned the shore. A conference was held in the boat. "Well," said the captain, "if no help is coming, we might better try to run through the surf right away. If we stay out here much longer we will be too weak to do anything for ourselves at all." The others silently acquiesced in this reasoning. The boat was headed for the beach. The correspondent wondered if none ever ascended the tall wind-tower, and if then they never looked seaward. This tower was a giant, standing with its back to the plight of the ants. It represented in a degree, to the correspondent, the serenity of nature amid the struggles of the individual—nature in the wind, and nature in the vision of men. She did not seem cruel to him then, nor beneficent, nor treacherous, nor wise. But she was indifferent, flatly indifferent. It is, perhaps, plausible that a man in this situation, impressed with the unconcern of the universe, should see the innumerable flaws of his life, and have them taste wickedly in his mind and wish for another chance. A distinction between right and wrong seems absurdly clear to him, then, in this new ignorance of the grave-edge, and he understands that if he were given another opportunity he would mend his conduct and his words, and be better and brighter during an introduction or at a tea.

204   "Now, boys," said the captain, "she is going to swamp sure. All we can do is to work her in as far as possible, and then when she swamps, pile out and scramble for the beach. Keep cool now, and don't jump until she swamps sure."

205   The oiler took the oars. Over his shoulders he scanned the surf. "Captain," he said, "I think I'd better bring her about, and keep her head-on to the seas and back her in."

206   "All right, Billie," said the captain. "Back her in." The oiler swung the boat then and, seated in the stern, the cook and the correspondent were

obliged to look over their shoulders to contemplate the lonely and indifferent shore.

207   The monstrous in-shore rollers heaved the boat high until the men were again enabled to see the white sheets of water scudding up the slanted beach. "We won't get in very close," said the captain. Each time a man could wrest his attention from the rollers, he turned his glance toward the shore, and in the expression of the eyes during this contemplation there was a singular quality. The correspondent, observing the others, knew that there were not afraid, but the full meaning of their glances was shrouded.

208   As for himself, he was too tired to grapple fundamentally with the fact. He tried to coerce his mind into thinking of it, but the mind was dominated at this time by the muscles, and the muscles said they did not care. It merely occurred to him that if he should drown it would be a shame.

209   There were no hurried words, no pallor, no plain agitation. The men simply looked at the shore. "Now, remember to get well clear of the boat when you jump," said the captain.

210   Seaward the crest of a roller suddenly fell with a thunderous crash, and the long white comber came roaring down upon the boat.

211   "Steady now," said the captain. The men were silent. They turned their eyes from the shore to the comber and waited. The boat slid up the incline, leaped at the furious top, bounced over it, and swung down the long back of the waves. Some water had been shipped and the cook bailed it out.

212   But the next crest crashed also. The tumbling, boiling flood of white water caught the boat and whirled it almost perpendicular. Water swarmed in from all sides. The correspondent had his hands on the gunwale at this time, and when the water entered at that place he swiftly withdrew his fingers, as if he objected to wetting them.

213   The little boat, drunken with this weight of water, reeled and snuggled deeper into the sea.

214   "Bail her out, cook! Bail her out," said the captain.

215   "All right, captain," said the cook.

216   "Now, boys, the next one will do for us, sure," said the oiler. "Mind to jump clear of the boat."

217   The third wave moved forward, huge, furious, implacable. It fairly swallowed the dingey, and almost simultaneously the men tumbled into the sea. A piece of life-belt had lain in the bottom of the boat, and as the correspondent went overboard he held this to his chest with his left hand.

218   The January water was icy, and he reflected immediately that it was colder than he had expected to find it off the coast of Florida. This appeared to his dazed mind as a fact important enough to be noted at the time. The coldness of the water was sad; it was tragic. This fact was somehow so

mixed and confused with his opinion of his own situation that it seemed a proper reason for tears. The water was cold.

219   When he came to the surface he was conscious of little but the noisy water. Afterward he saw his companions in the sea. The oiler was ahead in the race. He was swimming strongly and rapidly. Off to the correspondent's left, the cook's great white and corked back bulged out of the water, and in the rear the captain was hanging with his one good hand to the keel of the overturned dingey.

220   There is a certain immovable quality to a shore, and the correspondent wondered at it amid the confusion of the sea.

221   It seemed also very attractive, but the correspondent knew that it was a long journey, and he paddled leisurely. The piece of life-preserver lay under him, and sometimes he whirled down the incline of a wave as if he were on a hand-sled.

222   But finally he arrived at a place in the sea where travel was beset with difficulty. He did not pause swimming to inquire what manner of current had caught him, but there his progress ceased. The shore was set before him like a bit of scenery on a stage, and he looked at it and understood with his eyes each detail of it.

223   As the cook passed, much farther to the left, the captain was calling to him, "Turn over on your back, cook! Turn over on your back and use the oar."

224   "All right, sir." The cook turned on his back, and, paddling with an oar, went ahead as if he were a canoe.

225   Presently the boat also passed to the left of the correspondent with the captain clinging with one hand to the keel. He would have appeared like a man raising himself to look over a board fence, if it were not for the extraordinary gymnastics of the boat. The correspondent marveled that the captain could still hold to it.

226   They passed on, nearer to shore—the oiler, the cook, the captain—and following them went the water-jar, bouncing gaily over the seas.

227   The correspondent remained in the grip of this strange new enemy—a current. The shore, with its white slope of sand and its green bluff, topped with little silent cottages, was spread like a picture before him. It was very near to him then, but he was impressed as one who in a gallery looks at a scene from Brittany or Algiers.

228   He thought: "I am going to drown? Can it be possible? Can it be possible? Can it be possible?" Perhaps an individual must consider his own death to be the final phenomenon of nature.

229   But later a wave perhaps whirled him out of this small deadly current, for he found suddenly that he could again make progress toward the shore. Later still, he was aware that the captain, clinging with one hand to the keel of the dingey, had his face turned away from the shore and toward him, and was calling his name. "Come to the boat! Come to the boat!"

230   In his struggle to reach the captain and the boat, he reflected that when one gets properly wearied, drowning must really be a comfortable arrangement, a cessation of hostilities accompanied by a large degree of relief, and he was glad of it, for the main thing in his mind for some moments had been horror of the temporary agony. He did not wish to be hurt.

231   Presently he saw a man running along the shore. He was undressing with the most remarkable speed. Coat, trousers, shirt, everything flew magically off him.

232   "Come to the boat," called the captain.

233   "All right, captain." As the correspondent paddled, he saw the captain let himself down to bottom and leave the boat. Then the correspondent performed this one little marvel of the voyage. A large wave caught him and flung him with ease and supreme speed completely over the boat and far beyond it. It struck him even then as an event in gymnastics, and a true miracle of the sea. An overturned boat in the surf is not a plaything to a swimming man.

234   The correspondent arrived in water that reached only to his waist, but his condition did not enable him to stand for more than a moment. Each wave knocked him into a heap, and the under-tow pulled at him.

235   Then he saw the man who had been running and undressing, and undressing and running, come bounding into the water. He dragged ashore the cook, and then waded toward the captain, but the captain waved him away, and sent him to the correspondent. He was naked, naked as a tree in winter, but a halo was about his head, and he shone like a saint. He gave a strong pull, and a long drag, and a bully heave at the correspondent's hand. The correspondent, schooled in the minor formulae, said: "Thanks, old man." But suddenly the man cried: "What's that?" He pointed a swift finger. The correspondent said: "Go."

236   In the shallows, face downward, lay the oiler. His forehead touched sand that was periodically, between each wave, clear of the sea.

237   The correspondent did not know all that transpired afterward. When he achieved safe ground he fell, striking the sand with each particular part of his body. It was as if he had dropped from a roof, but the thud was grateful to him.

238   It seems that instantly the beach was populated with men, with blankets, clothes, and flasks, and women with coffee-pots and all the remedies sacred to their minds. The welcome of the land to the men from the sea was warm and generous, but a still and dripping shape was carried slowly up the beach, and the land's welcome for it could only be the different and sinister hospitality of the grave.

239   When it came night, the white waves paced to and fro in the moonlight, and the wind brought the sound of the great sea's voice to the men on shore, and they felt that they could then be interpreters.

1: NEWS STORY VERSUS FICTION

Read one or more of the accounts of the shipwreck. Compare the fictional account with the news stories mentioned above. Use the columns below to note the similarities and differences.

"The Open Boat"	Non-Fiction Accounts

Characters/People

_____

_____

_____

Plot/Events

_____

_____

_____

Scene

_____

_____

_____

Language

_____

_____

_____

Other

_____

_____

_____

2: SYNOPSIS

A **synopsis** is a brief summary of the main events of the story. Prepare a brief synopsis of "The Open Boat."

3: THE SCENE OF THE ACTION

To place yourself in this story, notice all the adjectives Crane uses to show you the sea, the sky, the men, and the other elements of the story. As a beginning, notice the adjectives below.

slaty

gruesome

bluish

cold

Make a list of the most powerful adjectives. Look up their meanings and discuss how those adjectives affect you. As you look up these adjectives, notice what impression each adds to the impression of the scene you had before you included that adjective in your mental picture. How does it change the scene of the story as you see or imagine it in your mind's eye?

▲·▲·▲·▲·▲·▲·▲·▲·▲·▲·▲·▲·▲·▲·▲·▲·▲·▲·▲·

C. IMAGES AND IMAGE CLUSTERS

You have noticed words in this book used as part of plot, the story itself; as the style or personality of the author arranged in words; as character, words used to describe human beings; and as many other aspects. In Chapter Seven ("The Storm") and in Chapter Thirteen ("Guests of the Nation"), you explored words used as images.

Recall what an **image** is. An image paints a picture, usually a picture of the physical world that will appeal to or attract one or more of your senses (sight, hearing, touch, taste, smell). The target of an image, which is usually as specific and exact as possible, is not a reader's thoughts but his or her senses.

In "The Open Boat" Crane relied heavily on groups or clusters of images. Before you begin to trace them, however, work first with one image alone.

4A: AN IMAGE ON A POSTCARD

Below you will find five images Crane used in "The Open Boat." Read each carefully and find it in the story. Read the paragraph in which it appears. Then, using Crane's image as a start, write a postcard to a friend. In the postcard, with Crane's image as your inspiration, describe the feeling the image conveys to you. Write no more than 50 words.

*Model **Image and Postcard:***

Crane's Image: "*The craft pranced and reared and plunged like an animal.*"

Postcard: **Dear Denise,**

 I was at sea yesterday in a boat that acted like a horse. Its front lifted very high one minute, like a proud stallion, and then suddenly dropped as if scared by something it saw.

Here are your five images. (The numbers after the sentence refer to sections of the story). Now write your postcards.

1. By the very last star of truth, it is easier to steal eggs from under a hen than it was to change seats in the dingey. (II)

2. Occasionally a great spread of water, like white flames, swarmed into her. (II)

3. The roar of the surf was plain, and sometimes they could see the white lip of a wave as it spun up the beach. (IV)

4. The wind had a voice as it came over the waves, and it was sadder than the end. (V)

5. The wind came stronger, and sometimes a wave suddenly raged out like a mountain cat.... (VI)

4B:

Read your postcards to the entire class. As you listen, notice and write down the various images that your classmates have used to create a larger picture in their postcards.

5: IMAGE CLUSTERS

Now it is time to study the larger world of image clusters. Review the story and find one particular image that you like or that affects you very strongly. Then follow that image throughout the whole story, making a list of the characteristics Crane associates with that image. See what happens to the image. How does its meaning change? With what other images is it repeatedly associated? How do your feelings about it change? Make the image your close friend; try to know it not only on the surface but completely, from the first time you see it to the last time it appears. Finally, think about how the movement of the image relates to the movement of the entire story. By reviewing the "histories" of all the image clusters in "The Open Boat," you will have a good overview of one important aspect of the story.

▲ ▪ ▲ ▪ ▲ ▪ ▲ ▪ ▲ ▪ ▲

D. SYMBOLS

Oranges, strawberries, and storms are symbols which appeared in the first stories you read in this book, "The Strawberry Season," "A Bag of Oranges," and "The Storm." Most stories have some symbolic dimension, although it is not always formally noticed or discussed.

A symbol is not born a symbol but usually begins as an ordinary detail, even a fact.

6: RESOURCES FOR SYMBOLS

Make a list of some of the many details in "The Open Boat." Don't evaluate them at all; simply brainstorm or list them as you find them in the story or as you remember them.

Here are a few details to help you start. Then you continue.

horizon

sky

waves

sea gulls

Now examine your list and make a second, short list.

This list is the best source of the story's symbols. One guide to judging the importance of a symbol is to notice if it appears throughout the entire story or, on the other hand, if it is mentioned only once or twice and then disappears. The short list details symbols which appear large enough in the story and consistently enough to be studied as symbols. Discuss the short list of symbols you have made.

7: FINAL WORD ON SYMBOLS

In a longer story such as "The Open Boat" or in a novel, the symbols are often more fully developed than they can be in shorter works. Compare the symbols in "The Open Boat" with symbols you have seen in "The Strawberry Season," "A Bag of Oranges," "The Storm," and "The Boarding House." In which story that you have previously studied are the symbols most similar to those in the Stephen Crane work? What are the similarities? Can an entire story, an account of four men shipwrecked at sea wanting to be rescued, itself be symbolic?

When an entire story has a symbolic dimension and includes an entire system of symbols complete in itself, it is called an **allegory**. Each symbol would have an exact meaning in the overall system of the story's symbolism. Does "The Open Boat" have such a complete symbolic system that it can be called an allegory?

▲·▲·▲·▲·▲·▲·▲·▲·

E. STRUCTURE

"The Open Boat" offers not one or two but many distinct positions from which to observe its structure. You will be able to add your own insights into Crane's **form** (another word for structure) in this story. Do one, some, or all of the activities below, keeping your eye on the movement or direction of the entire story.

8: PHOTOS OF MY SHIPWRECK AT SEA

Imagine that you have collected photographs of the shipwreck and all the action of the story from the boat, the shore, and, with a helicopter, the air. You have more than twenty-five photographs. Use a 3" x 5" card to represent each photograph. Number and identify each one. First arrange them in the order the events occurred. Then arrange them according to other possible sequences, such as (1) closeness to and distance from the safe shore, (2) day and night, and (3) other important aspects of the story. Keep shuffling the cards into different possible structures. Which ones satisfy you most? Why? Is there one sequence of photographs that seems better than Crane's actual sequence? Show your photograph "album" to your classmates and compare "albums."
Model:
Photograph 1: A sea gull is sitting on the captain's head. The captain is sitting without moving because if he waves the gull away, the boat may turn over.

Now create your "album."

9: PROGRESSION OF IMAGES

Images "progress" and accumulate more and more meaning throughout a story. Choose one image and compare its meaning at the beginning, middle, and end of the story. How does the meaning of the image change at each of these markers? How has the image "grown" from the start to the end of the story? Review some of the images you noticed earlier.

10: FOUR MEN IN A BOAT

"The Open Boat" is essentially the account of four men—a cook, an oiler, a correspondent, and a captain—trying to reach the safety of the shore in a small boat. Each man brings to the experience a unique background, lives the events uniquely, and arrives uniquely on shore. Follow the stories of each character and compare the movement or structure of each story to the other. What specific similarities and differences do you find in each character's story?

List in chronological (time) order the major events of each character's story under his name.

Cook	Oiler	Correspondent	Captain

11: CRANE'S SEVEN SECTIONS

In "The Open Boat" Crane separated and numbered each distinct section. As a class, or in seven groups (each representing one section of the story) chosen by the class or by your teacher, look closely at each section. What makes one section different from the others? How does each section move the story ahead yet not lose the sensitive connection to the previous sections. Finally, does the arrangement (I, II, etc.) make sense to you?

12: REWRITING THE STORY

You are hired by Stephen Crane as his literary advisor. He has completed a story, "The Open Boat," but feels dissatisfied with the structure. He is busy with another story, so he has asked you to make suggestions on how to rewrite the story, especially how to reorder the events and even the sections. How would you reorder the story? Which actions would you put first, halfway, and last? Reorder the events according to your concept of the story.

Now, it is your turn. Suggest two additional ways to look at the structure of "The Open Boat" and see how they change your understanding and appreciation of the story.

▲˙▲˙▲˙▲˙▲˙

F. VOICE

Voice, including the pace, the softness or loudness, the warmth or coolness of the words, as well as the closeness or distance of the narrator or author to the audience, binds the various parts of the story. The best way to understand and appreciate voice is to examine it in some passages from the stories themselves.

18: THE VOICES OF "THE OPEN BOAT"

In "The Open Boat" Crane uses many voices. In these voices he tries to capture the situation of four men shipwrecked at sea whose moods, hopes, disappointment, and despair, change from hour to hour. Study the five passages from "The Open Boat" given below. Consider the syntax (sentence structure and length) and word order, word choice, word form choice (nouns, verbs, adjectives, or adverbs), sounds of the words, the subjects of sentences (noun, pronouns, etc.), repetition, and any other aspects of language you feel are part of voice. Then, using only **adjectives** (warm, cold, friendly, distant, harsh, etc.) describe the voice in each passage.

Note: The numbers following the pages refer to the sections of the story from which the passages are taken.

Passage 1: A singular disadvantage of the sea lies in the fact that after successfully surmounting one wave you discover that there is another behind it just as important and just as nervously anxious to do something effective in the way of swamping boats. In a ten-foot dingey one can get an idea of the resources of the sea in the line of waves that is not probable to the average experience which is never at sea in a dingey. (I)

Passage 2: The brown mats of seaweed that appeared from time to time were like islands, bits of earth. They were travelling, apparently, neither one way nor the other. They were, to all intents, stationary. They informed the men in the boat that it was making progress slowly toward the land. (II)

Passage 3: It would be difficult to describe the subtle brotherhood of men that was here established on the seas. No one said that it was so. No one mentioned it. But it dwelt in the boat, and each man felt it warm him. They were a captain, an oiler, a cook, and a correspondent, and they were friends, friends in a more curiously iron-bound degree than may be common. (III)

Passage 4: A broad stretch of lowly coast lay before the eyes of the men. It was of low dunes topped with dark vegetation. The roar of the surf was plain, and sometimes they could see the white lip of a wave as it spun up the beach. A tiny house was blocked out black upon the sky. Southward, the slim lighthouse lifted its little grey length. (IV)

Passage 5: "If I am going to be drowned—if I am going to be drowned—if I am going to be drowned, why, in the name of the seven mad gods who rule the sea, was I allowed to come thus far and contemplate sand and trees?" (IV)

Passage 6: During this dismal night, it may be remarked that a man would conclude that it was really the intention of the seven mad gods to drown him, despite the abominable injustice of it. For it was certainly an abominable injustice to drown a man who had worked so hard, so hard. (VI)

▲·▲

G. CHARACTER AND POINT OF VIEW

14: APPLYING TWO ENTRANCES ON YOUR OWN

You have probably realized by now that "The Open Boat" is a story one can reread and restudy for a lifetime without discovering all of its richness. Moreover, in addition to the approaches we have used—setting, imagery, and the like—many other approaches would bring forth other dimensions of the story. For example, characterization and point of view are two approaches with which you have had much experience in this book. With your classmates, decide on which aspects of characterization and point of view can best help you understand "The Open Boat." Then you will be as ready as possible to review the story as a whole, in short, to look into the **theme** of the work.

▲·▲·▲·▲·▲·▲

H. THEME

Asking questions about the story is an interesting and effective way to discover its themes. In fact, an interesting question can itself stand as a statement of theme.

When you begin to study a story, your questions are often about facts (What happened at the market in "A Bag of Oranges?) or questions about feelings (How does the father in "The Use of Force" feel about the doctor?). At the end of your study of a story, however, the questions should be quite different. You already know more of the realistic basis of the story and understand the concepts of character, location, language, images, and symbols. You can now ask profound questions about the essential meaning of the work.

What are your questions about "The Open Boat"? The ingredients of Crane's tale are sea, land, sky, four men in a boat, a lighthouse, a man on the shore, the colors of things, the words of the men, and, finally, a force, call it Fate or Nature. These aspects will appear in your questions.

15. SAMPLE QUESTIONS

Read the two sample questions below.

Why does the correspondent suddenly remember a poem about a soldier who was dying in Algiers?

What is the meaning of the imaginary thoughts of the men "Yes, but I love myself"?

16: THEMATIC QUESTIONS

Ask three questions about the theme of "The Open Boat." As you discuss the questions asked, write down possible theme statements. Do not eliminate any possible themes.

▲ ▪ ▲ ▪

I. CLOSING THOUGHTS AND FUTURE OPENINGS

Carefully asking the questions and avoiding the urge for definite answers, patiently listening, and working through the various dimensions of theme is quite difficult. Yet it will finally feel quite satisfying. Here Crane himself has pointed the way. After the men's difficult struggle with the elements—sea, sky, land that approaches and seems to disappear, shadowy figures on shore, even sharks—the survivors have understood something. Of them, Crane, says at the close of the story, "When it came night, the white waves paced to and fro in the moonlight, and the wind brought the sound of the great sea's voice to the men on the shore, and they felt that they could then be interpreters." May no less be said of you, the appreciative, persevering, and courageous reader of fiction.

APPENDIX I
APPEARANCE OF TERMS BY CHAPTER

Allegory: 17

Allusions: 13, 14, 16

Character: 2, 3, 4, 5, 6, 7, 8, 9, 10, 11, 12, 14, 16, 17, 18

Conflict: 10, 11, 14

Congruent patterns: 16

Epiphanies: 16

Foil: 11

Foreshadowing (*see* Structure)

Guidelines for Reading Fiction: 2

Images and image clusters: 7, 11, 13, 18

Language and style: 5, 7, 10, 11, 12

Motifs: 14

Myth and ritual: 8

Pace: 13, 17

Plot: 2, 3, 4, 5

Point of view: 6, 10, 11, 12, 14, 15, 18

Setting: 2, 3, 4, 7, 10, 12, 14, 17

Slice of life: 4, 10

Structure: 6, 7, 8, 9, 10, 11, 12, 16, 17, 18

Style (*see also* Language and Style): 7, 9, 10, 11, 12, 15, 17

Subplot: 4

Symbolic language and associations: 6, 7, 9, 10, 14, 15, 17, 18

Theme: 4 5, 6, 7, 9, 10, 12, 13, 17, 18

Time: 3

Tone: 15, 17

Voice: 17, 18

APPENDIX II
SELECTED ARTICLES ON THE USE OF LITERATURE IN ESL/EFL

I. Studies of Individual Works and Classroom Applications

Ashmead, J. (1965). Whitman's "Wintry Locomotive," export model. In V. F. Allen (Ed.), *On teaching English to speakers of other languages: Papers read at the TESOL conference, May 8-9, l964, Tuscon, Arizona* (pp. 154-158). Champaign, Ill.: National Council of Teachers of English.

Gatbonton, E., & Tucker, G. R. (1971). Cultural orientation and the study of literature. *TESOL Quarterly,* 5, 137–143. (Culture gaps as barriers to understanding literature in English are explained in a report on an experiment with Filipino high-school students.)

Kerschgens, E. (1978). James Baldwin and the race problem in the USA. *Praxis des Neusprachlichen Unterrichts,* 24, 312–316. (A study of students in grades 11–13 and their reaction to four Baldwin texts.)

Kujoory, P. (1978). Iranian students and western cultural concepts in literature. *English Language Teaching Journal,* 32, 221–225. (Three novels [*The Old Man and the Sea, To Kill a Mockingbird,* and *One Flew over the Cuckoo's Nest*] and their difficulty for Iranian students because of lack of knowledge about the target culture with suggestions for solutions.)

Mc Conochie, J., & Sage, H. (1985). Since feeling is first: Thoughts on sharing poetry in the ESOL classroom. *English Teaching Forum,* 23, 2–5. Reprinted in *Perspectives* (Italy), 9, 3 (October 1985), 13–19.

Ramsaran, S. (1983). Poetry in the language classroom. *ELT Journal*, 37, 36–43. (A study of some specific poems successful with ESL/EFL students, especially helpful syntactically.)

Sage, H. (1987). *Incorporating literature in ESL instruction.* Washington, D.C.: The Center for Applied Linguistics/Prentice Hall. (Explains in depth how to teach Robert Hayden's poem, "Those Winter Sundays" and Stephen Crane's "The Open Boat.")

Spinelli, E., and Williams, S. S. (1981). From language to literature: Figurative language in the college foreign language class. *Foreign Language Annals*, 14, 37–43. (Includes techniques and principles for teaching figurative language and suggests a bridge from expository reading to literature in the foreign language class.)

Spuler, R. (1981). Concrete poetry and elementary language study. *Teaching Language through Literature*, 20, 36–37. (Advantages of using poetry as preparation for study of other literature, especially in developing student sensitivity to language.)

Watts, M. (1981). Writing poetry and learning English. *English Language Teaching Journal*, 35, 444–450. (Describes a project with poetry and grammar in Ghana.)

II. Studies on the Place of Literature in Language Teaching

Balakian, A. (1977). Teaching language and literature. *Teaching Language through Literature*, 16, 1–5. (Discusses language as communication and creation and which should come first.)

Charlesworth, R. S. (1978). The role of literature in the teaching of English as a second language or dialect. *English Quarterly*, 11, 157-177. (Explains why literature has been neglected in an ESL/EFL environment.)

Di Pietro, R.J. (1982). The multi-ethnicity of American literature: A neglected resource for the EFL teacher. In M. Hines & W. Rutherford (Eds.). *On TESOL '81* (pp. 215–229). Washington, D.C.: Teachers of English to Speakers of Other Languages.

Povey, J. F. (1967). Literature in TESL programs: The language and the culture. *TESOL Quarterly*, 1, 40–46. (Suggests that literature is a link to the culture which supports the expression of any language.)

Scott, C. T. (1964). Literature and the ESL program. *The Modern Language Journal*, 48, 489–493. (Illustrates why literature is a good way to promote the goal of cultural orientation.)

Topping, D. M. (1968). Linguistics or literature. *TESOL Quarterly*, 2, 95–100. (Argues against the use of literature for ESL students.)

Widdowson, H. (1982). The use of literature. In M. Hines & W. Rutherford (Eds.), *On TESOL '81* (pp. 203–214). Washington, D.C.: Teachers of English to Speakers of Other Languages.

Widdowson, H. (1983). Talking shop: On literature and ELT. *ELT Journal*, 37, 30–35. (Details the relationship between ordinary and literary discourse.)

III. Studies of the Selecting and Editing of Literature for Classroom Use

Adeyanju, T. K. (1978). Teaching literature and human values in ESL: Objectives and selection. *English Language Teaching Journal*, 32, 133–138. (Enumerates some criteria in selecting literature to teach to ESL/EFL students.)

Harris, A. S., & Harris, A. S. (1967). A selected bibliography of American literature for TESOL. *TESOL Quarterly*, 1, 53–62. (A very early listing and attempt to classify fiction for ESL/EFL use according to grammar and structure.)

Marckwardt, A. H. (1978) *The place of literature in the teaching of English as a second or foreign language.* Honolulu: East-West Center.

Potter, J. (1983). Reading for pleasure with an intermediate level of English. *MEX-TESOL Journal*, 7, 9–21.

Povey, J. F. (1967). Literature in TESL programs: The language and the culture. *TESOL Quarterly*, 1, 40–46. (Describes what one should consider in selecting literature to teach ESL/EFL students.)

Slager, W. R. (1965). Introducing *Literature in English:* Problems in selecting and editing. In V. F. Allen (Ed.), *On teaching English to speakers of other languages: Papers read at the TESOL conference, Tuscon, Arizona, May 8-9, 1964.* (pp. 128–132) Champaign, Ill.: National Council of Teachers of English.

Wolf, D. (1984). Research currents about language skills from narration. *Language Arts*, 61, 844–850. (What the study of narrative in particular offers children.)

IV. Studies of Principles of Language Teaching

Di Pietro, R. J. (1983). From literature to discourse: Interaction with texts in the ESL/EFL classroom. *Canadian Modern Language Review*, 40, 44–50.

Mc Kay, S. (1982). Review of Louise M. Rosenblatt's *The reader, the text, the poem; The transactional theory of the literary work. TESOL Quarterly*, 16, 529–536.

Widdowson, H. (1982). The use of literature. In M. Hines & W. Rutherford (Eds.), *On TESOL '81* (pp. 203–214). Washington, D.C.: Teachers of English to Speakers of Other Languages. (Presents a broad perspective on literature in language learning.)

COPYRIGHTS AND ACKNOWLEDGMENTS

◆◆◆◆◆◆◆◆◆
PHOTOS

Page xxii: Michael Dwyer/Stock, Boston.

Page 25: Philippe Heckly.

Page 30: UPI/Bettman Newsphotos.

Page 48: Archive Photos/Herbert.

Page 64: Owen Franken/Stock, Boston.

Page 76: © David Strickler/The Image Works.

Page 92: Peter Menzel/Stock, Boston.

Page 156: Michael Dwyer/Stock, Boston.

Page 172: UPI/Bettman.

Page 190: *Top:* Lionel Delevingne/Stock, Boston. *Bottom:* Dave Fwierkofz.

Page 210: Photofest.

Page 226: AP/Wide World Photos.

Page 240: Archive Photos/Lambert.

Page 251: Michael Dwyer/Stock, Boston.